SERMON GUIDES
for preaching in
Easter, Ascension,
and
Pentecost

Edited by

C. W. Burger
B. A. Müller
D. J. Smit

WILLIAM B. EERDMANS PUBLISHING COMPANY
GRAND RAPIDS, MICHIGAN

Copyright © 1988 by Wm. B. Eerdmans Publishing Co.
255 Jefferson Ave. S.E., Grand Rapids, Mich. 49503

Library of Congress Cataloging-in-Publication Data:

Sermon guides for preaching during Easter, Ascension, and Pentecost.

1. Preaching   2. Bible—Homiletical use.
3. Church year sermons—Outlines, syllabi, etc.
I. Burger, C. W.   II. Müller, B. A.   III. Smit, D. J.
BV4221.S4   1988   251'.02   88-3574

ISBN 0-8028-0283-4

Contents

Preface

When we started this series of "guidelines for preaching" several years ago, we never imagined the demand for this kind of literature. What we did realize—because we had discovered it in our own ministries—was that the task of preaching is a difficult one for a variety of reasons. Among the most difficult factors is the process of writing—or preparing to write—the sermon.

More often than not, preachers simply cannot find the time to do all the necessary preparatory work—the work they have been trained to do. Moreover, the books available on their study shelves do not get them very far in producing a finished sermon. Technical commentaries are a great help, but usually only in the first part of the homiletical process, namely the attempt to understand the text itself. We don't expect an exegete or a commentary to proceed further than that—but the preacher must! In the final stages of sermon preparation, preachers therefore often have to "go it alone," relying on their own originality, creativity, and experience. The average preacher often feels unable to produce a meaningful sermon, particularly on difficult texts, and particularly when he or she is pressed by the many other duties of a parish pastor. Consequently some preachers take refuge in relying on the hackneyed "easy" texts, or unearth their own earlier sermons, or even turn to published collections of sermons. While we have a high regard for good collections of sermons, we feel that a way must be found to help ministers in their task of producing a fresh sermon—fresh from a deep study of the Word and fresh in its application to immediate issues.

Our basic aim has been to help preachers write sermons of their own that are theologically sound and exegetically "true." Our means of achieving this was to start a kind of "exchange program." We asked some friends who were interested to take responsibility for specific pericopes, to study the material available, to analyse the exegetical issues at stake in the commentaries and other exegeses, to look for the doctrinal issues involved (and refer to helpful literature on those issues), to try to obtain some interesting and thought-provoking ideas from the history of the interpretation of a given pericope (the so-called *Wirkungsgeschichte*, or "the history of its effects"), to gather some associated references from liturgical, inspirational, or philosophical literature—and to exchange all this material among ourselves. The contributors do not claim to be extraordinary preachers, but wanted to serve the proclamation of the Word by sharing their theological groundwork and studies with others.

Our idea was never to prepare sermons for one another, because we are convinced that the final prophetic responsibility to preach the Word in a very specific context, to specific people in a specific congregation with very specific fears and dreams is something that can never be done by someone else, in general, context-less and time-less. We have tried to produce instead a series of sermon "enablers" to be used in diverse situations, denominations, cultures, and countries. Preachers will still have to write each sermon themselves, addressing it to the existential situation of their congregations.

To make our findings available to as many people as possible, we decided to publish our work. We also decided to organize it around the church year; even in churches that do not adhere to a lectionary with prescribed pericopes, many preachers try in general to follow the church year, but often find it difficult, especially in some parts of the year.

Our original South African publishers were willing to take the risk with a small number of copies. We were completely overwhelmed by the response. The first printing was sold out almost immediately, and the public reaction was most enthusiastic. It is not necessary to tell the whole story, but with seven Afrikaans volumes already in print and several others in preparation, the books are still very popular in South Africa.

Each of the sermon guides is divided into three parts. The first part is exegetical. We do not want to try to replace the preacher's own exegesis, but simply try to take the text seriously and to work with the available literature in order to try to find the basic thrust of each pericope. We can demonstrate alternate views from the available literature and point out potential mistakes in interpretation or superficial deductions to be avoided. Where no real difficulties of interpretation present themselves, this section will be short; some texts will require more extensive discussion. The intention is always to get at the central message and the most likely lines of communication presented by the text for further meditation and eventual application.

The second part is hermeneutical. Here we address the doctrinal issues raised in the pericope and may refer to literary works, relevant quotations, or, where they are available, to published sermons. We have found many German and Dutch publications very useful, and we frequently cite them. It is not our intention that our readers must also use them; we intend simply to spark off ideas and arouse the imagination with literature often not available to the parish pastor. In this section, we discuss ways in which the text can be applied in a modern context, point out misconceptions that need to be corrected, and warn preachers about the dangers of wornout applications, jargon, and subtle forms of spiritualizing or allegorizing.

In the third, or homiletical, part we offer our own suggestion for a possible sermon—but again, because we firmly believe that preaching must be prophetic, to the point, contextual, and the product of the preacher's own efforts, we do not write complete sermons. What we offer instead is an outline, usually with more than one option at various points along the way. Our intention is to help preachers from the text to the sermon—and from the sermon to the pulpit!

We also provide a select bibliography with each pericope. In this English language edition, although the bibliographies retain some of the more prominent foreign language literature, they have been shaped to focus on significant and available literature in English.

Our authors do not advance the tenets of a specific school of thought or a particular theology. They merely share the conviction that the proclamation of the church is very important and must be performed as responsibly as possible. They have been willing to work hard and to share the results of their efforts in order to assist others also struggling with this responsibility. Their knowledge of English, German, Dutch, and Afrikaans theological literature gives the reader access to a representative sampling of theological approaches to a given text, both those the reader already knows and some that are new to him or her. This groundwork is the necessary background for a good sermon. In truth, we can say that the book breathes an air of ecumenicity—in our opinion, the only air in which a sermon can be born and developed to maturity!

Our choice of texts deserves some explanation. We have arranged the pericopes in three cycles of eight Sundays each: Easter Sunday, the first, second, third, and fourth Sundays after Easter, Ascension Day (appropriate also for the fifth Sunday after Easter), the Sunday after Ascension (i.e., the sixth after Easter), and Pentecost. Although none of the cycles adheres to a particular year from the *New Common Lectionary*, the book can indeed be used by any minister who does follow the lectionary. Of the twenty-three texts in this volume (one text is applied to two Sundays), seventeen are prescribed by the lectionary for use during the period from Easter Vigil to Pentecost. Those seventeen texts are actually suggested in the lectionary for thirty-three occasions during the three-year cycle, so a preacher using this book will find numerous occasions to use the pericopes it contains.

Of the remaining six texts, three are prescribed by the lectionary elsewhere in the church year. We maintain that all six, however, are ideally suited for preaching on resurrection themes during the seasons of Easter, Ascension, and Pentecost: Psalm 87 (the universal mission of God's glorious Zion, suited for the Sunday following Ascension or even for Pentecost); Ecclesiastes 9:7-10 (the intriguing comparison of the vain life under the sun and the inevitable emptiness of Sheol); John 11:25- 26 (Jesus' claim that he is the resurrection and the life when Lazarus is still in the tomb); 1 Corinthians 15:29-34 and 1 Corinthians 15:50-58 (both important parts of the well-known chapter on the resurrection); and 1 Thessalonians 4:13-18 (Paul's admonition not to grieve as those who have no hope and his imagery of the Lord's coming again). The appropriateness of these texts for this time during the church year is abundantly clear.

We offer this volume in the sincere hope that it will help other preachers to proclaim the Word of God as it is contained in the preaching text: this is what every sermon must do, for any generation and for any denomination.

C. W. BURGER
B. A. MÜLLER
D. J. SMIT

Preaching around the Calendar

The resurrection of the crucified Christ is the point on which the weekly and annual cycles of the Christian calendar turn. In fact, it supplies the clue to the whole history of salvation and indeed the cosmos. Every Sunday and every Easter Day is a commemoration and celebration of the resurrection of Jesus and an anticipation of the day when the same Lord will come again in glory to judge the living and the dead and finally establish God's definitive and universal kingdom.[1]

Sunday

Let us begin by looking at Sunday. It was "on the first day of the week" that the tomb of Jesus was found empty (Matt. 28:1; Mark 16:2; Luke 24:1; John 20:1) and the risen Lord interpreted the Scriptures to the two on the road to Emmaus and revealed himself to them, and later to his other disciples, at table (Luke 24:13-32, 33-49). In Paul's time, the Christians at Ephesus gathered on "the first day of the week" to hear the apostle preach and to break bread (Acts 20:7-11). A century later, Justin Martyr reports that Christians from town and country gather together in one place "on the day of the sun" in order to hear the Scriptures read and expounded and to make eucharist: "We assemble on Sunday because it is the first day, that on which God transformed the darkness and matter to create the world, and also because Jesus Christ our Savior rose from the dead on the same day (*First Apology,* 67). The contemporary Epistle of Barnabas, taking the recurrent first day as also the eighth, speaks of "celebrating with gladness the eighth day, in which Jesus rose from the dead," "the beginning of a new world" (15:8-9) or, as Basil of Caesarea put it in the fourth century, "the image of the age to come" (*On the Holy Spirit,* 27). All these themes are resumed in Charles Wesley's hymn "For the Lord's Day":

> Come, let us with our Lord arise,
> Our Lord, who made both earth and skies;

1

Who died to save the world he made,
And rose triumphant from the dead;
He rose, the Prince of life and peace,
And stamped the day for ever his. . . .

Then let us render him his own,
With solemn prayer approach the throne,
With meekness hear the gospel word,
With thanks his dying love record;
Our joyful hearts and voices raise,
And fill his courts with songs of praise.

When the followers of Jesus assemble "in his name," they find the risen Lord present "in their midst" (cf. Matt. 18:20). For the preacher in particular, this is the ground and realization of the promise that, when the gospel is proclaimed, "whoever hears you, hears me" (Luke 10:16). All faithful preaching of "Christ crucified" (1 Cor. 1:23) is the gift of Christ's enabling presence and a means by which the living Lord continues to speak to his people and to the world. Even when the resurrection is not specially emphasized (and we shall see later that it is quite appropriate for the preacher to focus on other events in the Lord's career over the course of the year), every sermon is implicitly a testimony to the resurrection and an offer of eternal life to those who through Christ come to God in repentance, trust, and obedience. That the Christian assembly, and the preaching which is a constitutive element in it, regularly take place on a Sunday is an expression, in the symbolism of cosmic and historical time, of the foundational, continuing, and yet-to-be-fulfilled importance of the resurrection of the crucified Christ to the gospel, the history of salvation, and the destiny of the world.

The Eastern Orthodox think of every Sunday as "a little Easter." In reverse, Athanasius of Alexandria had already called the fifty days of the Easter season "one great Sunday." Let us look for a moment at Easter as the church's yearly focus on Christ's death and resurrection.

Easter

The Christian Passover

"Christ our passover has been sacrificed for us" (1 Cor. 5:7; cf. John 13:1, 19:36). The earliest Christian Pascha appears to have been a unitary commemoration and celebration of Christ's death and resurrection. In the Asian churches the feast was kept each year on 14 Nisan; in

Rome, on the following Sunday. The Roman practice won out by the third or fourth century. The Easter night of Saturday to Sunday, during which the paschal vigil was held, remained in that time of keen eschatological expectation the favored moment for the Lord's final advent. The Old Testament prophecies, whose reading formed the scriptural core of the vigil service, had found their first fulfillment in the death and resurrection of Christ, and now their universal consummation was awaited. Good Friday, which emerged into prominence with the more chronologically, geographically, and even dramatically oriented liturgical events of Holy Week around the sites of Jerusalem in the later fourth century,[2] had some earlier grounding in the weekly observance of Fridays as a fast day.[3] Palm Sunday, and then Maundy Thursday, are purely annual occasions, in which the historical commemoration of the detailed events of Jesus' entry into Jeruslaem and the Last Supper is the dominant content.

Eastertide

From Tertullian we know also that, as early as the second century, Easter extended forward into a "most joyful season" of fity days.[4] During the entire seven weeks of Eastertide, Christians did not kneel for prayer but rather stood in order to mark the heavenly location of believers in the risen and exalted Christ, in anticipation of the general resurrection; nor did they fast, for they were enjoying a foretaste of the heavenly banquet with the messianic bridegroom. Easter was the season of the Alleluia, a hopeful sign of the time when "we shall do nothing but praise God" (Augustine).[5] The oldest practice of the church draws heavily on the Fourth Gospel, the Acts of the Apostles, and the Apocalypse for scriptural readings during "the great fifty days": the followers of Christ, rejoicing in the gift of the other Paraclete, the Spirit of truth, spread the good news of salvation and taste the life of heaven.

Pentecost

The fiftieth day of Easter retained the name that could also designate the whole period: Pentecost. The first evidence we have of a special feast to "seal" the pentecostal period comes from the fourth century.[6] In dependence on Acts 2:1ff., the gift of the Holy Spirit to the 120 is commemorated and the Spirit's abiding presence in the life and witness of the church is celebrated. Our oldest testimony to the feast links the descent of the Spirit to the ascent of Christ, and preachers continued to make the connection.[7] A separate observance of the Ascension on the fortieth day (cf. Acts 1:3) is, however, attested only a little later than the evidence for the feast of Pentecost of the fiftieth. It may be that first Pentecost, and then Ascension as a distinct feast, together with the development of Holy Week, all mark a growing tendency to historicism in the church's liturgical sense, where the church of the earliest centuries had held the death, resurrection, and exaltation of Christ closer together in a single mystery whose evangelistic and eschatological import was brought home to the assembled believers by the Holy Spirit.

The permanent contribution to the Easter/Pentecost season to the method and message of the preacher resides in its insistence on the theological inseparability of Christ and the Spirit. The Spirit of truth, the other Paraclete, brings to remembrance all that Jesus has said (John 14:26), takes the things of Christ and declares them (16:14), vivifies the flesh which even in the case of the Incarnate Word is of no avail on its own (6:63). When Peter preaches under the Holy Spirit's inspiration, it is Christ crucified and risen that he proclaims, and baptism in the name of Jesus Christ is promised to bring the gift of the Holy Spirit (Acts 2:14ff., 38). It is only by the Holy Spirit that one can confess "Jesus is Lord" (1 Cor. 12:3), and when the Spirit is given to believers, it is to transform them into the likeness of their Lord (2 Cor. 3:18; cf. Gal. 5:5-6, 13-25). The Spirit enables Christ's fellow-heirs to call God "Abba" (Rom. 8:14ff.; Gal. 4:6). It is through Christ that we have heard the gospel, become believers, and been sealed with the Holy Spirit as the pledge of our inheritance unto a day of redemption (Eph. 1:13-14, 4:30). "If the Spirit of him who raised Jesus from the dead dwells in you, he who raised Christ Jesus from the dead will give life to your mortal bodies also through his Spirit which dwells in you" (Rom. 8:11). What is thematically celebrated in "the great fifty days" governs the message and method of all faithful preaching.

Beginning locally before the year 1000, the Western church has kept the first Sunday after Pentecost as Trinity Sunday. This more "dogmatic" feast can serve at least two purposes: it is a reminder that the work of our salvation—the self-giving incarnation and passion of the Son, his exaltation and continuing intercession, and the mission of the Spirit—is grounded in the eternal mystery of God; and it also allows us to rejoice in the fact that Christian worship is no less than a creaturely sharing in the life and communion of the Triune God.

Lent

The calendrical influence of Easter extends also backwards through Lent. In the patristic church, the Paschal vigil was the high moment for the administration of baptism into the death and resurrection of Christ. The climactic rites of Christian initiation described in the so-called *Apostolic Tradition of Hippolytus* belong to the great service of Easter Eve. After a preparatory catechumenate of several years, the learners finally emerged as "the elect," and in the weeks immediately preceding Easter they underwent decisive instruction in the faith, summarized at last in the creed and in the Lord's Prayer, and the candidates were solemnly exorcized in order to "make room" for the Holy Spirit who would henceforth fill their lives. Our season of Lent originated in the final weeks of preparation for baptism. It became also the season when penitents were made ready to have their baptismal privileges restored to them. Because we never outgrow our baptism, and indeed all of us continue throughout this life to struggle in grace to master the remnants of sin, it eventually came to be regarded as a salutary practice for all believers to "remake" their own baptismal preparations each year during Lent. In our own time, the Roman Catholic Church, in a widely imitated step, has introduced into its Paschal liturgy a "renewal of baptismal vows." Traditional Scripture readings for Lent relate the story of redemption and include Old Testament types of baptism as well as Gospel episodes which have baptismal resonances. The preacher has the opportunity to recall Christians to their baptismal foundations, somewhat in the way the apostle Paul grounded his exhortations and ethical instructions in the decisive act of grace which baptism signifies (e.g. Rom. 6; 1 Cor. 6:11, 12:12-13; Col. 2:11–3:17).

There is, however, a secondary pivot in what may perhaps be thought of as the irregular ellipse of the church year, namely the incarnation of the Word. It is to Christmas as a focal celebration that we now look.

Christmas

The Savior's Birth

When Jesus saw the light of day, it was in fact rather the world that was being illuminated by the incarnation of the divine Word. The birth of the eternal Son of God from a human mother was the early dawn of a new day, the drawing near of "the Sun of righteousness" (Mal. 4:2). Although Scripture does not help us to determine Christ's nativity on December 25 (Rome) or January 6 (Egypt), it was doubtless influenced along one track or another by the natural practice of observing the winter solstice as the point at which "the sun begins again to grow." Eventually the Roman date won out. That the present-day Slavonic Orthodox appear to celebrate Christmas on a different date (thirteen days after what the rest of the world calls December 25) is only due to their refusal to make the "secular" transition from the Julian to the Gregorian calendar.

Epiphany

Some other aspects of Christ's "manifestation" to the world were left to a January season of Epiphany (Greek *epiphaneia;* Latin *manifestatio*): his showing to the Gentiles (the Western church placed the visit of the Magi on January 6, whereas the East associates it directly with Christmas), his public appearance as the divine Son (the Eastern church places Christ's baptism on January 6, and the Western church traditionally kept January 13), and the shining forth of his glory at the wedding feast of Cana (the second Sunday after Epiphany in the West). An ancient Latin Epiphany antiphon weaves these themes together beautifully:

> Today the heavenly Bridegroom weds his Church,
> since Christ has washed away her sins in the Jordan;
> the wise men hasten with their gifts to the royal wedding,
> and the guests are made glad by the water turned to wine.

A hymn by Christopher Wordsworth prolongs this threefold manifestation into Christ's ultimate epiphany:

> Sun and moon shall darkened be,
> Stars shall fall, the heavens shall flee;
> Christ will then like lightning shine.
> All will see his glorious sign;
> All will then the trumpet hear,
> All will see the Judge appear:
> Thou by all wilt be confest,
> God in Man made manifest.
>
> Grant us grace to see thee, Lord,
> Mirrored in thy holy word;
> May we imitate thee now,
> And be pure, as pure art thou;

That we like to thee may be
At thy great Epiphany;
And may praise thee, ever blest,
God in Man made manifest.[8]

The preacher's task is to allow the glory of God to be seen in the face of Christ Jesus (2 Cor. 4:6), so that, being by that beholding changed from glory into glory (3:18), the righteous by faith may at the last shine like the sun (Matt. 13:43).

Advent

Epiphany became, after Easter and Pentecost, the next most favored moment for Christian baptism; and the preceding season of Advent, which is confined to Western Christianity, may in that respect have had origins similar to Lent. The liturgical themes of Advent, however, offer only a few hints of preparation for individual baptism and seem rather to envisage more directly the first and final comings of Christ. They encourage Christians to relive the Old Testament expectations that they believe were fulfilled at Bethlehem and, simultaneously, to prepare themselves for the Lord's return at the consummation. Isaiah is a favored source of Scripture lessons, since the book lends itself to a "stereoscopic" reading that sees the prophecies as both realized in Christ and yet still outstanding until the End.

The preacher will use the season of Advent not only to build up to the celebration of Christmas but also, following medieval practice, to confront the "four last things" of death and judgment, heaven and hell. This is the existential application to each individual of Christ's awaited coming again in glory to judge the quick and the dead (cf. 2 Cor. 5:10).

Two traditional feasts related to the date of Christmas are the Annunciation (March 25, nine months before December 25; cf. Luke 1:26-38) and the Presentation of Christ in the Temple (February 2, forty days after Christmas; cf. Luke 2:22-40).

The Rest of the Year

If we were to draw the "irregular ellipse" of the church's year, we should find the line fading into brokenness shortly after the feast of the Epiphany (January 6) until just before Lent (for many centuries the West had the pre-Lenten Sundays of Septuagesima, Sexagesima, and Quinquagesima), and then again from Pentecost or Trinity Sunday until just before Advent (the twentieth-century Roman feast of Christ the King, now placed on the Sunday immediately preceding Advent, is but the most recent instance of anticipating the season). For long the "green" Sundays—the most "neutral" color for liturgical vestments—were numbered "after Epiphany" and "after Pentecost" or "after Trinity." Beyond the first week or two, these scarcely constituted coherent seasons, although there may still be continuing tendencies to thematize the earthly life and ministry of Jesus particularly in the former case, and the ongoing life and mission of the church in the second. The current Roman Catholic bluntly designates these periods as "ordinary time" *(per annum)*.

"Ordinary Sundays" remain, however, precisely *Sundays*. That fact calls the preacher to bring the Scripture readings and the sermon into relation to the pivotal event and mystery of Christ's death and resurrection.

Lectionaries

Lectionaries do not fall directly from heaven. Rather they codify and promote patterns in the liturgical reading of Scripture that have commended themselves to the church over a greater or lesser extent of time, space, and confessional tradition. They are necessary because it is impossible to read the whole of the Bible in a particular service of worship; they are valuable in so far as they allow the broad range of the biblical witness to be heard. Lectionaries perpetually exhibit a certain tension between the reading of entire biblical books in course *(lectio continua)* and the eclectic selection of passages from the canon that are appropriate to particular times and occasions. The more definite the theological or christological content of a feast or season, the more likely are the lessons from the Old Testament and the New (Epistle and Gospel) to be arranged for their typological and thematic point and counterpoint; this is a strong testimony to belief in the unity of the Scripture, although there is a danger that the Old Testament in particular will be used for snippets to match the New. On the other hand, the individual books of the Bible have a greater chance of communicating their characteristic message when they are read more continuously. Mixed cases are found in, say, the semicontinuous reading of Isaiah in Advent, or of St. John, the Acts, and the Revelation in Eastertide.

The many coincidences of lectionary patterns over time, space and confessional boundaries bear witness to a remarkably common sense among Christians as to what Scriptures belong when, if the full range of redemptive history is to be commemorated, celebrated, and anticipated over a regularly recurring period (hitherto usually a year). In recent decades, various ecumenical efforts have been made to bring the various confessional practices into even greater harmony. In Britain, *The Calendar and Lectionary* (1967) of the semi-official Joint Liturgical Group, which spreads the readings over a two-year period, has exercised great influence on the official revisions of Anglican and Protestant churches. Unfortunately, this pioneering work has tended to isolate the British, since churches in other areas, particularly of the English-speaking world, have preferred to base themselves on the three-year Sunday and festive lectionary of the postconciliar Roman Catholic Church (*Lectionary for Mass,* 1969). In particular, the pattern of "naming" the three years after the Gospels of Matthew, Mark, and Luke has proved popular. In some respects, however, the Roman lectionary has undergone adaptation in its reception by others. Thus the American Consultation on Common Texts, in order to void the sometimes strained typologies of the Roman Old Testament snippets, has attempted a more continuous reading of the Old Testament in each of the three years in the Sundays after Pentecost, with only a rough typological correspondence between the Pentateuch and Matthew, the Davidic narrative and Mark, and the Prophets and Luke.

Protestant preachers in many regions and denominations are increasingly finding it a boon to have the scriptural matter of their sermons "provided" for them through the use of a lectionary. If, as Karl Barth almost implied on a couple of occasions, one should preach with the Bible in one hand and the newspaper in the other,[9] the use of a lectionary offers a better chance for the Scriptures to norm our current perceptions of the world and human affairs, rather than the other way around. This is not to say that a particular event may not sometimes impel the preacher to turn to another Scripture for the sermon, but the congregation ought not to be robbed of the steady and consistent reading of the Scriptures in the worship assembly as a long-term formative factor in the shaping of their perspectives upon reality and action.

We thereby come close to one final theme that has tentatively surfaced at a number of points in our discussion and now needs to be dug out: the theme of history and mystery, of time and eschatology.

History and Eschatology

It is sometimes argued that the fourth century marked a dramatically new phase in the Christian understanding of history and this temporal world.[10] Certainly it is no accident that this century—that of Constantine's conversion—provides our first evidence for an annual Holy Week (Palm Sunday, Maundy Thursday, Good Friday), a feast on the Day of Pentecost (and soon a separate Ascension Day), and a celebration of the Savior's birthday and public appearance (with Christmas and Epiphany becoming distinct feasts). Yet it may be a mistake to discern a drastic change rather than a more subtle and gradual shift of emphasis.[11] There was no sudden decline from *kairos* into *chronos* (to use a distinction beloved of an older biblical theology). The church's constantinian "settlement into the world" was foreshadowed, if H. Conzelmann's exegesis of Luke-Acts in *Die Mitte der Zeit* has value at all, in the Lucan accommodation to the delay of the Parousia.

There was probably from the first a touch of historical commemoration in the early designation, as we saw of Wednesday and Friday as weekly fastdays. The weekly Sunday and the yearly Easter, both inferable from the New Testament writings, commemorate the raising of Jesus from the dead, which was considered as *at least* an historical event. The resurrection was, of course, *more*. That is why Christian worship is always also a celebration of Christ's presence and an anticipation of the Lord's return. With Christ the final kingdom began its irruption into this world, and all our created time has become, as the Orthodox theologian Olivier Clément puts it, "porous" to God.[12] Every Sunday, in particular, is a declaration of the eschatological qualification brought to time and history by the resurrection of the crucified Christ from the dead.

Our time, though so qualified, is not abolished. The Savior himself "needed"—we can infer after the event—the years of his earthly life, from the moment of his conception to the day of his ascension, for the multi-faceted work of redemption. Moreover, the mystery of God's design for the world apparently includes the centuries that have since passed. And still the Parousia has not taken place. What is worked out in time and history will belong, we conclude, to the final kingdom of God, however marvellous the transformation it will undergo in the general resurrection which Christ's presaged. If the Creator's saving purpose accommodates itself to time and history in these ways, it is entirely appropriate to commemorate, celebrate, and anticipate it in the temporal symbolism which the church's calendar represents. That is in no way to deny the openness of all Christian worship and the whole of Christian existence to the entire mystery of God.[13]

GEOFFREY WAINWRIGHT

Notes

1. The present brief survey aims simply to indicate the theological importance both of the principle of a Christian calendar and of the main features of the church year; it is intended particularly for Protestant preachers who are beginning to rediscover the riches of traditional usage in these respects. The really seminal book in the English-speaking world has been A. A. McArthur, *The Evolution of the Christian Year* (London: SCM Press, 1953). The computational hypotheses of T. J. Talley, *The Origins of the Liturgical Year* (New York: Pueblo, 1986), have not yet been subjected to scholarly scrutiny. Current Roman Catholic scholarship and practice is represented by A. Adam, *Das Kirchenjahr mitfeiern: seine Geschichte und Bedeutung nach der Liturgieerneuerung* (Freiburg in Breisgau: Herder, 1979; ET *The Liturgical Year* [New York: Pueblo, 1981]), and very concisely in the same author's *Grundriss Liturgie* (Freiburg in Breisgau: Herder, 1985), pp. 256-295. The most useful Eastern study for our purposes is probably G. Barrois, *Scripture Readings in Orthodox Worship* (Crestwood, N.Y.: St. Vladimir's Seminary Press, 1977).

2. See J. Wilkinson, *Egeria's Travels to the Holy Land* (Warminster: Aris and Phillips, rev. edition 1981); also J. G. Davies, *Holy Week: A Short History* (Richmond, Va: John Knox Press, 1963).

3. See Didache 8:1, and Tertullian, *On Fasts,* 2. The other weekly fast day was Wednesday. The *Didascalia Apostolorum,* 21, links these days with Judas's betrayal and Jesus' crucifixion.

4. Tertullian, *On Baptism,* 19, and in other places.

5. Augustine, Letter 55 (to Januarius), 15, 28 (Migne, *PL* 33, 218); cf. Sermon 254, 4 (Migne, *PL* 38, 1184).

6. Eusebius of Caesarea, *Life of Constantine* IV, 64 (Migne, *PG* 20, 1220). The one major flaw in McArthur's study (see note 1) is to see a feast of the fiftieth day, as distinct from the whole fifty days, already in Tertullian.

7. For example, Maximus of Turin, Homily 60 (Migne, *PL* 57, 370), and Peter Chrysologus, Sermon 85/3 (*Corpus Christianorum,* series latina 24, p. 528).

8. An Anglican bishop, Christopher Wordsworth (1807-85) was prompted to bring out the eschatological dimension by the Epistle (1 John 3:1-8) and Gospel (Matt. 24:23-31) appointed in the Book of Common Prayer for the sixth Sunday after Epiphany, the last possible end of an Epiphany "season." His hymn begins "Songs of thankfulness and praise."

9. See Karl Barth, *The Epistle to the Romans* (ET London: Oxford, 1935),

p. 425, and *Dogmatics in Outline* (ET London: SCM, 1949), p. 33. Barth's point in the first context is closeness to life, in the second the need for a translation from "the language of Canaan."

10. See especially G. Dix, *The Shape of the Liturgy* (London: Dacre Press [A. & C. Black], 1945), chapter 11: "The sanctification of time."

11. A recent nuanced discussion of this complex question is found in R. F. Taft, "Historicism Revisited" in *Studia Liturgica* 14 (1982), pp. 97-109.

12. O. Clément, *Transfigurer le temps: notes sur le temps à la lumière de la tradition orthodoxe* (Neuchâtel: Delachaux & Niestlé, 1959). See also my chapter on "Sacramental Time" in G. Wainwright, *The Ecumenical Moment* (Grand Rapids: Eerdmans, 1983), pp. 120-133.

13. The relations between history and eschatology, as expressed in commemoration, celebration, and anticipation, could also be studied in connection with saints' days, the "sanctorale." Reasons of space have led to our concentration on the "temporale," which is theologically more fundamental. For hints on a proper place for the saints in Protestant worship see G. Wainwright, *Doxology* (New York: Oxford University Press, 1980), pp. 109-112.

Preaching during Easter

1. This introduction is divided into two sections. In the first part some of the difficulties surrounding the proclamation of the resurrection are discussed. In the second part the content of the Easter message is examined, looking at themes that are present in the New Testament itself and in the history of its interpretation. It is possible therefore to start with the second section without reading the first.

I. The Importance, Difficulties, and Correct Mode of Easter Proclamation

The Importance of the Resurrection

2. The gospel of Jesus Christ is the gospel of resurrection. The resurrection is the heart of all Christian proclamation, faith, life, and theology. In a very real way all Christian proclamation is therefore proclamation of the resurrection. Easter is the "origin as well as the content of all Christian preaching" (Josuttis). On the one hand, it is justifiable to say that the Christian proclamation, when viewed from a historical perspective, only started with the events of Easter. It is only since Easter that the Christian message and therefore Christian proclamation really exists. On the other hand, it is equally true that, when viewed from a systematic perspective, the Easter message forms the most fundamental supposition of all Christian preaching and is its very heart. Without Christ's resurrection, all Christian proclamation would be void and worthless. All Christian preaching remains, directly or indirectly, a further explication of the original message of and witness to the resurrection of Christ.

A variety of quotations from well-known literature can serve to demonstrate this. All Christian proclamation bears the character of Easter (Kamphaus). Every Sunday is therefore nothing less than a new Easter Day in miniature (Van Ruler). Easter is "the liberation to the word" (Josuttis), i.e. the legitimation and authority of the Christian wit-

ness. The meaning and the truth of all Christian ministry is situated in
the presence of the living and exalted Lord himself (Kamphaus). This
already applies to New Testament preaching. The four Gospels are
Easter narratives with elaborate introductions (Rengstorf, alluding to
the well-known formulation of Kähler). "Nowhere in the Bible can we
find anything comparable to these last chapters of the Gospels. . . .
They strike the key-note on which the gospel must always be proclaimed" (Noordmans). The resurrection plays a fundamental role in all
New Testament writings and forms the focus of everything they proclaim (Wilckens). Without the resurrection of Jesus Christ there would
be no church and consequently no preaching (Marxsen). The church
ceases to be the church whenever it begins to keep silent about the proclamation of Easter (Josuttis). "The resurrection is the *punctum stantis
et cadentis,* the very touchstone, of the Christian faith and of the
genuineness of Jesus Christ as well. Without it there would be no
Christ" (Boff). It serves as a testimony to Luther's profound personal
insight in the center, the heart, the deepest foundation of Christian proclamation and truth when it is recounted how he, in moments of great affliction from without and within, wrote in big letters on his desk: *"Vivit!
Er lebt!"* ("He lives!")

The Embarrassment of Easter Proclamation

3. In view of this fundamental role that the resurrection plays in
the message of the gospel, it is almost astounding to see how little of
this is reflected in the practice of Christian preaching, faith, life, and
theology.

It shows very clearly in preaching. In the Western church's liturgical year, seven weeks are faithfully devoted to the preaching of Lent.
The same prominence, however, has not been given to the resurrection
during the weeks that follow Easter Sunday. In very early Christianity
it was completely different. The festive celebration of Easter was very
important. At cock-crow, the fasting and vigil of the night suddenly
turned into jubilation and ecstasy—the lights were kindled, and baptism was administered. Even the forty days preceding Easter were often
not devoted to Lenten preaching as it is widely practiced today, but to
the proclamation of the resurrection. At present, the preaching of the
resurrection, instead of being central and festive, is meager and problematic. Virtually all literature on the preaching of the resurrection, exegetical as well as homiletical, accepts its problematic nature as given

and therefore proceeds from it. Berkhof, for example, discusses the "embarrassment" of Western preaching, which he attributes to the fact that Westerners "have no Easter message at all"!

This embarrassment is, however, only the symptom of a much more profound issue, namely that the resurrection does not play a fundamental role in the entirety of Christian life and thought. In Catholic theology this "stepmotherly treatment" (Gesché) has been widely acknowledged in recent years.[1] The same, however, also applies to Protestant theology.[2] Numerous theories exist on the reasons for this phenomenon.

a. Some explain it *psychologically,* referring to "Western sobriety" (Berkhof) and the accompanying lack of ability to "celebrate" truly and to experience the essence of liturgical realities (Nörenberg; cf. the number of recent publications promoting the elements of "festivity" and "celebration," e.g., Moltmann, Cox, et al.).

b. Many others ascribe it to the process of secularization, which results in modern-day listeners no longer possessing any "obvious point of contact" with the message of the resurrection (Josuttis). This is closely related to the widespread conviction that influences present Western exegesis so strongly, namely that the earlier (i.e. New Testament) "worldview" has become outdated and is no longer capable of conveying the "meaning" or "actual kerygma" of the Easter message. This worldview is regarded as the real cause of the "embarrassment" surrounding the resurrection and the "stepmotherly treatment" it receives.

That opinion is expressed in a very representative way by Marxsen, who sees the physical resurrection as "an interpretament," i.e. one possible interpretation alongside of others already present even within the New Testament itself. According to him, it is not even the best interpretation available. In this view, it is possible to explain the reality or meaning of the "resurrection of Jesus" without referring to a physical resurrection, and such commentators hold that this interpretation is more appropriate than the specific interpretation that we find in the New Testament.

c. Still others ascribe this lack of interest in the resurrection to historical developments within theological traditions. Already at a very early stage of soteriology, emphasis was laid either on the suffering and the cross (the Latin Fathers) or on the incarnation (the Greek Fathers). According to both of these traditions (and their combinations), the resurrection plays only a subordinate role. It either serves as the confirmation that God the Father has accepted the voluntary sacrifice of the Son (Latin), or as the final proof for Christ's divinity (Greek). In both of these traditions the fundamental role of the resurrection in the New Testament is no longer operative.

This developed further with the Arian struggle and the decisions of Nicea, after which the divinity of Christ became a widespread and dominant idea, extending also to popular piety. It became increasingly difficult to attach much value to the resurrection. Rather than being something new, surprising, and wonderful, it became almost incomprehensible and confusing for many people. It came to be regarded as an almost inevitable consequence of Christ's divinity, so that the emphasis in Scripture on this powerful act of God, as well as the accompanying conviction that in the resurrection Christ had been made someone, had been given a special name, and had been appointed to a new and unique position of authority and honor became a cause of embarrassment for some classical expositors. These developments can still be seen in some versions of the doctrine of Christ's humiliation and exaltation, in which the treatment is overly logical and overly systematic. The resurrection is then robbed of much of its centrality and uniqueness.

The final result of these developments has been that within traditional theology the resurrection is often only discussed in one of three contexts (Gesché). It is sometimes used in apologetics (or fundamental theology) to prove Christ's divinity, and/or the legitimacy of his mission, and/or even the truth of Scripture. It is also sometimes used within christology to prove the perfection of his divine nature. And it is sometimes used in soteriology as the "noetic" affirmation of the salvific meaning of the cross, i.e. it does not add anything new but only "explains" the cross. It is clearly not possible for the preacher to establish the central role of the resurrection in the New Testament traditions along any of these lines of argument. In these contexts, the resurrection becomes only one more truth in addition to others, instead of "the center and source of light" of the Christian faith, "the organizing principle," "the central root of all truth" in Christianity, from which everything else radiates (Scheffczyk).

d. Some theologians maintain that the daily experience of suffering may make people more susceptible to the message of the cross than to a message of joy and victory and life. People may simply not have the antennae to receive the resurrection message; it may not strike any chord in their everyday experience. That may be the reason many people view life as a process of extended suffering, like a "long good Friday," rather than as the "theater of his glory," where his power and his victory can already be experienced. They feel more at home during the Lenten worship of the church than during the celebration of Easter.

e. Others draw attention to still another fundamental cause of embarrassment, the strangeness of this message itself. It was, after all, a stumbling block for the Jews (cf. the mockery of the Sadducees). According to the false preachers in Corinth the resurrection was not humanly possible. For the Greeks on the Areopagus it was the ultimate offense. Even for the earliest witnesses, the women and the disciples, it caused, more than anything else, fear and trembling! Something of this embarrassment—almost apprehension—was probably at work when Barth, after thoroughly exegeting 1 Corinthians 15, asked Thurneysen to preach in his place. Barth explained that this chapter turned him into an invalid!

Our problem with the resurrection, according to Noordmans, is actually no problem; the reverse is really the case: if we had no problem with this message, *that* would be cause for alarm! In a meditation on the words of the angel, "Do not be afraid" (Matt. 28:5), he writes that on Easter morning an encounter took place between two worlds, the world in which we live and the world for which we hope. Noordmans notes that in the biblical narratives, the first thing that seems to always strike those who enter our world "from the other side" is our fear of what we call eternity. Consequently this is the first thing dealt with during such encounters. When reading the resurrection narratives, we time and again experience the same anxiety that the first witnesses experienced, simply because we, too, do not know what to think or say about it.

> This phenomenon in itself does not necessarily prove a lack of faith. The opposite attitude would rather have been alarming, i.e. if the resurrection were accepted as such an obvious and normal fact that there no longer remained any room for the astonishment of the evangelists. The real stumbling block when the congregation celebrates Easter is consequently not so much intellectual doubt but fear. We fear an invasion of God into our lives. . . . It sounds strange to say this, but this fear is a fear of the joy which is proclaimed to us on Easter. We see how even the women and the disciples repeatedly shrank back from this joy. There is hardly another issue on which the Gospels are so clear and so

unanimous.

According to the Bible, *this* is the biggest problem we have with the resurrection. We feel distressed, not because we do not understand it, but because we fear this absolute joy. We have learned to love our troubles. Some people even seem to find the very essence of human existence in our troubles and anxieties. We have trained ourselves to hide and to seek cover and now we want to use all these shelters which we have built, simply because we have them and we are so accustomed to them. Our hearts do not know what it means to be safe and saved where the last enemy, death itself, has been conquered. And for that reason we do not understand what life really is. Will the walls of our hearts be able to stand the inpouring of eternal joy? That is the question which truly forms the sting in our fear of Easter.[3]

Attempts to Overcome the Embarrassment

4. Whatever the causes for this embarrassment may be, it is simply a fact beyond any doubt that Easter preaching has suffered and still suffers from severe uncertainty and attenuation. Preachers, in different traditions and divergent contexts, often do not know how to handle this strange and powerful message. An important result is that several attempts are commonly made to counter these difficulties by adapting the message to something more easily understood and accepted. It is possible to list a variety of these attempts.

a. One well-known way of evading the "paradoxical commission" of Easter proclamation—"witnessing boldly against the power of death" (Josuttis)—is to try to make this message more comprehensible and credible by harmonizing it with the world of human experience. This search often produces miscellaneous "analogies" between ordinary human life and the gospel of the resurrection. Especially in Anglo-Saxon preaching this is a popular method. The point of the resurrection is then frequently changed into an (albeit powerful) illustration of general truths or principles, e.g., that "good always triumphs over evil" or that "life always blooms again after death," as the succession of the seasons also shows. In the Northern hemisphere Easter often coincides with the beginning of spring, which makes this kind of argument even more attractive. Easter is therefore often celebrated as a symbol of the recurring start of new life in the natural world (and almost nothing more), an interpretation which, of course, makes it more comprehensible and acceptable, but which also radically distorts the original meaning of the New Testament's proclamation.

It is within such a context that Noordmans' well-known remark must be seen, namely that "true proclamation of Christ's resurrection resembles a philosophical discourse on 'flesh and spirit' as little as a flash of lightning resembles fog!"[4] Especially in German homiletical literature, strong warnings are issued against this type of preaching, for losing the uniqueness of the event of Christ's resurrection, and for exchanging its final and once-and-for-all significance for general truths originating from ordinary human experience or speculative discussions.

Scheffczyk warns that modern theology is continuously faced with this same temptation—to change this message into something that fits human experience better. He is of the opinion that systematic theology often fails to appreciate the real depth of Christ's resurrection, e.g., when Jesus is seen merely as an ethical example, only as "the man for others" (Bonhoeffer), or only as "the bearer of a new freedom" (Van Buren), or only as "the one who, out of a revolutionary love for humankind, is willing and able to die without fear" (Pesch). According to Noordmans, all these and similar interpretations remain stuck within the domain of human possibilities only. If the reality of the resurrection is lacking simply because people find it too difficult to believe, it is not the real gospel of Jesus Christ. According to him, this is a choice—between an acceptable message of ethical, human possibilities and a message that recognizes the reality of the resurrection—that modern theology and the church simply cannot evade.[5]

b. Another widespread type of Easter proclamation is what Berkhof calls the "just as/so also" method (the "evenals-zoo-ook-methode"). This represents yet another attempt to push the unique, once-for-all character of Christ's resurrection to the background and to put the emphasis on an existential or personal repetition of the events and experiences described in the biblical narratives. Members of present-day congregations are summoned to place themselves in the position of the characters in the narratives in order to share their experiences of Jesus. Just as they met, saw, heard, and experienced Jesus, so also can—and must—we still meet, see, hear, and experience Jesus. Just as the women, Peter, Mary, the disciples, and the pilgrims on their way to Emmaus, so also must we search for Jesus in order to meet him as they did.

One is justified in saying that the recent awakening in Catholic ranks concerning the Easter proclamation very often, unfortunately, does not show much difference from this method. Much attention is devoted to the study of the Easter preaching of the oldest Christian literature and the Fathers, e.g. the Easter sermons of Melito of Sardes, Hippolyte of Rome, Zeno of Verona, Pope Leo the Great, etc. In practice, however, this often only results in propagating an existential re-enactment of the "mysteries of the life of Jesus." In the cult-mystery of the Easter night, the participants experience salvation in Christ in the mystical way of the early church (cf. Rahner).

It is indeed important to acknowledge that this new attention to the resurrection within Catholic circles represents a serious attempt to improve on previous Easter preaching. In an instructive investigation, Kamphaus thoroughly analyzed this Catholic preaching, and the results can probably be applied to Protestant preaching as well.[6] He examined 1,500 Catholic sermons, all of them in German and all of them written since World War II. He came to the conclusion that only fifteen of them show signs of serious exegesis! The common form was "reporting," in which the biblical narrative was simply retold in an existential manner, with lots of detail and imagination. Very often small parts of the narrative are isolated (without regard to the thrust or structure of the pericope). The purpose is to encourage Christians to practice specific aspects of a Christian lifestyle. For example, the words "stay with us, for it is toward evening" of the disciples of Emmaus easily lead to meditations on the meaning of evening (the end of the day; the beginning of darkness; the time of rest; etc.) and the importance of evening prayer.

According to Berkhof,[7] these unfruitful methods must be replaced with a "because-therefore" method—seeing Christ's resurrection and his appearances not as timeless, mystical experiences to be repeated through the ages, but as definite events in the history of salvation. *Because* Christ was resurrected by God, *therefore* a new stage in the history of salvation has come into effect. Only with such a method, Berkhof believes, will it be possible to view the resurrection properly as a salvific event of which the fruit, results, or implications can now be proclaimed in order to be heard as good news, as promises, and as gospel.

Should One Preach on the Difficulties Raised by the Historical Nature of the Resurrection?

5. Because it is now commonly acknowledged that the most legitimate way of proclaiming Easter is to proclaim the salvific fact of Jesus' resurrection and its implications, the problems concerning this type of

preaching have in recent years been focused, sometimes almost exclusively, on the question of the legitimacy and the limits of the historical-critical method in this regard and the role it may or even must play in the Easter proclamation.

One can find almost no exegetical literature on the resurrection (including commentaries, monographs, articles, and theologies) that does not deal with the questions raised by these investigations. For very obvious reasons, the issues involved in the use of these methods come to the surface when the resurrection is being discussed in a more serious and fundamental way than it is done anywhere else. The resurrection forms the ultimate test case for these methods. Can the truth of the resurrection be proclaimed with any degree of intellectual honesty when the suppositions of normal historical analysis are taken into account? And vice versa: Is ordinary historical research capable of dealing with religious claims that God has acted within human history?

Naturally, there is no consensus of opinion in the exegetical literature on this point, except for some vague generalities, such as that "something" indeed happened. Even Marxsen, in some ways perhaps the most important figure in the present debate, agrees to this when he opens his now renowned work with the reminder that nobody disagrees with the claim that Jesus rose from the dead. The only question is, he continues, what that means!

Another vague generality is that the ancient worldview of the New Testament is outdated and not an integral part of the kerygma of the resurrection itself. The result is that it is not necessary to accept and believe in this worldview by means of a blind *sacrificium intellectus,* a sacrifice of reason. Again the real question, however, remains. How are we to distinguish between the real kerygma and the outdated worldview! The important question for the minister, preaching to the assembled congregation, is, of course, how to evaluate and use the available literature with its conflicting results and its often radically opposed, but perhaps concealed, presuppositions.

The reader is often warned against two extreme positions, though different authors use different expressions to describe these dangers. O'Collins speaks of "underbelief" and "overbelief," both of which must be avoided.[8] Kamphaus says that it is wrong simply to say that one does not want to shock the congregation's childlike, innocent faith and then to carry on in a naive way as if no problems exist, but that it is equally wrong to find some kind of selfish pleasure simply in the "de-

stroying of false ideas"![9] Kremer warns that all forms of language or
ideas that can create misunderstanding have to be avoided, but that,
simultaneously, the message should be proclaimed unabridged and in
its fullness, even though it may cause annoyance to some listeners.[10]

On the one hand, one may therefore say that the preacher should
try to avoid any unnecessary offense or false stumbling blocks. The
gospel, and especially the gospel of the resurrection, is meant to have
a redemptive and liberating effect on people and should never be experienced as something burdensome or oppressive! For that reason, it
should also be proclaimed in a comprehensible and credible manner.
Naive and even primitive conceptions should not be confused with the
truth of the gospel.

The well-known maxim of the queen in Lewis Carrol's "Through
the Looking-glass and What Alice Found There" is not true of the
preaching of Easter: "Alice laughed. 'There's no use trying,' she said,
'One can't believe impossible things.'

"'I daresay you haven't had much practice,' said the Queen. 'When
I was your age, I always did it for half-an-hour a day. Why, sometimes
I've believed as many as six impossible things before breakfast!'"

The congregation should never experience this message as something that can only be accepted by way of intellectual gymnastics and a
tour de force of the will! In this connection it may therefore be of great
help if the preacher could, in the words of Josuttis, visibly demonstrate
his or her "solidarity" with the questions, problems, and even doubts of
the congregation. The preacher should not be ashamed of the problems
and the congregation's difficulties, and should never try to gloss over
it with dogmatic slogans. Instead we should readily admit that this message is indeed strange and almost incredible. Josuttis adds that a congregation does not need "fascinating orators" on the pulpit, but instead
ordinary human beings who, like themselves, know something of the
radical seriousness of death—yet who can continue to witness that
Jesus was raised on our behalf.[11]

Josuttis consequently pleads that the preacher inform the congregation of the opinions and results of historical criticism, for the sake of
the church, for the sake of believers, and for the minister's own sake.
He is convinced that the irrational reaction that many church members
show toward modern theological viewpoints can be attributed to the
fact that for two centuries believers have been kept in the dark. They
have not been informed of the progress, the serious nature, and the im-

plications of the Enlightenment and the process of secularization. The main reason, he says, is that the church has for the most part been interested primarily in the upbuilding of groups of people whose existential and personal problems have not been of a primarily intellectual nature. According to him this has gradually resulted in an "emigration" of intellectuals from the church, a fact that the church can no longer neglect.

If Christian faith is degraded to the level of simple naiveté, the church will eventually become nothing more than the refuge of those who cannot cope with the responsibilities of modern life and who seek there a haven, free of problems. He also refers to the strange paradox that often the more pious people are, the more difficult it is to discuss matters of faith with them. "Where other people want to understand *(kennen)*, pious people want to confess *(bekennen)*. Where others want to discuss, they want to proclaim. Where others want to raise questions, they want to provide answers."[12]

On the other hand, it should also be kept in mind that Easter proclamation should not be seen as apologetic argument either. It is not an attempt to remove all intellectual and theoretical questions that people may have. It is not an attempt to convince people of the truth of the Christian message. Although all this is very important, the pulpit is not the place for that. Proclamation is much more a witness, the bringing of good news, than it is a rational or philosophical argument. "The preacher simply has to show his or her true colors!"[13]

"Although the preacher ought to be rational, serious, honest, and credible, the task is not to enter an apologetic discussion, but only to proclaim positively the good tidings as someone who believes it personally."[14] For this reason, both Dijk[15] and Berkhof[16] warn preachers not to get involved in such questions once he or she is on the pulpit. Josuttis also acknowledges that the worship service is not the ideal place to raise these questions, regardless of how important they may be. This assumes, of course, that these questions are not presently an issue in the particular congregation. Other, more suitable occasions for discussion are available within the church. It may be important to obtain reliable statistical information on the way the members of a specific congregation think about the resurrection. In several countries and churches, research of this nature has been done, with extremely interesting and useful results.[17]

The "Double Key" of Easter Proclamation

6. Finally, after looking at all the problems and questions surrounding present-day Easter proclamation, it is necessary to return to the central role of Christ's resurrection in the Christian gospel, and to remember that the tone or style of Easter preaching should never be negative and apologetic, but instead positive and certain, witnessing to the good news of God's love and power. This message concerns the very heart of the gospel, the central fact of salvation, proclaimed in all its richness! For this reason, it was customary during the Middle Ages to start the Easter message with a joke, in order to ridicule the final enemy, death! The congregation was to take sheer delight in Christ's sovereignty, and in the absurdity of the resistance against him still present in the world! This wonderful reminder should, however, not mislead anyone to the other extreme, to think that it is warranted to be triumphalistic in the Easter sermon.

Three well-known Dutch theologians who have written extensively on the resurrection may help us understand this strange dialectic in the tone of the church's Easter proclamation.

Van Ruler refers to this dialectic as the "dual key" in which the resurrection must be proclaimed—a major as well as a minor key. In a somewhat artificial way he even juxtaposes the sequences of Luke 24:6a (in some ancient manuscripts only) and Mark 16:6 in order to demonstrate this. Luke reads: "He is not here, but has risen," and Mark: "He has risen, he is not here." Van Ruler explains:

> The single gospel of Christ's resurrection has these different aspects . . . a positive and a negative side. There is something fundamentally positive in the message of Easter: *He has risen.* That is the rock that will make men stumble or the precious rock of salvation, but whichever way one looks at it, it is a rock. That is the positive, the unshakeable, immovable, unalterable *fact* from which there is no escape.
>
> There is, however, also something fundamentally negative in the Easter message: *He is not here.* Is this world, seen from Christ's perspective, anything more than a garden with an empty grave in it? He is not here; he has risen. That means: He has ascended. And that means: He is coming again. That is the Easter perspective on this world: it is enormously empty. In spite of all its splendour of spring, it has been given over for destruction, and this is symbolized by the negative "he is not here."

The emphasis, Van Ruler continues, can either be laid on the positive aspect first, as in Mark's rendering, or on the negative aspect, as in Luke's version.

The gospel of the resurrection can be proclaimed in these two opposing keys. Therefore, do not be afraid when the Easter gospel is heard in the minor key. Especially during Easter time, humanity's condition of sin and death is revealed to such an extent that the knowledge of sin and distress changes the whole world into a vale of tears. . . . He is not here—not in our small, pagan hearts, not in our Christian activities, not in this world, so intent on its own destruction. . . . On the other hand one should, however, not complain about superficiality when the Easter gospel is brought in the major key. For to what avail is all our knowledge of our sin and misery without the message of eternal life in the risen Christ? We must first and foremost have heard and understood the good news that he has been raised before the reality that he is not here can dawn upon us![18]

Noordmans frequently states that our "human weakness" comes to the fore very much during Easter. "Here everything is fear, hesitation, lack of faith, doubt." Easter, according to him, is often presented in the church as "the feast of jubilation," and rightly so, but then it is "a restrained joy, mixed with fear." The church year may never estrange people from everyday reality! "It is not correct if we are taught during our services of worship to close our eyes to life's realities. It is easy enough simply to raise the tone and volume of one's voice and proclamation, but in the end that does not really benefit anyone. It is just not enough now and then to add a 'Hallelujah!' and to increase the joy of Easter artificially by way of more celebrations and festivities."

There are, in Noordmans' opinion, two complementary reasons why Easter may never be a feast of "mere jubilation." On the one hand, he says, the work of the *Father* makes that impossible. From this work we are excluded to such an extent that we can only watch it with fear and trembling, so that "all thoughtless shouts of joy will surely die on our lips." On the other hand, the work of *Jesus* makes all heedless joy during Easter impossible. His work is precisely to reveal to us the real misery of creation and to send us, after his ascension, back into this miserable reality. Easter, by way of strange contrast, is the time when we are reminded more than ever of the harsh realities of life and of the distress of the world! That which applied to the women and the disciples after Jesus' resurrection should still apply to all of us today, when the message is correctly proclaimed.

Almost everywhere an almost childlike attentiveness prevails, a looking-on in awe, which should remain one of the permanent components of the proper fear-of-Easter and of the entire Christian life. It simply cannot be taken for granted that Jesus was raised from the dead. . . . First and foremost it is cause for a strange astonishment and wonder. The distance between their own existence of continuous flight and God's descending and approaching style was just too big.

Noordmans warns that this "holy fear" or "watching in awe" should never be lost, though he warns simultaneously against "unwarranted fear," which both Jesus and the angels often sought to expel.

We must come to understand that we are fleeing in the wrong direction when we are afraid of the power with which God is busy to recreate everything anew. For us it is indeed not easy to conquer our fear of God. We sometimes even prefer the silent orderliness of the grave, where nothing ever changes or becomes disturbed, to the unknown and therefore unpredictable reality of the resurrection and of life. One is able to locate the dead Jesus. One can find him where you expect him. He cannot surprise one any longer. One can do something for him and even buy him some spices. We are, however, less certain how to show our love when his place is empty. The grave is so small and so easy to understand, but the world so big and the living Lord so unfathomable in his ways. . . . Easter wants to help us conquer precisely *this* fear.[19]

Noordmans also refers elsewhere to "the clouds of Easter" obscuring "the light and the brightness of a sunny summer morning."[20] And to the "humble God" with his "inseparable connections between suffering, death, and resurrection, all linked together by the divine *dei* ('had to'),"[21] as well as to "embarrassed and perplexed Christians, knowing only too well that the coming of God's kingdom is not always a time for them to be proud, but often also a time during which their hearts may writhe and wince."[22] It is clear that in all these contexts he is underlining the "double key" in which Christians experience Easter.

In his moving book on the resurrection, Buskes writes in this same spirit. He argues that "a hallelujah-Christianity, which thinks it possible to leave behind the 'out of the depths I cry' of Psalm 130 by simply shouting 'Hallelujah!' all the time" is not legitimate.[23] It is true without any doubt that one should occasionally "distort dogma in preaching" (Noordmans)— for the sake of the truth! Truth's highest triumph lies in this kind of one-sidedness! It is impossible to see everything at once or to say everything at once. One does not proclaim everything every

Sunday. Especially with regard to the church year, this is very true. After having been "distorted" for seven weeks during Lent (without ever forgetting the resurrection), the dogma is "distorted" during and after Easter by the positive testimony of the victory over death, the "joyful 'nevertheless'" (K. M. Fischer), but now without forgetting the gravity and radical nature of death (and life!).

Triumphalism, which sometimes borders on frivolousness, is unconvincing under all circumstances, for it denies the realism of the gospel. "Capitulation" (Josuttis), on the other hand, which suffers from the desolateness of life to such an extent that it no longer feels the freedom to proclaim the victory of life over death, denies the truth of the gospel.

7. In summary, the message of the resurrection is both crucial and difficult to accept. For several reasons, the message must always be proclaimed in "a twofold key," full of joy, but never triumphalistic.

II. The Contents of Easter Proclamation

The Resurrection Message Includes Several Themes

8. During the last few years, much fruitful thought has been given to the content or meaning of the gospel of the resurrection, from exegetical as well as doctrinal points of view. Surely no single motif or aspect of meaning can exhaust the entire wealth of the gospel of resurrection. One should rather consider several motifs in combination.

One reads of "different aspects" (Rengstorf), "points of orientation for exegesis" (Klappert), divergent "approaches of understanding" (Gesché), a "multidimensional promise of God" (Wiederkehr), "models of interpretation" (O'Collins), a variety of "contexts" in which the resurrection can be understood (Geyer), "multi-dimensionality" (Klappert), several legitimate "anthropological approaches" (Kasper), resurrection as "the center radiating many truths" (Scheffczyk), and a "complex, polymorphous and diverse understanding of the mystery of Easter" (Gesché). Kuitert talks about "a multiplicity of legitimate contexts in which the story of the resurrection has to be told and retold," of a "multiple profiling" and of "miscellaneous foci" this one word of promise receives.

Which expression one prefers is not so important. It is more important that the different aspects are neither isolated from each other nor absolutized. Systematic theologians especially are tempted to look at the resurrection from only one viewpoint. Within such a one-sided framework it often happens that all other equally legitimate motifs or aspects are neglected or even denied. Naturally, in preaching, this systematic "compulsion" is not so strong! One could, once again with a certain measure of permissible "distortion," study the motif or motifs present in a particular pericope, in order to concentrate on these specific aspects in the proclamation. The proclamation deals with a particular pericope (and its thrust or message) and is not meant as a balanced, systematic treatise. Literature is abundantly available to help one in this. Any attempt to provide a systematic compilation of some of the most important motifs will, of course, be arbitrary (which explains the divergent variety of classifications in systematical works, monographs, lexicon articles, New Testament theologies, etc!) and inadequate (because of the fact that the deepest meaning of the resurrection itself will never be fully defined or exhausted).[24] However, such an attempt may be useful.

It Is Real!

9. A first, obvious aspect is the historical character, or what is sometimes called "the motif of reality" in the New Testament proclamation of Christ's resurrection, especially in some of the appearance narratives, but also elsewhere. Although it is true that the "historical" question is never the primary issue in the Bible (so that Barth and Rengstorf, for example, both work out the theological implications first, and after that the soteriological ones, and only then, as the presupposition of both the preceding, the aspect of the reality),[25] it undoubtedly is the aspect that ever since the Enlightenment has been the most prominent as a result of the Western historical-critical approach. For this reason it is also the aspect on which opinions differ most easily, about which misconceptions and accompanying resistances are evoked most easily, and consequently, it is the aspect which has to be formulated most accurately.

In the first place there is almost consensus on the fact that "something" definitely happened. Even Marxsen accepts this without reservation. The differences arise over exactly *what* happened, and how it can best be expressed or described today. The even more fundamental question, of course, is whether the means and methods of modern historical research are capable of judging what is supposed to have taken place!

Many exegetes (e.g., Marxsen) proceed from the assumption that from a methodological viewpoint there is absolutely no other honest, responsible, and scientific alternative to approaching the biblical witness concerning the resurrection with the modern means of historical research and historical criticism formulated classically in the three principles of historical criticism. Critics of this approach, however, point out that with such a starting point the conclusions are already given! According to this approach, they argue, everything simply must remain within the closed circle of immanence, of what can be repeated and demonstrated, of the fundamental similarity between all historical events, and of the analogy between events. The biblical testimony and the "reality" it proclaims is thus reduced in advance to something repeatable or something that must be generally accessible.

These critics sharply criticize such an approach, but are then themselves confronted with the dilemma as to whether it is still possible (for them) to talk about "historicity" when they refuse to accept these criteria, and what "historical" means under these circumstances. Was this "something" that happened "historical"—in the standard sense of the word, or was it something of a fundamentally different nature? Is it not somewhat confusing to deny historical research its rights, like Barth did, and still talk about the historicity of what happened?

In recent years, Pannenberg (as well as Von Campenhausen) has tried to argue that the resurrection (or at least the empty grave) is indeed provable by means of historical research, i.e. when one accepts the legitimacy of all these historical-critical criteria. But in the process he has changed the meaning of "historical," and does not provide logically compelling (historical) "proofs."

Furthermore, it is remarkable to note that the New Testament also does not claim that anyone saw or described the actual resurrection (i.e. what happened between God the Father and Jesus of Nazareth). Only later on, in an apocryphal gospel, is there an attempt to do this. In the New Testament one finds a double tradition, the (later) appearances of the (already resurrected) Jesus of Nazareth, and the empty grave. Although the opposite conviction is frequently asserted by many people (including some prominent exegetes, e.g., Pesch), it can be said with certainty that both these traditions are historically well founded. Neither of them, however, are presented as compulsory logical "proofs" for Christ's resurrection. On the contrary, the appearances quite clearly caused doubt, uncertainty, confusion, and even fear. And the fact of the empty grave was apparently also accepted by the Jews, but interpreted differently (as theft, Matt. 27:62-66 and 28:11-15, or as a mistake, John 20:15)!

One could therefore say that the actual event of the resurrection made some marks in human history, had historical effects or implications, but that all of these remain ambiguous, that is, that all of them could also be seen or interpreted differently so that they do not form compulsory proofs without faith. (This close connection with faith is exceptionally important for the New Testament and is treated later as a separate motif.) This historical impact was decisively important for the early church (as emphasized by Barth, Künneth, Berkouwer). They are not "proofs," but they are very essential "signs."[26]

What are the implications of this? On the one hand it means that the numerous psychological and other explanations of what happened have to be rejected, as is the case almost everywhere today. The "something" was not merely something that happened to the disciples (cf. Bultmann, Ebeling, Van Buren, et al.), but it was something *ante nos* and *extra nos* (O'Collins)—something *outside* of them and *outside* of us, something that happened to Jesus of Nazareth and in that sense was therefore "real" and "historical." To say that the concept of the empty grave is unnecessary and even a stumbling block for real Easter faith is therefore to deny this important motif of historicity and reality.[27]

On the other hand, the identity of the resurrected Lord with the deceased Jesus of Nazareth is for this reason vitally important to the church. In all the elaborate accounts of how the resurrected Lord ate and drank with them (Luke 24:39-43; John 21:9ff.), the main purpose is not merely to indicate that the body lived as it had lived before. (Note that in the immediate context one also finds deliberate descriptions of how he entered and went out through closed doors [Luke 24:36; John 20:19, 26].) The main purpose was to emphasize the identity of the resurrected Lord with the crucified Jesus (Klappert, Wilckens). With that, docetism and gnosticism are rejected, the essential basis is laid for the soteriological aspect of resurrection (also discussed in a separate paragraph), and, moreover, the point is made that God accepted and exalted the same Jesus they knew. This was the Jesus of the Gospels, the Jesus who taught and showed them how to live, the Jesus who gave himself in loving service to the sick and needy, and who came to proclaim God's love and forgiveness to publicans and sinners. In this way the proclamation of the resurrection makes the rest of the Gospels important!

Equally remarkable is the way the New Testament narratives treat both the nature of the resurrection events and the resurrected body. Jesus' resurrection was obviously something qualitatively different, something of a totally different nature, than, for example, the resurrection of Lazarus, of Jairus's daughter, or of those resuscitated in the Old Testament. Here it concerns a new act of creation on God's part, an eschatological event, the first-born from death, a "spiritual body" (Paul in 1 Cor. 15 about *our* resurrection), something that breaks open and surpasses the immanence of time and space, something new and unprecedented. It does *not* merely concern the revival of a deceased body to its former historical and earthly existence. Precisely on this issue, the preaching of the church often fails, and Christ's resurrection is presented so naively, so primitively that it causes offense and disbelief. In this sense, then, we are dealing with an eschatological event, rather than with a historical event. God's eschatological deed does have a historical impact, as shown already, but this impact remains ambiguous and is easily misunderstood. In this sense, the theological meaning of what happened is therefore of much greater importance than its historical or realistic aspects, although—as already argued—the latter forms the essential presupposition of the theological meaning.

The first witnesses, of course, experienced this strange, new, and totally inexpressible act of God concerning Jesus within their historical situation of space and time. They then tried to express this in concepts and expressions arising from their own frame of reference, from their own worldview, their own traditions, and from the ideas available to them. There are numerous studies about the meaning and origins of the various expressions they used (e.g., "risen," "resurrected," "raised," "has been seen," "has appeared," "showed/revealed himself," etc.). Especially Wilckens and Marxsen have devoted much attention to this.[28]

Wilckens maintains that expressions like "risen from the dead" are inseparable from apocalyptic thinking and should therefore be understood in that sense, even today. But Marxsen disagrees. He asserts that already in the New Testament one finds different interpretations for the actual event and that the idea of resurrection should no longer be considered the most appropriate interpretation, because it creates so much confusion. He argues that although it would seem *a* possible "interpretament" available to them in their worldview, this is no longer the case for modern people. It does not make immediate sense any longer

to say that "Jesus has been raised." We do not get the point. It only leads
to confusion, instead of defining or explaining something. It therefore
needs much explanation, and this shows that it is no longer a good approach for Christian proclamation. New and more meaningful ways of
expression must be found to say what the apostles wanted to say by
means of this now archaic metaphor.

In conclusion, the benefit of all the research done in recent decades
on this issue is undoubtedly that there exists at the moment a "remarkable consensus of opinion" (Fuller, O'Collins, Gesché) about the fact
that the resurrection of Jesus cannot merely be explained as something
subjective that happened to the disciples but that it was indeed something objective, historical, and real that happened between God the
Father and Jesus. At the same time, however, it has become more clear
that this "something" was an eschatological event and not merely ordinary human history, that it was something that indeed had historical effects, but which in itself was of a totally different nature and order than
ordinary history.

It is therefore often said that the event itself could not, in a manner
of speaking, have been captured by a camera. We are not dealing here
with *bruta facta,* with mere historical facts. For this reason it was and
still is impossible to understand all this without faith. This means that
the historical issue is a secondary issue and of secondary interest. Although this presupposition is decisive for understanding the truth of the
gospel of the resurrection, the primary issue still remains the (theological) question of the *context* in which the Bible proclaims this message. The purpose of the church's Easter proclamation could therefore
never be to defend the historicity as such, but only to proclaim the
meaning and implications of that which indeed happened. In a certain
sense this has brought an end to some extremely unfruitful research,
and in the latest literature more and more attention is given to the more
important question of the specific intent of the various pericopes in
which the resurrection is mentioned.

It Awakens Faith!

10. A second aspect is the role of faith in the proclamation of the
resurrection. Once again, two basic positions can be distinguished. On
the one hand, some people regard the events concerning the resurrection as the (objective) *ground* or foundation of Christian faith and therefore also as part of the content *(fides quae)* of faith. On the other hand,

some people, especially in existentialist ranks, regard the resurrection as the *description* of the (subjective) event when the disciples' faith or insight in the salvific meaning of either the cross or of Jesus' life and his "cause" flared up and lived on. According to this view, the resurrection is therefore not so much an addition to the content of faith but rather a description of the act of faith *(fides qua)*.

Traditionally the resurrection was considered a historical "fact" that seemingly could be demonstrated or proven by means of various arguments (which appealed to human reason and not to faith itself). The resurrection, considered the most extraordinary miracle of all, often served the purpose of grounding the faith or proving the truth of the Bible and the gospel. Especially in the traditional scholastic apologetics, the resurrection functioned in this way, as "confirmatory miracle." This point of view therefore represents the first of the two basic positions, and in its most extreme form: one accepted the truth of the resurrection in one or another form of *sacrificium intellectus,* and only then believed the rest of the gospel on this basis.

Such an extreme position, however, led to various reactions. Since the earliest times, objections have been raised against the Christian faith because the witnesses to the resurrection were themselves believers. It was argued that this seriously affected their credibility. One could, however, draw the opposite conclusion just as easily, namely that the nature of the gospel of the resurrection is such that it is aimed at faith. It creates faith and is not accessible without faith. This aspect, however, has led to the other extreme, the assertion that the resurrection is nothing other than the beginning of this faith itself.

Examples of this viewpoint can be found in Bultmann, Ebeling, Fuchs, Van Buren, Marxsen, Schillebeeckx, and Selby, with variations among them.[29] One has to acknowledge that they generally do not want to deny the possibility of an objective resurrection outside of faith; they rather want to protect and insure the nature of true faith, by maintaining that such an objective event is inaccessible without faith. Fuchs, for example, emphasizes that one should not talk in such a way about the basis or ground of faith that it would seem as if faith were redundant, unnecessary, or even easier, as if this basis or ground would be accessible without faith also or prior to faith. Geyer[30] points out that the actual difference between Barth and Bultmann was not the fact that the former was orthodox and the latter wanted to deny the resurrection, but rather that Barth wanted to emphasize the concrete objectivity of the basis of faith, while Bultmann, in order to let faith *remain* faith, wanted to deny that one could speak of such a basis without faith.

While the first basic position seeks to prevent the possibility that the "event" will be absorbed by its "meaning," the second position wants to prevent the possibility that the "event" may become isolated from its "meaning" and therefore become isolated from faith itself.

It is important to note that many preachers—though quite unintentionally!—treat the resurrection in exactly the same way as the existentialists. They are primarily concerned with an existential or personal experience, which people must have in the present time with the living Lord, almost similar to the experience that the original eyewitnesses had. Berkhof calls this type of proclamation the "just as/so also" method. The present experience of faith becomes, in a certain sense, the ground or basis for faith. It is with this sort of attitude that the well-known remark is sometimes made: "Is God dead? It is impossible. I have just talked to him." Such an experience can, of course, either be made individually, or in the congregation, in a situation of collective faith (Selby). Noordmans calls it a misunderstanding when people maintain that they believe in the resurrection "because they experience it themselves."[31]

It is obviously difficult to define the exact relation between history and faith. The reality of the resurrection can only be known through faith. It is *not* a basis or ground accessible without faith and thereby making faith unnecessary or easier. It cannot replace faith or prove it. Nor can it change faith into a kind of logical conclusion. Historical facts are merely "indicators and signs" (Kasper) for faith, but never "proofs." However, faith does not create this reality either, but this reality—including that of the living Lord through the Spirit—creates *faith*.

Klappert, agreeing with Barth, says that there exists an irreversible order between the events of resurrection, the proclamation concerning the resurrection, and the faith in the resurrection. "Der Osterglaube gründet in den Ostererscheinungen."[32] (Easter faith is based on the Easter appearances.) Everything depends, of course, on the exact meaning of the term *gründet*—"being based on," "being grounded in," "resting on." Jesus' resurrection, as an eschatological act of God, can indeed *never* be separated—by us!—from the beginning of the disciples' Easter faith (because we are not capable of going beyond their witness and examining the events themselves). But his resurrection should, notwithstanding, be very clearly distinguished from the disciples' faith.

These two are not identical. In this sense, faith *is* therefore dependent on the proclamation of the resurrection as part of the *content* of the Christian faith, of the *fides quae,* of the salvific facts.

It Leads to Mission!

11. The former aspect is closely connected with the missionary, apostolic, or kerygmatic motif one finds in the resurrection narratives. The close connection between the resurrection and the apostolate is already very noticeable in most of the appearance narratives in the Gospels. When the risen Lord appears to his disciples, he sends them out with a mission, with authority, and with the promise of his accompanying presence.[33] This happens time and again, with the woman, with Mary, with the whole group of disciples. Even the travelers to Emmaus are made into witnesses. It seems as if the risen Lord appears in order to send people both with a message and a witness, to tell and to proclaim.

Luther already emphasized this link between the events concerning Christ and the proclamation concerning him (and therefore faith in Christ).[34] The events are aimed at and they achieve their goal within proclamation and faith. Berkouwer also treats the apostolate as an integral part of the resurrection,[35] and Van Ruler talks about "the electing and official character" of the resurrection, because through these appearances the disciples were appointed as (official and elected) apostles.[36] Klappert calls the resurrection therefore "die Aufrichtung des Kerygmas" (the origin, the basis of all Christian proclamation), and he reckons it indeed possible and legitimate to argue that "das Osterereignis ist nicht ohne die Osterverkündigung" (the events of Easter do not exist without the proclamation of Easter).[37]

This aspect, however, has also been absolutized to very extreme positions (cf. Bultmann and later Marxsen). Bultmann's well-known thesis, later to be adopted and adapted by Marxsen, is that "Christ rose into the kerygma." By this they mean that the resurrection is nothing other than the fact that the disciples (noetically) *came to understand* the meaning of Jesus' cross (Bultmann), or the meaning of his entire life and "cause" (Marxsen). That means that ontologically nothing happened to the dead Jesus, but the disciples became aware of the salvific value of either his cross or his entire ministry. To believe in his resurrection is therefore exactly the same as to believe that Jesus' cause has not come to an end, but is still continued and making progress in the world. Jesus returns, or—one could say—rises continually, in the proclamation of this cause. Here the kerygma or apostolate is clearly no longer the fruit of the resurrection and commission of the risen Lord, but it is identical with the resurrection event itself.

One has to say that this is a distortion of a biblical motif, although it does contain an important element of truth. In the New Testament, the resurrection event precedes the kerygma and it also forms the *content* of the kerygma. The appearances at Easter indeed do not exist without the proclamation of Easter, but they exist in such a way that the former provide the basis and content for the latter. "Das Osterereignis begründet die Osterverkündigung,"[38] says Klappert. The proclamation originates in the self-revelation and self-expression of the risen Crucified One, who calls people to faith and to be witnesses and authorizes them to be apostles, precisely because they have become eyewitnesses of these appearances! The resurrection forms part of the content of the kerygma. It describes God's action in a new way, it proclaims God's salvation with a new meaning, and it brings hope for a new future.

It Reveals Something of God!

12. The fact that the resurrection defines God in a new way means that it has a revelational character, that it has theological implications in the strictest sense of the word, and that it makes a substantial contribution to Christian knowledge of God. This is very clear in the New Testament. The very first references to the resurrection (better: the raising) of Jesus are probably the short formulas scattered throughout the Epistles. Time and again, the adjectival subordinate clause "God . . . who raised Jesus" plays a very important role (cf. Rom. 4:17, 24; 8:11; 10:9; 2 Cor. 1:9; 4:14; Gal. 1:1; Eph. 1:20; Col. 2:12; Heb. 13:20; 1 Peter 1:21). Clearly this conviction formed an integral part of the first Christians' faith. They used this expression to name their God, to distinguish the God they believed in, to describe his will, his power, his activities, etc. It serves almost as a kind of definition.

German Protestants have often emphasized this link between Christ's resurrection and our knowledge of God, for example, Schniewind, Iwand, Klappert, Moltmann, et al.[39] Iwand, in a first part of his lectures on christology, describes the cross and the resurrection as the "self-definition of God" (an expression Klappert also adopts). He says that God reveals himself through these events "as the One who he really is. . . . There is no other God. I do not believe in the 'resurrection,' but I believe in the *God* who raised our Lord Jesus from the dead." The early church used this same fundamental and stereotypical description for God's "uniqueness and 'unheard-of' nature" (Klappert). In Catholic ranks Kasper emphasizes this very strongly.

> The Resurrection is so much God's work and so characteristic of him that it can be used as a sign by which God is recognized. . . . The formula, God "that raised from the dead Jesus our Lord" thus becomes immediately a New Testament predicate of God. . . . Jesus' Resurrection is . . . God's eschatological revelation of himself; here it is finally and unsurpassably revealed who God is. . . . Faith in Jesus Christ's Resurrection thus has its roots in the most fundamental confession of faith, faith in the creative potential and in the faithfulness of God. Finally it has its roots in faith in God's divinity. Conversely, it is equally true that God's divinity only shows itself conclusively in Jesus' Resurrection. The decision for or against Easter faith is not taken on the grounds of some miraculous event or other but on whether one is ready to see reality from God's viewpoint and to rely totally upon that God in living and in dying. . . . The Christian concept of God stands and falls with faith in the Resurrection. The Easter faith is therefore not a supplement to belief in God and in Jesus Christ, it is the entirety and essence of that belief.[40]

Van Ruler also frequently elaborates on this "significant connection" between the resurrection and the knowledge of God. According to him, Easter is not so much concerned with Jesus Christ and the fact that he rose from the dead, but rather with God and with the fact that *he* raised Jesus.

> And indeed: the entire matter of the resurrection rests not so much on the historical fact of Jesus Christ's resurrection, but much more powerfully on the knowledge of God, as it has already been given to Israel in the Old Testament. Finally even this centers on the crucial issue of who and what God really is.

He continues by saying that the basic idea of all attempts to understand God outside of the Bible is that divinity forms part of the continuous flow of reality, of life and death. In the Bible, however, God is Lord beyond all life and death, and that is the *essence,* the "divinity of God." Christian faith is to surrender to and to trust in *this* God, with the result that everything is denied when the resurrection is denied.[41]

Van Ruler is even more explicit when he talks about

... the most typical and the most characteristic aspect of God, namely God's "assistance." ... Whoever ... denies this mystery of the resurrection ... does not know God's power, and overlooks God's most distinctive characteristic, and serves another God than the God of the Bible. ... Practically everything, the entire biblical knowledge of God, is at stake here.[42]

He once again refers to these issues when he comments on unbelief regarding the resurrection:

In the entire gospel and in the entire Bible, and very centrally in the resurrection ... we are dealing with *God* himself. ... We are therefore actually protesting against God's most characteristic aspect. ... This God, who is not equal to fate, or to the process of life and death, or to the divinity of everything which exists and lives, *this* God ... he gives life, resurrects. ... That is his most characteristic feature. Precisely in *that* he is truly God and not equal to idols. Yes, from the knowledge of God that we receive from the Bible, the resurrection of Jesus Christ becomes perfectly obvious. And with that also our own resurrection.[43]

It Saves Us!

13. The resurrection also plays an important role in Christian soteriology, or the doctrine of redemption. The Heidelberg Catechism considers this fact, namely that "he has overcome death, so that he might make us share in the righteousness he won for us by his death" (Lord's Day 17, question and answer 45), to be the most important "benefit" of the resurrection.

In Catholic exegesis, especially since 1950, this aspect has been particularly stressed, especially in connection with similar emphases that Thomas had already laid.[44] In Protestant ranks, this has been discussed in detail by Barth and some of his disciples.

Barth discusses the resurrection under the title of "the verdict of the Father" (*CD* IV/1, par. 59.3). He views the resurrection as God's (new, second, separate) act by which he accepts the Crucified One, by which he grants justice to him, legitimates him, and by doing that makes reconciliation valid and effective for us. This differs radically from Bultmann's point of view, which regards the resurrection as an expression of the "Bedeutsamkeit," the significance or importance of the cross, in other words as something noetic only.

Barth sees the resurrection as a second, separate act of God. According to Barth, God changes the human situation to one of reconciliation by these two consecutive, different events of Jesus' death and resurrection.[45] People like Delling, Lohse, Kreck, Iwand, and Klappert tend to agree with this point of view.[46] Klappert calls the resurrection "die Inkraftsetzung der Versöhnung" (the putting into action effect of reconciliation).

In the New Testament, this important role of the resurrection in reconciliation or redemption is accentuated in several contexts and in different ways. In a series of expressions it is explicitly stated that Christ was raised "for our sake" or "for us" *(huper)*. On other occasions this same idea becomes clear within the argument of the specific context, namely that his resurrection was *pro nobis* and that we benefit directly from it (cf., e.g., the first verses of Rom. 6; 8:34; 10:9; 1 Cor. 6:14; 2 Cor. 4:14; 5:15; 1 Thess. 4:14; 1 Peter 3:21).[47] In addition to that, this idea is also present in the importance that is attached to meals in the reports about Christ's appearance after the resurrection (e.g. Luke 24:30ff.; John 21; Acts 1:4; 10:41; etc.).

Especially exegetes like Jeremias and Cullmann[48] have indicated that these meals were tokens of forgiveness and the renewal of communion. The resurrected Lord demonstrates by these signs that he forgives his unfaithful disciples and that he restores communion with them once again. This intimate relation between reconciliation and Christ's resurrection is, however, most explicitly formulated in the difficult,[49] but very important, Romans 4:25. It functions as key text, as a *locus classicus,* in this connection. Paul says there that Jesus "was put to death for our trespasses and raised for our justification."

It Raises Us into a New Lifestyle!

14. The motif that the resurrection presents new possibilities of life, that it at present already raises Christians into a new life, is very closely connected to this. Abundant information can be found in the New Testament, especially in contexts dealing with the nature of Christian baptism and its implications for the Christian life. It is also the second of the "benefits" mentioned by the Heidelberg Catechism (Lord's Day 17, question and answer 45).

Perhaps some of the most moving passages on this theme have been written by Van Ruler, especially in two different meditations on Galatians 2:20.[50] He says, among other things:

> It all starts when one becomes amazed at the fact that for some strange reason we "still" live in the flesh. . . . After Easter that should not be possible . . . ! There exists some kind of a discrepancy here. Something

must be wrong. Let it be wrong! Let it disturb me! The mere fact that I am now aware of this, the mere fact that it amazes me, the mere fact that I do not take this life-in-the-flesh for granted any longer, is already the a-b-c of the Christian attitude towards life! The life-in-the-flesh has now been undermined. Dynamite has been put under it. It has been put between brackets. Now I am continuously struggling with this. I continuously dispute what seems to be the most indisputable. I live "according to the style of humanity" (Calvin), yes, but at the same time I have been made to sit in heaven with him.

He frequently uses these expressions and calls this growing amazement at the fact that we still live in the flesh the "a-b-c of the Christian attitude towards life." That is, however, only the beginning. That is where the Christian life starts. Then, increasingly,

. . . the order is reversed more and more. At first, the ordinary life-in-the-flesh seems the obvious fact, the reality that we accept as normal and given, while the spiritual life in Christ is seen as something additional and strange. . . . Through an intense process of spiritual experience, however, under the discipline of the Word and the Spirit, things are gradually changed in the opposite direction. Now Christ's resurrection and the eternal life that has been granted to us by this resurrection, become the axiom, the normal and the given, the fundamental principle that does not have to be proven any longer, the most basic fact in which I am rooted and grounded. . . . Now the extent to which I still live in the flesh is seen as something additional, now I am continuously more and more amazed about that!

This process, in which the new life becomes the obvious one, is, however, still not the ultimate stage, but "only part of the beginning itself!" In our spiritual experiences, under the discipline of Word and Spirit, "the way *back* has to be found once again. The amazement and the wonder must now be translated into faith and love. . . . Only then do we really live 'in the hope of eternal life.' . . . Now I do not strive to give up anything that forms part of this earthly, 'fleshly' life."

In his typical style he then describes how such a "new life" (which has discovered the obviousness of the resurrection via the way of initial amazement about the fleshliness, only eventually to return to the life "in the flesh"), clings to and stays faithful to the brokenness, suffering, and horrors of our daily life. As in the New Testament, this "new life" or "the life of the resurrection" should consequently not be seen in a purely moralistic sense (as if the resurrection only enhances legalism and moral exertion), or in a purely mystical sense (as if the resurrection wants to alienate us from this life's concreteness, but it should rather be seen as a new vision on all things, a new starting point, a new root for human existence, a new perspective and a new meaning, but with that also as a new power, a new present reality, new possibilities of existence.

It Brings Hope for the Future!

15. The soteriological meaning of the resurrection, however, is also very closely related with its eschatological aspect. The motif of forgiveness is very closely connected with the motif of hope. In the Heidelberg Catechism, this is the third "benefit" mentioned, namely that his resurrection is "a guarantee of our glorious resurrection." It becomes very clear from several New Testament writings, e.g., the well-known argumentation in 1 Corinthians 15. It is very important, however, that the close tie between justification (soteriology) and hope (eschatology) be retained. They may not be severed from each other.

Ridderbos and Klappert have strongly emphasized this inseparable connection. Ridderbos describes Paul's entire theology as "resurrection-eschatology"[51] and points out that the resurrection as "breakthrough of the new aeon" should therefore not be understood only in forensic, ethical, or existential categories, but rather in a more comprehensive sense.[52] Klappert, in turn, warns that the resurrection is the "opening of a new future," because it is the affirmation or the putting-into-effect of the reconciliation. He stresses that the "nature of promise" of the resurrection should not be isolated from the aspect of reconciliation.[53]

In contrast with Moltmann, who is, together with Pannenberg and Kreck, one of the systematic theologians who work out this aspect of the resurrection in fine detail,[54] Klappert asks whether he does not perhaps absolutize the motif of hope (and mission) at the expense of the aspect of justification or reconciliation, which indeed forms the basis of both hope and mission.[55] Moltmann, in any case, stresses the fact that the resurrection can be understood only "in the mode of promise."

Its "Verheissungscharakter" (character of promise) must also be kept in mind in preaching. With the resurrection the case has not closed, but, on the contrary, has been forced open, has been opened up.[56] Now new possibilities exist. Everything is possible. Hope is meaningful. The future beckons. The future has been unlocked and is promised in Christ's resurrection. Heyns talks of an "imperfect past tense" and calls the resurrection an "open event."[57] The resurrection is indeed a "safeguard" and a "pledge." Christ is the first-born.

This promise includes both the individual and the collective future. Concerning the individual future, several related matters now become relevant, such as the nature of "death," life after death, the immortality of the soul, the interim period, the resurrection of the body, the function of apocalyptic language, the meaning of "heaven," etc. Concerning the collective future, Berkhof rightly points out that Christ's resurrection gives meaning to our interim lives in two ways. Viewed from a vertical perspective, it means that the center of our orientation and inspiration is situated beyond or outside this mortal world. Viewed from a horizontal perspective, it turns us into "aliens and exiles," into travelers and sojourners, whose real citizenship is somewhere else.

In practice, it leads to a dual attitude toward the present life: the vertical aspect brings freedom from care and perfect peace; the horizontal aspect brings anxiety about and resistance against the status quo and all its misery and sin. In this connection Berkhof uses the well-known word-play: "Jesus' being raised raises our spirits, his rising arouses in us a spirit of rebellion" (in Dutch: "De opwekking maakt ons opgewekt, de opstanding opstandig").[58] This aspect of the resurrection is, of course, also very prominent in political and liberation theology.[59]

In Conclusion

16. Obviously one could also mention other aspects.[60] Furthermore, it is also clear that all these motifs or aspects are not on the same level. Nevertheless, preaching will benefit when the preacher consciously and deliberately looks for the theological motif or motifs present in a specific pericope. Only in that way the most extreme forms of the "just as/so also" method, as well as other forms of ungrounded exegesis and application, can be avoided. There is illuminating literature available that can help one discern the motifs or theological importance of particular pericopes. At the same time one may not absolutize a single motif, because that may lead to an underestimate or denial of the variegated wealth of the gospel of resurrection.

D. J. SMIT

Notes

1. Cf. the thorough treatment by A. Gesché, "Die Auferstehung Jesu in der dogmatischen Theologie," in *Theologische Berichte* 2 (Benziger Verlag 1973), 275-324, in which he discusses five causes for the phenomenon in great detail. He develops his own point of view before expounding three new "gateways to understanding the resurrection," which, to his mind, will do better justice to the message of the resurrection than the traditional approaches. Cf., however, also L. Scheffczyk, *Auferstehung*. He points out the neglect of the resurrection in history and then attempts to construct anew an entire Christian theology, in a systematic way, from the "principle of the resurrection." See also R. Schnackenburg, *Ostern und der neue Mensch,* who says that for a variety of reasons the Easter message has only regained a new importance during this century, that is, after World War II; and G. O'Collins, *What Do They Say about the Resurrection?* for similar arguments.

2. One only has to look at some orthodox or traditional Reformed systematic works, e.g., J. A. Heyns, *Dogmatiek,* to see what part (in this case 1 page out of 418!), what place (only in the sixth subdivision of the tenth chapter!), and what function the resurrection has in the entire argumentation (very little), to determine that there is hardly anything left of the all-important role that the New Testament allocates to the message of the resurrection. This unfortunate state of affairs has only very recently started to change, especially in the ranks of Pannenberg and his associates, and in Moltmann.

3. Originally in *God's poorten,* pp. 66-68, now included in *Verzamelde Werken* 8, pp. 133-34. He then continues by pointing out the close connection between Easter and Pentecost, because the Spirit virtually first has to come and prepare our hearts for that eternal joy that we at present cannot endure. This is, of course, a very typical illustration of his overall theology, in which the event of Christ and with that also the resurrection itself is to a large extent subservient to the more central, new, and free action of the Spirit.

4. O. Noordmans, *Gestalte en Geest,* p. 180, or *Verzamelde Werken* 8, p. 318 hereafter referred to as *V.W.* 8.

5. L. Scheffczyk, op. cit., pp. 63-72.

6. F. Kamphaus, *Vor der Exegese zur Predigt: Über die Problematik einer schriftgemässen Verkündigung der Oster-, Wunder- und Kindheitsgeschichten,* 1968. The English translation is entitled: *The Gospels for Preachers and Teachers* (London: Sheed and Ward, 1974).

7. H. Berkhof, "De prediking in de paaschtijd," in *Handboek voor de Prediking,* p. 196.

8. G. O'Collins, op. cit., pp. 42-55.

9. F. Kamphaus, op. cit., introduction.

10. J. Kremer, *Das älteste Zeugnis von der Auferstehung Christi,* pp. 131-49.

11. M. Josuttis, "Theologische Erwägungen zur Osterpredigt," in *Festtage* (ed. H. Breit, K.-D. Nörenberg), p. 101.

12. M. Josuttis, op. cit., pp. 108-14.

13. K.-D. Nörenberg, "Ostern und die Verkündigung des Auferstandenen," in *Festtage* (ed. H. Breit, K.-D. Nörenberg), p. 131.

14. K.-M. Fischer, *Das Ostergeschehen,* pp. 105-9.

15. K. Dijk, *De Dienst der Prediking,* p. 343.

16. H. Berkhof, op. cit., 188-89. Cf. H. M. Kuitert, "Het geloof in de opstanding in de nieuwere theologie," in *GTT* 68 (1968), 78, who also points out the wholesome difference that exists between the chaotic circumstances in the fields of philosophy and theology on the one hand, and the life of the believing church on the other.

17. Cf., e.g., K.-D. Nörenberg, op. cit., especially pp. 124-36.

18. A. A. Van Ruler, *Het leven een feest,* pp. 62-64.

19. O. Noordmans, *Zondaar en Bedelaar,* pp. 60-67 (*V.W.* 8, pp. 46-50).

20. O. Noordmans, *Gestalte en Geest,* pp. 173-76 (*V.W.* 8, pp. 313-15).

21. Ibid., pp. 176-78, 207 (*V.W.* 8, pp. 315-17, 339). He describes the credo of the first Christians as a "faith-against-hope-in-hope" (cf. Rom. 4:18) and reminds us of Calvin who said "that amongst the many of those who proclaim Christ as king with pomp and splendor and exalt him with sublime eulogies, there is hardly one out of ten who is aware of the fact that grace befalls us because of his death" (*V.W.* 8, pp. 316-17).

22. Ibid., pp. 205-7 (*V.W.* 8, pp. 338-40). He warns against "an amiable enthusiasm and a benevolent optimism." Such people think and speak of the kingdom all too easily. He remarks that twentieth-century Christians have regained something of this "characteristic of perplexity and irresolution and have lost something of the self-confidence."

23. J. J. Buskes, *Opstanding,* p. 72.

24. Precisely because of the fact that these aspects are not on the same level and, in addition to that, are so closely related that they overlap in many respects, the literature shows a variety of attempts to make classifications. Some people simply enumerate a number of unconnected aspects without any system (e.g., K. Dijk, op. cit., p. 33, with seven items). Others base the classification on the questions they raise, or on the principle with which they work. In this way D. Wiederkehr, *Perspektiven der Eschatologie,* pp. 56ff. makes a fourfold division from the point of view of eschatology (the future is God's prerogative; the resurrection is God's demonstration of the future; the resurrection is an anticipation of the universal consummation; the resurrection is retrospective criticism and promise at the same time). W. Künneth, *Theologie der Auferstehung,* in his second volume, puts the question about the "doctrinal meaning" even more schematically, and consecutively deals with four aspects, namely God's action with Christ, God's action with the world, the presence of the risen Lord, and the final consummation of the reality of the resurrection in eschatology. K. Frör, *Wege zur Schriftauslegung,* pp. 357ff., uses temporal categories as principle of classification and arrives at the tripartition of everything which has happened in the past, everything which flows from it at present, and everything it still holds for the future. W. Kasper, *Jesus the Christ,* and J. Kremer, op. cit., pp. 88ff., stay closer to the biblical testimony and they work with an almost identical tripartition: the resur-

rection is an eschatological action of God's power; it is the exaltation of the Son; and it is a redeeming event (Kasper) because of the fact that he has become the first-born from death, and the life-giving Spirit (Kremer). H. Geyer: "The Resurrection of Jesus Christ: A Survey of the Debate in Present-Day Theology," in *The Significance of the Resurrection for Faith in Jesus Christ* (ed. C. F. D. Moule), pp. 105-36, makes a tripartition on the grounds of the different contexts in which the meaning of the resurrection may be looked for (namely the cross of Jesus; the life of the historical Jesus; apocalyptic thinking). H. Schlier, *Über die Auferstehung Jesu Christi*, pp. 51ff., deals, in one of the best summaries available, respectively, with the implications for Christ himself, the implications for the world, and the implications for human existence, each one with its own subdivisions. One also finds miscellaneous divergent classifications in systematical works. The following discussion is related to the five aspects with which B. Klappert deals in *Diskussion um Kreuz und Auferstehung*. It is, however, supplemented by the motif of revelation (in the same way that G. O'Collins also supplements Klappert), as well as the motif that Christ's resurrection calls for our own rising into a new life here and now already, i.e. the everyday, ethical implications of the resurrection message.

25. K. Barth, *CD* IV/1; K. Rengstorf, *Die Auferstehung Jesu,* in successive paragraphs, starting with the aspect of the "reality" only after that. Geyer, op. cit., also says that the historical issue is wrongly emphasized, because the theological issue concerning the meaning of the resurrection should really be the most decisive one. However, it is impossible to separate these two from each other.

26. W. Nauck, "Die Bedeutung des leeren Grabes für den Glauben an den Auferstandenen," *ZNW* 47 (1956), 243-67; K. Barth, *CD* IV/1; IV/2; III/2; K. H. Rengstorf, op. cit., pp. 61, 76-78; B. Klappert, op. cit., pp. 18ff.; L. Goppelt, "Das Osterkerygma heute," in *Luth. Monathefte* 3 (1964), 50-57; H. Schlier, op. cit., p. 28; G. Koch, *Die Auferstehung Jesu Christi*, p. 163. It is therefore slightly confusing when J. A. Heyns, op. cit., p. 266, talks about the appearances as "unshakable proofs." The various attempts to harmonize the information from the Gospels, to smooth out the apparent problems, and especially the attempt to "verify" the historicity of the resurrection are also not convincing. Well-known examples of this are: F. Morrison, *Who Moved the Stone?; J.* McDowell, *The Resurrection Factor;* and G. R. Habermas, *The Resurrection of Jesus: An Apologetic.* Perhaps the most convincing work in this style is K. Bürgener, *The Resurrection of Jesus Christ from the Dead.* M. Green, *The Day Death Died,* shows affinities with this type of view, but nevertheless shows more nuances. This is also true of G. E. Ladd, *I Believe in the Resurrection.* The latter, however, asserts, and rightly so: "Only those who have reason to believe in the God to whom the Bible witnesses can accept the witness of the Gospels, *viz.* that God raised Jesus from the dead" (p. 102). A. A. Van Ruler, *De dood wordt overwonnen,* thus writes that "one can only talk about a message and not about proofs, because proofs can only remain in the sphere of the possible and the essential" (p. 51). For us, "in our present condition there is something inconceivable and unimaginable here.... For us,

there *has* to be something ridiculous about it, about the salvation that God promises us in Jesus' resurrection" (p. 113).

27. Through the ages many such theories came into being. The most important one is probably the "subjective theory of vision" (which has existed already
since W. Milligan, 1927, but with a number of variations by J. Weiss, M. Enslin)
and the "objective theory of vision." J. McDowell, op. cit., pp. 75ff., deals with
five natural explanations that deny the empty grave (among which are the wrong-
grave-theory of K. Lake, 1912, the unknown-grave-theory, the view that the biblical narratives are legends, as well as various forms of hallucination-theories) and
four natural explanations that accept the empty grave (among which are the theft
theories, the "swoon" theory or the "resuscitation theory," which used to be popular especially among eighteenth-century rationalists, as well as the well-known
"Passover plot" idea of H. Schoenfield). Although most of these are rejected almost universally today, there still continues, especially in German ranks, a penetrating discussion of the so-called "origin of the Easter faith," in which it is
frequently asked whether the empty grave could be seen as a *conditio sine qua non*
for real faith in the resurrection. People like R. Pesch, H.-W. Bartsch,
P. Stuhlmacher, M. Hengel, W. Kasper, K. H. Schelke, H. U. von Balthasar,
L. Scheffczyk, K. Lehmann, and others have, up to very recent times, contributed
to this discussion.

28. Some of the best-known sources are: U. Wilckens: "Der Ursprung der
Überlieferung der Erscheinungen des Auferstandenen," in *Dogma und Denkstruk-
turen* (publication in Honour of Schlink); "The Tradition-History of the Resurrec-
tion of Jesus," in *The Significance of the Message of the Resurrection for Faith in
Jesus Christ* (ed. C. F. D. Moule), pp. 51-76; W. Marxsen, "The Resurrection of
Jesus as a Historical and Theological Problem," in *The Significance of the Mes-
sage of the Resurrection for Faith in Jesus Christ* (ed. C. F. D. Moule), pp. 15-50;
The Resurrection of Jesus of Nazareth.

29. Their viewpoints are developed and discussed in a variety of writings.
Some of the most interesting ones are Fuchs's discussion with Künneth, *Die
Auferstehung Jesu Christi von den Toten: Dokumentation eines Streitsgesprächs,*
and E. Schillebeeckx's *Interim Report on the Books Jesus and Christ* (with the
significant title of the German translation, *Die Auferstehung als Grund der
Erlösung* = "The Resurrection as Basis for Salvation"), as well as P. Selby, *Look
for the Living,* in which he describes the fellowship within the church as the place
where the living Lord is experienced.

30. H.-G. Geyer, op. cit., pp. 105-36.

31. O. Noordmans, *Zondaar en Bedelaar,* p. 58 (*V.W.* 8, p. 45).

32. B. Klappert, op. cit., pp. 34-40.

33. Cf. Matthew 28:16-20, Luke 24:36-49, John 20:19-23 and 21:1-17, as
well as the role of the resurrection in legitimating Paul's apostleship in 1 Corinthians 15:1-11 and also Romans 1:5 and Galatians 2:8. Some interesting exegetical
work has been done in this connection by C. H. Dodd, "The Appearances of the
Risen Christ," in *Studies in the Gospels* (ed. D. E. Nineham), pp. 9-35; D. W.
Palmer, "The Resurrection of Jesus and the Mission of the Church," in *Reconcil-*

iation and Hope (dedicated to L. L. Morris), pp. 205-23; P. Benoit, *The Passion and Resurrection of Jesus Christ;* R. E. Brown, *The Virginal Conception and Bodily Resurrection of Jesus.* Almost all of them distinguish between two traditions of appearances, namely "concise" and "circumstantial" reports (in Dodd's words) or "narratives that contain a recognition" and "narratives that contain a mission" (in Benoit's formulation). According to them, the two most important motifs are therefore either the recognition of the resurrected Lord as the Crucified One himself, or the reception of his word or summons to witness (or, as in some cases, a combination of both).

34. B. Klappert, op. cit., pp. 31-32.

35. G. C. Berkouwer, *The Work of Christ.*

36. A. A. van Ruler, *De dood wordt overwonnen,* pp. 17-18.

37. B. Klappert, op. cit., pp. 29ff.

38. Ibid., pp. 29ff.

39. J. Schniewind, "Die Leugner der Auferstehung in Korinth," in *Nachgelassene Reden und Aufsätze,* pp. 110ff.; B. Klappert, op. cit., pp. 11ff.; H.-J. Iwand, his lectures on christology, included in B. Klappert, op. cit., pp. 44, 275ff.; J. Moltmann, "God and Resurrection," in *Hope and Planning,* pp. 31-55, as well as his *Crucified God* and later works. Barth also emphasized the revelatory aspect of the resurrection, especially in his early dialectical period, i.e. in his *Commentary on Romans* and again in his exegesis of 1 Corinthians 15 in *The Resurrection of the Dead.*

40. W. Kasper, op. cit., pp. 144-45.

41. A. A. van Ruler, op. cit., pp. 30-31.

42. A. A. van Ruler, *Het leven een feest,* pp. 64-66.

43. A. A. van Ruler, op. cit., pp. 74-76.

44. Cf. O'Collins, op. cit., pp. 16ff.

45. K. Barth, *CD* IV/1, as well as IV/2 and IV/3, par. 69.4. For a good exposition of the discussion between Barth and Bultmann, see B. Klappert, op. cit., pp. 53-145, and for a penetrating interpretation of Barth's own viewpoint, see B. Klappert, *Die Auferstehung des Gekreuzigten.* H. Geyer, op. cit., is of the opinion that the most crucial theological question concerning the resurrection is indeed this relation between the cross and the resurrection: whether the cross has to be seen as a type of catastrophe that is then cancelled and rectified by the resurrection, or whether there does exist some or other form of significant continuity. Cf. also C. F. D. Moule's introductory article, and G. Delling in "The Significance of the Resurrection of Jesus for Faith in Jesus Christ," p. 99, especially note 49, both of these in *The Significance of the Resurrection for Faith in Jesus Christ* (Moule et al.).

46. G. Delling, op. cit., pp. 93ff.; E. Lohse, *Märtyrer und Gottesknecht,* pp. 115ff.; B. Klappert, *Diskussion,* pp. 24ff. and pp. 298ff.; W. Kreck, "Der Gekreuzigte als der Sieger über den Tod," in *Die Zukunft der Gekommenen;* "Die Lehre von der Versöhnung" (on Barth); *TL* 85 (1960), 90ff.; H.-J. Iwand, op. cit., pp. 275-79.

47. R. E. Brown, op. cit.

48. J. Jeremias, *The Eucharistic Words of Jesus*. Also O. Cullmann and his scholars in several works.

49. G. E. Ladd, op. cit., p. 147 calls this "a rather difficult verse." And he adds: "The present author has puzzled long over the meaning of this verse."

50. A. A. van Ruler, "Ik leef nog in het vlees," in *Het leven een feest*, pp. 61-62, and "En voor zover ik nu nog in het vlees leef," pp. 68-72.

51. H. N. Ridderbos, *Paul*, p. 57.

52. Ibid., p. 55.

53. B. Klappert, op. cit., pp. 26-27.

54. J. Moltmann, *Theology of Hope*, especially the third chapter; W. Kreck, *Die Zukunft des Gekommenen;* W. Pannenberg, *cum suis,* occupy themselves elaborately, in various works, with the relation between resurrection and future. A. Gesché, op. cit., also mentions the eschatological element as being the element that ought to have preference and that ought to be the criterion from which all other aspects should be seen. His opinion is that eschatology presents the only real theological explanation of the resurrection, though he does not go into detail in this short article.

55. B. Klappert, op. cit., pp. 27-28. Perhaps it is possible to argue that Moltmann has tried to rectify or at least to complement this in his later works (e.g., *The Church in the Power of the Spirit*).

56. W. Kasper, op. cit., pp. 136ff., distinguishes between four approaches that interpret the resurrection from the angle of anthropology (Rahner, Boros, and Elert, as examples of an analysis of human freedom, which always strives after something absolute and eternal; Ratzinger, and one could also add Fuchs and Jüngel, who proceed from the assumption that love is stronger than death; Pannenberg sees the resurrection in the context of a phenomenology of hope; and Moltmann takes the view that justice will finally triumph). According to him, these approaches structurally resemble each other, because each time the question about the final purpose and meaning of human life cannot be answered satisfactorily from a historical point of view only, but calls for an eschatological realization. All these approaches furthermore implicitly argue that one is impelled, precisely by this question about the final meaning of human life, to anticipate an answer that will only be found at the end of history. At the moment it is therefore already possible and indeed meaningful to look for signs that strengthen this hope of realization and keep it awake, and in this connection Jesus' resurrection plays an important role.

57. J. A. Heyns, op. cit., p. 265.

58. H. Berkhof, *Christian Faith,* p. 314.

59. Reference can be made to J. Sobrino, *Christology at the Crossroads.* Although some of the other aspects also function in his work (e.g., that the resurrection is an event which reveals God, p. 240), the idea of hope is nevertheless very prominent, linking up with Moltmann. It is, however, a very specific type of hope. "The resultant faith cannot be adequately translated into anthropological hopes or some universal tendencies of history; it must be translated into a hope for some new justice in an unredeemed world. . . . The hermeneutic locale for under-

standing the resurrection of Jesus is not to be found simply in hope. It is to be found in the questioning search for justice in the history of suffering. . . . Basic discussion about Jesus' resurrection does not have to do with the possibility of envisioning it in physical, biological or historical terms. It has to do with the triumph of justice. Who will be victorious, the oppressor or the oppressed?" (p. 244). In this connection he, like Moltmann, emphasizes the cross as the horizon against which the resurrection receives meaning. The Easter message has nothing to do with the universal human possibility of resurrection that is affirmed or denied in faith or unbelief, but it has to do with the raising of the Crucified One by God himself, thereby creating a radical hope against all impossibilities and improbabilities. He also emphasizes, once again linking up with Moltmann, the promising and missionary nature of the resurrection. Finally, the praxis of actual love in the suffering world becomes the key to experiencing the resurrection in the right way. It also becomes the crucial question whether one really understands its meaning or, better still, whether one has really been grasped by it.

60. Thus B. Klappert, op. cit., pp. 43-44, mentions a "salvation-historical perspective" (i.e. concerned with the fulfillment of the promises of God), a "cosmocratic perspective" (which coheres with Christ's exaltation and power, as well as with the eventual realization of God's kingdom, cf. 1 Cor. 15:20ff., Phil. 2:6ff.), and also the "trinitarian relations" in which the resurrection is mentioned time and again. The implications of the resurrection for the life and person of Jesus himself could also be pointed out as yet a further important perspective. In the New Testament, this is often accentuated. In literature this theme is quite often discussed under the theme of Jesus' "legitimation" by God.

Pericopes Mainly from
the Synoptic Gospels and Acts

Easter Sunday:
Matthew 28:1-10

Bibliography

Commentaries

Beare, F. W. *The Gospel according to Matthew.* San Francisco: Harper & Row, 1981.

Gundry, R. H. *Matthew: A Commentary on His Literary and Theological Art.* Grand Rapids: Eerdmans, 1982.

Hill, D. *The Gospel of Matthew.* New Century Bible. London: Marshall, Morgan & Scott, 1972. Grand Rapids: Eerdmans, 1981.

Lewis, J. P. *The Gospel according to Matthew, Part 2 (13:53–28:20).* Austin: Sweet, 1976.

Nielsen, J. T. *Het Evangelie naar Mattheüs.* Nijkerk: Callenbach, 1971.

Senior, D. *Invitation to Mattthew.* Garden City: Image Books, 1971.

Tasker, R. V. G. *The Gospel according to St. Matthew.* Grand Rapids: Eerdmans, 1961.

Homiletical

Kamphaus, F. *The Gospels for Preachers and Teachers,* 22-24. London: Sheed and Ward, 1974.

Noordmans, O. *Verzamelde Werken.* Vol. 8, 43-53. Kampen: Kok, 1980.

Velema, W. H. *Tussen Tekst en Preek,* 81-84. Kampen: Kok, 1976.

Additional

Barth, K. *Dogmatics in Outline,* 121-23. New York: Philosophical Library, 1947.

Berkouwer, G. C. *The Work of Christ,* 181-201. Grand Rapids: Eerdmans, 1965.

Fiorenza, E. S. *In Memory of Her: A Feminist Theological Reconstruction of Christian Origins*. New York: Crossroad, 1984.

Moltmann-Wendel, E., *The Women around Jesus*. New York: Crossroad, 1982.

I. Exegetical

1. One can, of course, use any of the Gospels for a sermon on the resurrection. In each case, however, it is very important to keep in mind the context of the Gospel and also the function of the resurrection account in that Gospel. In our opinion, Matthew's Gospel has an advantage here in that it places the resurrection within the context of several attempts, before as well as after Jesus' resurrection, to discredit both the event and belief in the event. Furthermore, Matthew's narrative has been a prescribed text for Easter in the Lutheran lectionary, and has now been included in Year A of the *Common Lectionary*, again for Easter itself.

2. Exegetically, this is not a difficult pericope. A few remarks may prove helpful:

a. There are many opinions as to the precise time of the women's visit to the tomb. This does not, however, affect the message of the account.

In the RSV the time seems to be early on Sunday morning. Some exegetes, however, hold that the visit took place on the evening of the Sabbath (Saturday). The problem arises from the fact that *sabbaton* can mean "sabbath" as well as "week," and that "after the sabbath" may refer to the evening of the Sabbath, since the Jewish Sabbath ends at sunset. Some exegetes who believe the visit occurred on the evening of the Sabbath explain this seeming difference between the Gospels as due to the fact that in the initial account, Mark's Gospel, we read "on the first day." Some have interpreted this as the evening of the Sabbath, while others have understood it as the morning of the following day. It does, however, seem a more convincing interpretation (along with, e.g., Ridderbos and Grosheide) that Matthew, with his threefold indication—"after the Sabbath," "toward the dawn," "of the first day"— is referring to Sunday morning.

b. It is remarkable that so often women were witnesses of the great events of salvation. For example, women were prominent at the crucifixion and burial of Jesus. Especially in recent exegesis attention has often been focused on the crucial role of women in Jesus' earthly ministry and in early Christianity. Of course, the fact that they are the first witnesses to the resurrection plays an important role in this reconstruction. Most of the attention here, however, has been given to the versions of Mark and John. (Cf., e.g., the works of Fiorenza.)

Matthew simply indicates that the women wanted to "see the sepulchre." Evidently they wanted to mourn for Jesus. Matthew does not mention the anointing with spices, as does Mark. It is very clear from this and from the rest of the narrative that the women in no way expected, or even remotely dreamed of, a possible resurrection. Velema remarks that if things had depended on the women (and for that matter on the disciples), Easter would never have occurred. They wanted to open the tomb, yes, but only to close it again.

c. The earthquake (v. 2) is another detail not mentioned in Mark. As in the case of the crucifixion (27:51), the earthquake signifies the omnipotence of God, the announcement of a powerful divine deed. The angel's presence makes the event infinitely more glorious. After all, the resurrection of the Crucified One does indeed hit this world, in which death reigns as by an eternal law, like an earthquake! "The earthquake in the text symbolizes a much more powerful earthquake, by means of which Jesus' resurrection causes the old world of sin and death to tremble" (Bauer).

It is important to note that there is no causal relationship between the earthquake and the resurrection. The earthquake is merely a sign. In fact, the first few verses of this pericope contain only descriptions of the signs accompanying Jesus' resurrection. The resurrection itself is not described. Such an account is not possible, for the resurrection is something totally beyond description. Neither the witnesses at the grave nor the evangelists themselves are able to say anything about it. Whereas the crucifixion and the burial were historical, visible events, the resurrection represents a completely different kind of "history," of which God alone is cognizant.

d. The reaction of the guards (v. 4) is an example of divine irony. All human efforts to keep Jesus in his grave (27:62-66) are rendered null and void by the revelation of God's omnipotence. "Those who should guard the Dead One, become like dead men, and the Dead One, who should have been guarded, enters life" (Grundmann). However, the revelation of Jesus' glory is a source of terror only to his opponents. For those who seek him, it signifies salvation. "For them, it is a message of life unto life, whereas for the guards it is a message of death unto death" (Iwand).

e. The message of the angel (v. 6) may be the central verse in this pericope. God himself elucidates the events through his messenger. Indeed, these words can be uttered only from heaven. No human being is able to deliver this evidence about the victory of the crucified Jesus over death. The angel allays the women's fear with an unexpected message of joy: "He is not here; for he has risen." With one phrase, "he has risen from the dead" (v. 7), the kingdom of God breaks through in all its power and glory!

The angel understands the reason for the women's visit, but announces that they are at the wrong place. It is significant that the angel starts by countering the women's expectations: "He is not here." Jesus is not to be found in death. He is not merely another figure in history and now alive only in their memories of his life and crucifixion. Jesus is alive: the empty tomb is the visible evidence. The angel invites the women to see for themselves, to confirm the truth of his message.

f. This victory of Jesus must be proclaimed. Hence the women are instructed to go and tell the disciples that he has risen from the dead. It is significant that the message has to be told first of all to the disciples. They who have followed him during his lifetime and who have seen God's great deeds, though they often have not understood them, must now also become witnesses of his resurrection. And later they would be the ones to proclaim his resurrection to the world (28:16-20). This link between the resurrection and proclamation in early Christianity is of the utmost importance.

g. In verses 8-10 Matthew once again deviates from Mark's account. Mark's version ends with the women so terrified by these strange events that they do not tell anyone, at least initially. Matthew, however, describes the women's emotion as containing elements of both fear and great joy. Koopmans remarks that it is this twofold emotion that proves they have truly understood the gospel of Easter. They are terrified, for they are witnesses that death's power has been broken and that their Master has suddenly and forcefully proven that he is indeed the Son of God. And yet their joy is overwhelming: Jesus is alive!

h. Jesus' appearance to them on their way to tell the disciples is found only in Matthew's Gospel. Attempts have been made to identify this appearance as Jesus' meeting Mary Magdalene as narrated by John. And yet it seems as if we can accept this as an independent appearance.

They meet the resurrected Jesus "on their way of obedience" (Koopmans), and Jesus convinces them that the resurrected One is indeed the crucified Savior. This identification is of course not only of great importance to their experience and faith, but it is also vital to the Easter message. Jesus' resurrection is the outcome of a powerful struggle with death and evil, a struggle in which God himself is at stake. The heart of the gospel lies in and depends upon the fact that the Resurrected One is none other than the crucified Jesus. This appearance is also important in that Jesus repeats the angel's command to the women, thereby confirming the close connection between his resurrection and proclamation.

II. Hermeneutical

1. The primary question here for many exegetes is that of historicity. The widespread effects of the Enlightenment, of secularization in general, and of textual criticism have all contributed to making a sermon on such historical accounts very difficult. Jesus' resurrection as an actual physical event is questioned more and more. It is not possible to deal here with this question in any depth. (See also the introduction to this volume.) A few brief remarks follow.

Beckmann, for example, is of the opinion that a sermon about the historical text is one of the most difficult assignments a preacher is ever confronted with. The conflict over the "possibility," "reality," and "nature" of the resurrection has often focused on the "empty grave." In textual criticism and among many of the more recent exegetes the empty grave is seen as a legend without historical substance or kerygmatic value. In this view faith does not depend on the fact that the grave was indeed empty.

It must be stated emphatically that the question of historicity has no place on the pulpit. It is something a preacher should have settled in his mind prior to delivering the sermon. An Easter sermon should always be a personal and joyous testimony and never a somber, apocalyptic, and semiscientific discussion of metaphysical theories!

Furthermore, it is worth noting Berkouwer's comment that it is scarcely comprehensible that one can speak of the living Lord without attaching any value to the empty grave. The resurrection (and the kerygma that goes with it) has definitely been emptied of its content when interpreted in a way that has nothing to do with the corporeality of the crucified and deceased Jesus. It is not so much a matter of the relationship between resurrection and projection, but rather between resurrection and disbelief! Admittedly, the empty grave is no rational proof of the resurrection. That this is not the intent of the angel in inviting the women to "come, see the place where he lay" is very important to keep in mind during an Easter sermon. On the other hand, this does not in any way deny the significance of the empty grave. The historical nature of Jesus' resurrection is indeed indicated by the empty grave. However, the resurrection, not the empty grave, is the central fact of salvation.

2. One should also note the important place of faith in the resurrection narrative. Since the empty grave does not furnish rational proof that Jesus arose, the message of the resurrection presupposed faith from the very beginning. This is of course crucial for a sermon on the historical account. The angel's message calls for faith. The resurrection is, finally, a mystery, a miracle. And miracles can always be interpreted in different ways. Certainly in this most powerful act of all, God remains a mystery and faith remains the necessary prerequisite for recognizing it as indeed an act of God. Hence Jesus does not appear to Pilate, but to his disciples. For the same reason the travelers to Emmaus do not recognize Jesus immediately. And neither the earthquake nor the stone rolled away lead to faith in Jesus. As in the case of the empty grave, they became striking signs only through the message of the resurrection, through the words spoken by the angel. A sermon on the historical text is therefore not primarily the proclamation of the empty grave. Even when faced with this mighty act of God, the message from the angel and the summons to faith remain the elements of prime importance.

3. The contrast between belief and unbelief is accentuated by the context of this narrative in Matthew's Gospel. After this account, he tells of the "story" afterward spread among the Jews concerning the guards at the grave. Earlier, in his account of the suffering and death of Jesus, Matthew repeatedly calls attention to the unbelief of the Jews. This unbelief is now carried to the extreme in their total rejection of the resurrection and their attempts to discredit the believers.

Today also, humanity is doing everything in its power to destroy Jesus, and if that does not succeed, it tries to discredit faith in him. Jesus fell into the hands of the Jews through the vehicle of money, and his resurrection is denied by means of bribery. All these attempts, however, are ironic. In spreading false rumors, the high priests become witnesses of the fact that Jesus had actually risen! Contrary to their intention, they become part of the message!

4. In spite of the importance of historicity, faith, and belief versus disbelief, the heart of a resurrection sermon must be the fact that the resurrection represents a final happening, a breakthrough, in the history of redemption. The heart of the Easter message must be: "He is not here; for he has risen." In Jesus' resurrection, God himself enters human history. In the events of Good Friday, humanity is judged and all attempts to escape the dilemma of our alienation from God are blocked. Only a mystery can still help here. This mystery occurs on the morning of the resurrection. God's promise is fulfilled, and the kingdom of God breaks through finally and irrevocably in Jesus' victory over death. Jesus has won the struggle against evil and has risen "beyond death" (Van Ruler). With this victory a totally new and final phase of history has begun for humanity.

This salvation history deed has enormous implications. As in the case of the cross, the resurrection takes place *pro me, pro nobis,* "for me, for us." The resurrection is indeed "God's amen and humanity's hallelujah" (Gebhardt). Easter summons us to rejoice. Accordingly, an important part of an Easter sermon would be to point out that the joy of Easter may never be less than the joy of Christmas. Easter is the true climax of the gospel!

To believe in the resurrection is to escape the bond of sin and death. Easter signifies a new life for the Lord *and* for his followers. On Easter morning we experience anew, just as the women did, that "the stone has been removed" (Koopmans). The stone of sin has been removed from our lives. The stone that made it impossible for us to love God and our neighbors has been removed. The stone of our sinful past has been removed.

As Barth says: Easter is

> the proclamation of a victory already won. The war is at an end, even though here and there troops are still shooting, because they have not yet heard about the capitulation. The game is won, even though the player can still play a few more moves. Actually he has already been checkmated. The clock has run down, even though the pendulum still swings a few times this way and that. It is in this interim space that we are living: the old is past, behold all things are new. The Easter message tells us that our enemies, sin, the curse and death, are defeated. Ultimately they can no longer start mischief. They still behave as though

the game were not decided, the battle not fought; we must still reckon with them, but fundamentally we must cease to fear them any more.

5. So for the Christian, the resurrection means a new life. Equally important, this new life implies a command for the congregation. The resurrection has ethical implications. We must walk in this new life. Faith in Jesus' resurrection makes us part of the history of the resurrected Lord. To truly meet the Risen One means to accept his commission to bring his message to the whole world.

A congregation that celebrates the resurrection may never take refuge in their faith and forget about the world. It may never sleep and dream, nor doubt and capitulate, it must always be alert, it must struggle and witness, it must live as people who are busy erecting victory signs for the King of kings. The larger context in Matthew's Gospel is once again instructive. Specifically, the pericope that concludes his Gospel is important here. Matthew sketches the resurrection and its significance in bold strokes, in broad outline form. From the resurrection he passes directly to the unlimited, cosmic perspective that has been opened by Jesus' death and resurrection (28:18-20). Matthew's account of the resurrection concludes with Jesus' commission to his followers to proclaim the gospel of his victory worldwide, to "all nations" and "to the close of the age," with the promise that he is with those who obey his command.

III. Homiletical

1. One could begin a sermon on this text by describing Mary Magdalene and "the other" Mary's state of mind on that first Easter morning. When they visited the grave, they were dejected. Jesus now lived on in memory only. They expected nothing at all. They had lost all hope.

Quite often we, too, are like that. Although we have much knowledge about Jesus' resurrection, this is often not real enough to change our feelings of hopelessness. We so often do not experience the power of his resurrection; and, time and again, we do not really expect anything from the living Jesus. The experience of Jesus is often little more than merely remembering historical events.

2. But the events in our text were, and still are, the proclamation of joy: he has risen! Matthew proclaims Jesus' resurrection and his victory over sin and death as a powerful act of God. The earthquake, the angel, and the empty grave are signs of this glorious power—

wonderful signs to the eyes of faith. God demonstrated his power over evil and over all human attempts to oppose him or tie him down. Even the sealing of the tomb did not help. The guards, who were supposed to see that it stayed sealed, trembled and became like dead men.

This is the joyous message the angel proclaimed on Easter morning. And this is still the gospel of Easter: Jesus is alive! The kingdom of God had irrevocably broken through! Easter is a feast of joy, a feast of victory—the climax of the gospel of Jesus. On this day all doubt and fear should be transformed to faith and joy!

3. One could then show that this event calls for faith, especially within the context of Matthew's description of the unbelief of the Jews. Faith means that we recognize in Jesus' resurrection the breakthrough of God's new world. And, accordingly, that we also allow God to break into our lives with his renewing power. On Easter morning, faith means that we appropriate the power of Jesus' resurrection as the source of our power. "God's amen is at the same time humanity's hallelujah!"

4. Finally, it can be pointed out that resurrection faith, if it is understood and lived correctly, should lead to the further proclamation of the gospel of the resurrected Jesus, through word and deed, through witness and action, mission and ministry. The Gospel of Matthew puts this beyond all doubt. Resurrection faith means being a witness of the resurrection. It means living in the light of "Go therefore" and of "Lo, I am with you always." It means looking forward with fear and great joy to the last redemptive act of the God of surprise, when we too shall hear: "Welcome, brothers and sisters!"

J. J. E. KOORNHOF

First Sunday after Easter: Luke 24:13-35

Bibliography

Commentaries

Geldenhuys, N. *Commentary on the Gospel of Luke.* Grand Rapids: Eerdmans, 1952.

Morris, L. *The Gospel according to St. Luke.* Tyndale New Testament Commentaries. Grand Rapids: Eerdmans, 1974.

Rienecker, F. *Das Evangelium des Lukas.* Wuppertal: Brockhaus, 1959.

Van der Sprenkel, S. F. H. J. *Het Evangelie van Lucas.* The Hague: Boekencentrum, 1964.

Homiletical

Fuller, R. H. *The Formation of the Resurrection Narratives,* 168-88. New York: Macmillan, 1971.

Koopmans, J. *Kleine Pestille,* 68-71. Goudrian: De Groot, 1971.

Noordmans, O. *Verzamelde Werken.* Vol. 8, 309-46.

Additional

Evans, C. F. *Resurrection and the New Testament.* Studies in Biblical Theology. London: SCM, 1970.

Kelsey, M. *Resurrection: Release from Oppression.* New York: Paulist, 1985.

Küng, H. *On Being a Christian,* 343-410. Garden City: Doubleday, 1976.

Minear, Paul S. *To Die and to Live: Christ's Resurrection and Christian Vocation.* New York: Seabury, 1977.

Perrin, N. *The Resurrection according to Matthew, Mark, and Luke.* Philadelphia: Fortress, 1977.

Smith, R. *Easter Gospels: The Resurrection of Jesus according to the Four Evangelists.* Minneapolis: Augsburg, 1983.

Spong, J. S. *The Easter Moment.* New York: Seabury, 1980.

Van Unnik, W. C. "A Storm Center in Contemporary Scholarship," in *Studies in Luke-Acts,* 15-32. Edited by L. E. Keck and J. L. Martyn. Nashville/New York: Abingdon, 1966.

I. Exegetical

1. This narrative about two men on their way to Emmaus is related only by Luke. It forms the long middle section of chapter 24, the chapter on the resurrection. Most exegetes see the genre of this narrative as very important, although they differ fundamentally in their theories.

Questions about its historicity (the location of Emmaus, etc.) and especially about similarities—with popular legends (Bultmann, Betz), Old Testament epiphanies (Breit), other Old Testament passages (Groenewald), Greek mythology (Ehrhardt), other passages in the Gospels (e.g., feeding of the masses [Roloff]), passages in Acts (e.g., Philip and the Ethiopian eunuch [Marshall, Dupont])—are discussed everywhere.

Some see this as a narrative composed by Luke himself, with a specific purpose in mind. Thus we read of: the "catechetical nature of the pericope" (Benoit), "a narration with didactic purport" (Wanke), a narrative constructed around "historical remnants" (Ernst), "things which cannot be expressed abstractly, but can only be put into words in a narrative form" (Lohfink), an "edifying or moving story" (Dupont), and a narrative that deliberately teaches specific truths (Léon-Dufour). Others approach this passage from a traditional-historical view, seeking to separate the genuine Lukan parts from the rest (Dibelius, Schubert—followed by Hahn and Wanke). Still others approach the text by means of structural analysis (Schnider-Stenger, Boismard, Léon-Dufour, J. d'Arc, Meynet, Van Iersel, Hamel).

2. The important question that all these approaches seek to answer is this: What is written here? What is the purport or thrust of this section? The answers are incredibly diverse:

a. In his article on structural analyses of this pericope during the past decade, Van Iersel examines five attempts, and then adds his own. Schnider/Stenger, for this issue linking up with Schubert, assume a chiastic construction for this narrative, but are rather vague about the exact turning point.

Four French authors have also analyzed the lexical structure according to a chiastic, or concentric, construction, each one coming to a different conclusion. Boismard regards verse 30 and the breaking of the bread as the moment of recognition. Léon-Dufour holds this moment is to be found in the words "he was alive" in verse 23. Jeanne d'Arc believes it to be in verse 26: "Was it not necessary that the Christ should suffer these things and enter into his glory?" Meynet claims that the center of the lexical structure is to be found in verse 23: "who said that he was alive." But he adds that this may indeed differ from the intent of the narrative structure—an issue on which he and Van Iersel differ sharply.

Van Iersel then presents an ingenious but unconvincing argument that the turning point of the epic structure lies in verses 28-29. According to him, the travelers are tested in three ways: the "qualifying test" (vv. 15ff.) is whether they will recognize him. In this they fail. The "main test" comes in verses 28-29. Jesus is in a state of need, because he has no shelter for the night. They give him shelter, although he is a stranger, so they pass this test. Then comes the "glorifying test" (vv. 30-31); they recognize him (vv. 30-31) when he breaks the bread. According to Van Iersel, the point of this narrative is exactly the same as that in Matthew 25:31-46, namely that they *show love* to Jesus when they show love to this stranger! Van Iersel consequently strongly defends a sermon in this vein by Gregory the Great. He criticizes d'Arc, who saw only a "moral lesson concerning hospitality" in Gregory's sermon, arguing that this is indeed the point.

Hamel also makes a structural analysis of sorts when he speaks of an "artistic construction in seven parts." He too detects a chiastic arrangement, with verses 25-27 (Jesus "interpreted . . . the scriptures") as the turning point. In his directives for preaching, however, he does not adhere to this analysis. Instead, he demands attention to the confession in verse 34. According to him, this is unjustly neglected by most preachers.

b. Another common approach is to assume that Luke is answering a very existential question: How can those who have not personally "seen" the resurrected Jesus still believe in him? How can they experience him? In this view, the purpose of the narrative is to show that seeing the empty grave, or listening to the witnesses (vv. 22-24), or even being present at one of the appearances of the resurrected Jesus does not necessarily lead to faith. Accordingly, those who experienced these things do not have any special advantage. It is indeed possible for those living in the "period of the church" (Conzelmann), who have not shared in these experiences, to believe. Through the ages and yet today, that which leads to true faith has been and is now available to everyone in doubt.

There are three major ways Christ reveals himself as the living Lord to the two men on the road to Emmaus and to all desperate people today. The first means is through the opening of Scripture. The second way is the breaking of the bread, seen as the Lord's Supper, and with the latter seen as the way Christ reveals himself yet today. Numerous exegetes, in combining these two possibilities, hold that this narrative demonstrates how Christ is actually present in word and sacrament. A third possibility is that verses 33-34 indicate that Christ also reveals himself in the public worship of the church (Hamel). Often all three possibilities are combined.

c. In his short summary of the intent of this passage, Geldenhuys interprets it as an admonition that we should also invite Jesus into our lives. "If the men of Emmaus had not invited Jesus into their home, He would have passed on, and how poor would their lives have been then! . . . How often does He address us also on life's way? And He still desires to enter where He is invited."

d. Marshall sees the narrative as a historical account rather than one with an intentional message. He believes that the *fact* of the resurrection is guaranteed in these verses, pointing out that it was expected (Old Testament promises and Jesus' own words) and that the resurrected Lord *appeared* to witnesses and was recognized as none other than Jesus himself. The two important issues, then, according to Marshall, are that the reality of the resurrection is demonstrated and that the Risen One is identified as Jesus of Nazareth. He considers Jesus' presence in the worship of the church as only a "secondary" motif in this pericope.

3. For more detail, commentaries can be used. The role of Jerusalem (in the entire theology of Luke, as well as at the beginning and again at the end of this narrative) is meaningful. Explanation of why they could not recognize Jesus at first, and why they did eventually recognize him when he broke the bread could also be helpful.

The textual variants of verse 4 are also important. Codex D, as well as Origen, change the *legontas* into *legontes,* putting the confession into the mouths of the travelers. This completely changes the importance. So instead of them being welcomed in this "congregation" by this group's confession that Jesus had indeed risen, these two men become witnesses of the resurrection to them. Hamel quite correctly points out that although this change of text is rejected almost universally in theory, in practice these verses are interpreted and preached as if this reading is indeed correct! This pericope then becomes a history or an object lesson in which "two questioning followers are changed by Jesus into faithful messengers proclaiming his resurrection."

II. Hermeneutical

1. It is interesting to note the wide variety of sermons on this pericope.

a. One of the most common approaches is to give an almost didactic exposition about the three ways one can still meet Christ today as the living Lord. Proclamation, sacrament (the Lord's Supper), and public worship are then presented, either separately or in combination, as the ways of encountering the Lord.

For example, Dinkler: "The Easter faith is bestowed in the Easter experience . . . in Word, sacrament and the worship of the congregation." A similar example is Stählin's sermon on "the first example of Christian worship." He presents four parts: "the lost faith of the disciples; their initiation into the divine plan; their recognition of the mystery of his eternal presence in the celebration of his supper; and our continuous prayer for his Holy Spirit."

b. Closely related to this and equally popular is the view that this story is a timeless "history of the heart" (Trillhaas), a history in which all share, through all ages. Numerous illustrations are available.

Dehn writes that it is the task of the preacher to "lead the congregation on the inner journey of the travelers to Emmaus, from their folly and slowness of heart, to their joyful confession that the Lord has truly risen." He states that all of us walk the same road and that they—just like us—have reached Easter certainty by faith alone (in the proclaimed Word, and through the living Lord) and not because they have seen. He sketches the inner disposition of the two disciples in a very moving way, especially their not understanding why he had to die and rise again, and adds that we, too, often struggle with this question. Emphatic declarations from the pulpit that Christ had to die and rise may be only signs of the preacher's personal compassion. Little is achieved by the mere repetition of evangelical phrases and orthodox doctrines of reconciliation, accompanied by pious phraseology. Members of the congregation may well accept all these historical truths and orthodox doctrines, but still "their hearts may not burn." They may still be without hope.

Moreover, Dehn says, in every congregation there exists an undogmatic theological liberalism that is not interested in Jesus' death and resurrection but only in "an ethical Christianity of the deed." In this view, Jesus' death only becomes understandable as the fulfillment of a genuine human life. Jesus held fast to his convictions and was willing to sacrifice for a worthy cause. And the resurrection only symbolizes a general truth, for example, that good will never be conquered, for in spite of the tremendous power of evil, the good will survive and overcome every time. He contends that many church members today do not understand the gospel of Easter and that their eyes are "kept from recognizing him" for who he really is. So the congregation has to be led to faith along the same existential path that these travelers to Emmaus walked.

Lilje treats this pericope in a similar way, although one has to remember that his discussion is a meditation rather than a sermon. In his preface, he explains that the meditation is based on his being imprisoned by the Gestapo on account of his "confession of our living Lord, who accompanies us, even when our eyes are too blind to notice his presence." His meditation begins: "A completely ruined world lies behind these two people. . . . All of a sudden they had lost everything which gave their lives a meaning and content." The author's identification with these two travelers is very apparent. In a deeply personal way, he describes how, during the Second World War, he did not have any other words from the Scriptures to cling to than "for thy sake we are being killed all the day long, we are regarded as sheep to be slaughtered" (Rom. 8:36). He explains that at some point in life every Christian comes to this place in their relationship to God, with nothing else left. In prison, he experienced such godforsakenness that at times he thought he would never again be able to speak honestly about God's goodness and mercy. When, however, he meditates on the fact that there are many shocking experiences such as his own all over the world, he realizes that people in such hopeless situations can still identify with the travelers to Emmaus. In the midst of all their questions there shines the faint ray of God's holy *dei* ("must"). This in turn reminds him of Meister Eckhard's observation that the horse that carries us most quickly to perfection is suffering. He concludes his meditation by noting that after recognizing Jesus the two travelers did not even think about the dark and dangerous road, because they knew where they belonged: with the brothers and sisters! "The diabolic danger of every temptation is that it tries to alienate us from others, to sever us from the fellowship of the church, to make us isolated and alone."

Gollwitzer also claims, in a certain sense, that the temptation we share with these travelers is the key to this pericope.

> It is the deepest affliction possible. . . . The doubt whether there really is a God and whether Jesus really spoke the truth—these are but small temptations! One only gets to know real, severe temptation when we stand in the midst of this history of hope, when we have become a prisoner of hope, when we do not have any doubts about God and Jesus . . . and when, unexpectedly, the final and gravest doubt attacks me, namely, that Jesus has perhaps withdrawn his promises, that he has allowed us to push him away from us, that he is finished with us. . . . This last temptation is so serious, because it makes such good sense! . . .
>
> With this most extreme despair, not about Jesus, but about themselves and about the entire world, these two followers walked along. . . . And perhaps the most glorious part of this story is what happened to them before they recognized or knew Jesus. When we find ourselves in the deepest affliction, Jesus is already right next to us. . . . From then on these travelers and we know: it may sometimes seem as if all our hopes and dreams have been killed, it may seem as if God has totally turned away his face from us, it may seem as if Christ is not available to us any more, it may seem as if Jesus and his Word and the Holy Scriptures have totally died to us . . . and yet, in reality, Jesus has already been on the way with us for a long time.

The message of the gospel proclaims that darkness has been caught up with and has been erased. It is now outdated, extinguished, past. This is the gospel of the resurrection.

c. In seeing this as a history of the heart, one has to make some distinctions. Hamel quite correctly remarks that it is "more than problematic" to make the story merely a timeless history of the heart that must be repeated over and over. The story presents the objective fact of a single, unique appearance of the resurrected Jesus to two men, in a dramatic and well-constructed narrative. At the same time, however, one has to admit that it seems the narrator wants to hold up Jesus as the living Lord before desperate Christians of all times. Accordingly, this narrative on the one hand presents us with the objectivity of the self-revelation of the resurrected Jesus, but on the other hand, this same message serves as subjective consolation for desperate, hopeless people. It is not, says Hamel, simply the history of our hearts, but also the "histories of our temptations." It is indeed meant to encourage our hearts and to bring us to new faith and hope. In this truth, according to him, lies the legitimacy of this very popular kind of preaching.

Many preachers, then, see temptation, despair, and hopelessness as the hermeneutical key. G. J. A. Jonker writes that the Resurrected One bestows new hope, hope of a totally different nature and order than the travelers had known previously. According to him, the theme is therefore two kinds of hope. Bornkamm emphasizes the hopelessness, consternation, and desolation of the travelers. (In a word-play, he speaks about the dead hopes of the living, while the dead one is actually the Living One!) Weber speaks of the "motif of the antithesis" in the Gospels, the strange but striking theme that Jesus' actions do not seem to be directed at those who are prepared for them, but rather at the helpless and the seemingly unworthy. This is very true of the resurrection appearances. We do not read that the early church expected the resurrection. Faith is under no circumstances a prerequisite for an encounter with the resurrected Jesus. The process is rather reversed—time and again faith is the result of such an encounter! According to Weber, this motif is expanded in the last two Gospels with "a certain joy of narration." According to him, the preacher today has to bear in mind the distress, embarrassment, and lack of faith of worshipers and should proclaim that Jesus lives, by pointing to the Scriptures. (With respect to the meal, he remarks that Augustine regarded it as the Holy Communion, that Luther did not refer to this question at all, and that Calvin explicitly denied it.)

d. In the homiletical and meditative literature also, numerous divergent approaches can be found. Many of these focus on only one component of the narrative, but others attempt to explain this pericope in its entirety.

Especially in older sermons, attempts were often made at verse 27 to identify Old Testament texts that Jesus could have used, and to enumerate and interpret them.

The inability of the travelers to recognize Jesus is often attributed to their false political expectations about the Messiah.

Luther used this pericope to argue that all proper exposition of Scriptures must, in the final analysis, be exposition by the Spirit of Christ himself. Only Christ himself can "interpret in all the scriptures the things concerning himself."

Schleiermacher's theme at verses 30-32 is "the connection or link that exists between the effects of Scripture and the immediate effects of the Redeemer." He concludes by appealing that we share with others the inner experiences and blessings we receive from the Lord.

This pericope is often used as an appeal to hospitality and generosity, which will then be blessed (see the reference to Gregory the Great earlier).

Kamphaus points out that in German Catholic preaching these verses, and particularly verse 29, are frequently used as an admonition to persevere in the practice of evening prayer. See also the application by Geldenhuys, that we should invite Jesus in to stay with us.

De Vries meditates on the words "but him they did not see" in verse 24, concluding that it is necessary to have insight into the heart of Scripture.

De Klerk treats verse 34, with the title: Peter—met secretly. He says that we should recognize ourselves in Peter, as sinners and as people who have been forgiven. The message here, then, is an invitation and a promise to penitent sinners. Koopmans also focuses on the appearance to Simon, speaking of Jesus being "resurrected for the sake of our justification."

Westermann draws a parallel between Jesus' walk with these two men and his obscurity during his earthly ministry, an ordinary man among the people and yet a prophet. He suggests this story also reminds us of how Jesus communicated with people, how he had to deal with a lack of understanding throughout his ministry, and how he only became fully known after his ascension. He warns those who doubt the truth of the resurrection not to isolate Jesus' resurrection from his earthly life, explaining that false conclusions can arise out of this. He encourages us rather to reflect on and believe in the entirety of Jesus' life and works, including the resurrection and the appearances.

Zippert uses the theme "Jesus keeps the conversation going." He looks at the significance of daily experience, especially our conversations. Even though a conversation may sometimes seem empty and in vain, it may be that someone says just the right words, words that comfort us and that result in the Resurrected One appearing to us. The worship service, holy communion, yes, even conversations and everyday experiences can be transformed into sacraments or symbols of God's nearness, if we only persevere. We, too, should "keep the conversation going."

Rössler tells us that personal histories of the heart cannot be "exchanged," but can only be experienced personally and subjectively. The Christian assurance of faith is not based on external or objective factors, or on that which is said by others, but it is ultimately based on existential, personal trust.

III. Homiletical

Perhaps it is best to approach this passage as a historical narrative, but one with a message to desperate people—people without any hope that Christ is alive and abides with us (see Marshall's exegesis [I, 2d] and Weber's guidelines [II, 1c]). Preaching, the Lord's Supper, and the communion of the saints could then be raised as subordinate themes, as the ways Christ assures us even today of his presence.

1. First, one could start by simply telling this moving story. Two travelers meet a stranger and tell him about Jesus and the remarkable events of the past few days. They tell him they "had hoped" (v. 21). It may seem to us as if they have lost all hope, but this is not true. They were still talking about him and thinking about him. They even told this stranger about him. They had not totally abandoned all hope, yet it was not real, living, joyful hope anymore. Their despair was a result of the circumstances, the realities, the facts. They were torn between hope and reality.

That is often the case with us as well. We cannot and do not want to abandon all hope. But in the final analysis we *have* already given up hope, because we are telling ourselves that we need to be "realistic" about things. In a more pastoral section, several variations of this sort of "realism" can then be described.

There are several things that confuse these strangers—and us (vv. 22-24), several indications that our realism may be mistaken, that we may perhaps be wrong. But we somehow ignore these evidences and try to live according to the rules of what we can see and touch.

2. Second, one can point out that God did not forsake these two confused disciples. Jesus walked with them and he did admonish them about their foolishness and slowness of heart, but he did not reject them.

He patiently led them to the moment when their eyes would be opened to see the invisible. In this connection, one perhaps may use the important distinction that Luther (and Calvin) made between reason and faith, according to which reason is the faculty that enables us to see the visible things, realistically, and faith is the possibility, given by God himself, to see the invisible as well, and to reckon with this reality also.

In this passage it is very ironic that the travelers were telling our Lord about two women who had "seen" Jesus and about others who had not "seen" him, while they themselves were seeing him and yet could not "see" him! Only the eyes of faith can see the living Jesus next to us. Scripture, the Supper, and the fellowship of the church could be raised here as being the most important means Christ uses to open our eyes. One can especially stress that they had to come to know the mysterious divine *dei* or "necessity" (v. 26) behind the suffering and death of Jesus. Real hope does not derive God's nearness from what we can see and touch; it takes into account the living and meaningful presence of God, right through everything, and sometimes concealed far beyond everything, often in direct contradiction to the visible. What we call realism is often only blind unbelief. Faith means taking into account the living Christ and organizing one's life accordingly.

3. In conclusion, one could point out the miraculous fact that this hope is never put to shame. Whoever ventures on this way will certainly see it confirmed. The travelers to Emmaus hurried back to Jerusalem, perhaps thinking about the difficulty of convincing the (unbelieving) disciples that they had seen Jesus. (For what "proof" did they have—just like us today—other than that their hearts "burned" within them and that "he was known to them in the breaking of the bread"?) When they arrived, however, they found people who were also rejoicing: "The Lord has risen indeed, and has appeared to Simon!"

D. J. SMIT

Second Sunday after Easter: Luke 24:36-49

Bibliography

Commentaries

Geldenhuys, N. *Commentary on the Gospel of Luke*. Grand Rapids: Eerdmans, 1952.

Morris, L. *The Gospel according to St. Luke*. Tyndale New Testament Commentaries. Grand Rapids: Eerdmans, 1974.

Rienecker, F. *Das Evangelium des Lukas*. Wuppertal: Brockhaus, 1959.

Van der Sprenkel, S. F. H. J. *Het Evangelie van Lucas*. The Hague: Boekencentrum, 1964.

Homiletical

Kingsbury, J. D. In *Interpretation: A Journal of Bible and Theology* 35 (1981): 170-74.

Noordmans, O. *Verzamelde Werken*. Vol. 8, 317-19. Kampen: Kok, 1980.

Velema, W. H. *Tussen Tekst en Preek,* 89-92. Kampen: Kok, 1976.

Additional

Evans, C. F. *Resurrection and the New Testament,* 92-115. London: SCM, 1970.

Küng, H. *The Christian Challenge,* 209-53. Garden City: Doubleday, 1979.

Minear, P. S. *To Die & To Live: Christ's Resurrection and Christian Vocation,* 39-65. New York: Seabury, 1977.

Perrin, N. *The Resurrection according to Matthew, Mark, and Luke.* Philadelphia: Fortress, 1977.

I. Exegetical

1. Luke's resurrection narrative is to a great extent autonomous. There are three stories in all: the women at the empty tomb (24:1-12), the appearance of Jesus to the two men from Emmaus (24:13-35), and his appearance to the disciples (24:36-49). The other Gospels also relate the first of the three stories (Matt. 28:1-10; Mark 16:1-8; John 20:1-9), but the last two stories one finds only in Luke.

Three prominent aspects appear in Luke's resurrection account. First, in line with the structure of his Gospel, Luke focuses on Jerusalem. He does not mention Jesus' appearances in Galilee. Second, Scripture plays a very important role (24:27, 32, 44-47). Third, he emphasizes Christ's physical resurrection. Some consider the emphasis on Scripture as the central motif in Luke's portrayal of the resurrection. Resurrection then means "opening their minds to understand the Scriptures" (v. 45): "The risen Jesus enables the disciples to perceive that God's plan of salvation, attested to in the Scriptures, attains its fulfillment in him, the crucified and the risen Messiah, in whom God exercises his end-time rule and proffers salvation to humankind" (Kingsbury).

2. This pericope is subdivided by most commentators (Marshall, Morris, and others) into the appearance (vv. 36-43) and the mission (vv. 44-49). Still, it is possible and perhaps even desirable to treat it as a single unit.

For a complete verse-by-verse exegesis, the commentaries must be consulted. There are a few fairly controversial (but, fortunately, not fundamental) problems of textual criticism (vv. 36, 40, 42) and also certain difficulties with translation (vv. 44, 46) that must receive attention.

a. In verses 36-43, Luke clearly wants to emphasize that Christ has actually risen physically. The question is whether Luke, with his "foremost reason of fidelity to his sources" (Caird), also has other motives for this emphasis. Most commentators see a strong apologetic motive, in opposition to possible Docetic views, for instance. Caird thinks this emphasis on the physical details is important because to the Jewish mind it would be proof of the truth and reality of Christ's resurrection.

When Christ, in verses 39 and 40, shows his hands and feet to his disciples, he not only wants to convince them of his *physical* presence, however, but very specifically of *his* physical presence. Nearly all the commentators see the issue at stake in John 20:25-27 (the mark of the nails) as the recognition that the Resurrected One is Jesus himself.

> And now the main thing is that they must know that they . . . are dealing with the same Jesus whom they heard delivering the Sermon on the Mount on the shore of Tiberias; who sailed with them on the lake; who told his parables; who healed the sick. The same Jesus who suffered, was crucified and buried. With an eye to the future, their first and foremost need was to know that this same Jesus was still with them and would stay with them. (Noordmans)

Everything Jesus does is aimed at awakening faith and assurance in the confused disciples (note the strongly psychological description: "startled," "frightened," "troubled," "doubts rise in your minds."

b. The second part of this pericope (vv. 44-49) is of special importance. Not only does it form the link between the Gospel of Luke and Acts, but it also includes nearly all of the central themes of Luke's theology (cf. Kingsbury: "[1] God as the author of salvation; [2] Jesus Christ as the one in whom God effects salvation; [3] the disciples as witnesses of salvation; [4] the Spirit as the power that will enable the disciples . . . to become the proclaimers of salvation"). In verses 44-46 we have a repetition of what happened to the two men on their way to Emmaus: Scripture is explained as pointing to Christ, and the listeners' minds are opened to understand the Word. In verses 47-49, however, there is a new element not present in the Emmaus pericope. God's plan for the salvation of the world (cf. the universalism of Luke) is announced and unfolded. In the name of Christ and in the power of the Spirit, the disciples will preach repentance and forgiveness of sins to all nations.

3. An apt summary of the events in this pericope is: The risen Lord comes to meet his frightened and disbelieving disciples to bring them from doubt to faith, in order to recruit them as witnesses and to call them to preach the gospel.

II. Hermeneutical

1. In resurrection sermons it is most important to keep doctrine and Scripture in the proper relationship. This relationship can be distorted in a number of ways. Because the physical resurrection of Christ is unacceptable to the rational mind, it sometimes happens that a preacher shrugs his shoulders about the historical doctrine, and resorts to the so-

called Easter kerygma. On the other hand, there is a type of preaching that completely disregards the text and its message and "defends" the historical facts of the resurrection. A better way is to expound the specific message of the text. In line with what the Heidelberg Catechism does, the preacher must repeatedly look for the "benefit" of the resurrection.

2. Edmund Schlink sees the message of this passage in the comforting and pastoral behavior of Christ. After his resurrection he returns to his disciples.

> He has not conquered sinners and the world, only to leave them behind now. He has not risen for his own sake. He does not cling to his resurrection as though it were stolen goods, to possess and enjoy it and not to share it. Soon after he has dethroned death, the risen Lord turns to those who killed him and who forsook him in his death. Soon after he has conquered the world and its hatred and enmity, the Lord spreads out his hands to offer this same world the fruit of his resurrection.

In a striking passage Schlink then shows how the love of Christ for his disciples and his turning toward them in love reach a climax when he asks for food (v. 41) and eats it (v. 43).

> Here the exalted Lord is busy again humbling himself because of his disciples. He does not need this food, but eats it only because of them. This is grace in action. As real as this food, so real is God's grace! Christ, the new human being, is not ashamed to eat the fruits of an "old" world together with "old" human beings.

This is grace. Furthermore, it is important to realize that these tokens not only bear witness to his love and grace, but are primarily meant to show that he lives, that he has risen from the dead, and that he is truly present with his disciples.

3. Luke's emphasis on the link between the resurrection and Scripture can also be used as a starting point for a sermon. To celebrate Easter means to learn to read, says Velema. He then refers to the double movement in Luke 24 from Scripture to the recognition of Christ (cf. the travelers to Emmaus, vv. 13-35) and from the encounter with Christ to Scripture (vv. 36-49). "To celebrate Easter means to understand the Scriptures and thus to meet Jesus. But it also means to meet Jesus and thus to understand the Scriptures. We must not neglect either of these" (Velema). Gollwitzer points out that when Christ returns to his disciples, he does not give them an eyewitness account of his experiences,

but "he leads them in a Bible study." Here, says Gollwitzer, we see the secret and the power of the resurrection faith. In the same way that Jesus simply explained his own history to the disciples, according to the Scriptures the church should also continue to tell Jesus' story. It pleases God "to do unheard of things by means of something as simple as a story and as debatable as witness." This witness, based on Scripture, is the key, "the strongest weapon of the church."

4. Luther writes that the problem with the doctrine of Christ's death and resurrection is that it lies outside our experience. "If we therefore wish to understand it and to experience something of it . . . then we must all—I for myself, you for yourself, and everybody for himself—believe in the forgiveness of sins." With these words of Luther as a key, Steck tries to explain the message of Luke 26:36-49.

a. Can such an approach be justified? In the popular creed, the forgiveness of sins is usually linked to Christ's crucifixion and death only. This is why a direct connection between resurrection and forgiveness seems somewhat strange. This, however, certainly does not mean that it is incongruous. In Romans 4:25 Paul connects the resurrection with justification when he states that "Jesus our Lord . . . was delivered over to death for our sins and was raised to life for our justification." Although there is some difference of opinion about the interpretation of this difficult text, it is generally regarded as the *locus classicus* for the idea of the resurrection as the effectuation of the atonement. When the Father raises Christ, he proves that he accepts Christ's self-sacrifice for the sin of the world, and that, therefore, the fruit of the death of Christ (i.e., justification and forgiveness) is truly valid. (Cf. Heidelberg Catechism, Lord's Day 17 on the benefits of Christ's resurrection: "by his resurrection he has overcome death, so that he might make us share in the righteousness he won for us by his death.")

Klappert also refers to the so-called Easter meals of Jesus with his disciples after the resurrection (Luke 24:30ff.; John 21:4-11; Acts 10:41) as a further confirmation of the link between resurrection and forgiveness. "The resurrection narratives are in essence 'histories of forgiveness.'" In the Bible, eating together means fellowship. When, after his resurrection, Jesus therefore eats with the disciples who had forsaken and denied him, this demonstrates that he has forgiven them and that he resumes and continues his fellowship with them.

b. This connection between resurrection and justification is also clear in our text. Christ's resurrection prepares the way for the fulfillment of the promise to the nations, and thus for the preaching of the gospel of forgiveness and repentance. "To open up this way to repentance and forgiveness of sins, the Holy One of God had to die. The fact that this way is now open to everybody is confirmed by the living presence of the risen Lord in whom God himself confirms the fruit of his death" (Joest, commenting on v. 47).

Steck explains that with this kind of approach to a very difficult issue (namely, the historical resurrection) he is not trying to escape into an easier and more existential matter, the forgiveness of sins. "That is probably the reason why the Lord takes so much trouble to make this article clear and comprehensible to us: the coming of his Son, the cross, the resurrection, the witness of the disciples—everything is put into effect to give us assurance and to help us to believe this difficult article about the forgiveness of sins." In a world filled with relentless demands and laws it is our privilege to bring the message of a merciful God!

5. A few interesting sermon outlines from the homiletical literature can be mentioned.

Joest follows the story line of the pericope and suggests: (1) the living Lord assures the disciples of his supportive presence; (2) he opens their minds to understand the Scriptures; (c) he calls them to be witnesses.

Schmithals discusses three aspects of Christ's physical resurrection: (1) the soteriological significance (life only via death); (2) the eschatological significance (God calls the nations); and (3) the ethical significance (new life).

Velema preaches about the three "musts" of Easter: (1) Christ must suffer; (2) Christ must rise; and (3) in his Name, repentance and forgiveness must now be preached.

Wilcock detects in the second part of the pericope (vv. 44-49) four guiding lights Christ uses to indicate to his disciples the way to the future: (1) a biblical theology (v. 46); (2) an evangelistic program (v. 47); (3) an apostolic authority (v. 48); and (4) a spiritual dynamic (v. 49).

Bauer uses a four-point scheme: (1) As Jesus in the past appeared to his disciples as the living Christ, so today we experience his living presence only in the communion of saints, when he meets us through his Word and the sacraments. (2) When he addresses us in the worship service and when we speak to him in prayer, our certainty grows that he is still alive. (3) As Jesus in the past preached God's plan of salvation to the world, so still today he brings peace in our disturbed lives through his Word. (4) As our faith grows out of the witness of the apostles to his resurrection, so it is our task to pass on our faith to anxious and despondent people, so that they too can live.

III. Homiletical

A suggested sermon outline:

1. One can start by pointing out to the congregation Christ's comforting attitude toward his disciples (cf. I, 2a, and especially II, 2 for details that can be used in this regard).

2. This loving, merciful attitude culminates in the message of the forgiveness of sins. To explain, one can first refer to the general connection between the resurrection and forgiveness (cf. II, 4a, for details), and then to the connection between the two within this pericope (cf. II, 4b: Jesus forgives his disciples and makes them witnesses to, and preachers of, the forgiveness of sins).

3. The radical nature of this forgiveness can then be explained.

Forgiveness of sins is often misunderstood. Some think forgiveness means that in the long run sin is not so bad or as awful. This is a fatal misunderstanding of the message of the church. Sin *is* terrible. It is a destructive power that can ruin the lives of people. A second general misunderstanding is that forgiveness means that we have a chance to make amends or to compensate for our sins: sin is terrible, some people would say, but the good news is that Jesus gives us a chance to even matters up. Forgiveness of sins in the name of Christ is, however, far more than this. It means that forgiveness does not depend on what we do, but on what Christ has done. Sin, which ruled our lives like a tyrant, which made us chained slaves and wanted to destroy and wreck our lives, has finally lost its power, being destroyed by Christ. Through his cross and resurrection, Christ became the Conqueror. Perhaps few people wrote more movingly about this radical victory of Christ over sin than Barth. In his theology, Christ's cross and resurrection together proclaim "the triumph of God's grace." Through Christ's victory, sin has truly become "das Nichtige" (nothingness)—a conquered and beaten enemy, finished and done for. Because Christ rose, the church can tell people: Peace unto you! You have no need to be so afraid. The enemy has been beaten. Because Jesus has risen, you have been liberated and you can go out free. Your sins are forgiven!

4. Lastly, the congregation must know that, according to verse 47,

not only forgiveness must be preached but also repentance. Forgiveness always goes hand in hand with repentance (change, transformation). Repentance should, however, never be interpreted in such a way that change becomes the condition for forgiveness. Change is only "the way" we can obtain forgiveness (Velema), though it is also the *only* way!

Isn't it possible that one can gain forgiveness in another, easier way? No, in any case not Christ's forgiveness. Why not? Because the Lord who rose and conquered is the same who died and had to pay the price for our sins (cf. I, 2). The connection between forgiveness and repentance is very closely linked with the connection between the resurrection and the cross.

Steck tells a beautiful anecdote that illustrates this. It is the story of a Bishop Martin. Once the devil appeared to Martin in the form of the Savior himself, full of glory and splendor. The devil started speaking to the bishop in quite a flattering way: "Martin, you have served me so faithfully that I could not do otherwise but pay you a visit. Do you see now how I love you? I appear to you before I appear to anybody else!"

Martin asked: "But, tell me, who are you?"

The devil answered: "I am your Savior, Jesus."

"Where are your wounds?" asked Martin.

"Oh," answered the devil, "I do not come from the cross right now. I come from heaven, in my glory."

The bishop replied: "Go away from before my eyes. You are the devil. A Savior without wounds I may not see. The only Savior I acknowledge and profess is the one who can show the signs of his suffering!"

Forgiveness without repentance is the gospel of hell. The only Savior who can truly forgive and save is the one who can show his wounds. He also asks for repentance. Forgiveness? Yes, completely! But never without repentance.

C. W. BURGER

Third Sunday after Easter:
Psalm 16:8

Bibliography

Commentaries

Craigie, P. C. *Psalms 1-50*. Word Biblical Commentary. Vol. 19. Waco: Word, 1983.

Hubbard, D. A. *Psalms for all Seasons*. Grand Rapids: Eerdmans, 1971.

Kidner, D. *Psalms 1-72*. London/Downers Grove: InterVarsity, 1973.

Ridderbos, N. H. *De Psalmen*. Korte Verklaring der Heilige Schrift. Vol. 1. Kampen: Kok, 1962.

Van der Ploeg, J. P. M., O.P. *Psalmen*. Roermond: Romen, 1971.

Homiletical

Kraus, H. J. In *Herr tue meine Lippen auf*, vol. 5, 257-65 (on Ps. 16:8-11). Wuppertal-Bormen: Müller, 1961.

Van Ruler, A. A. *Over de Psalmen Gesproken: Meditaties over de Psalmen*, 44-47. Nijkerk: Callenbach, 1973.

Additional

Boers, H. W. "Psalm 16 and the Historical Origin of the Christian Faith." *Zeitschrift für die Neutestamentliche Wissenschaft* 60 (1969): 105-10.

Goppelt, L. *Typos: The Typological Interpretation of the Old Testament in the New*. Grand Rapids: Eerdmans, 1982.

I. Exegetical

1. In the presence of God the believer experiences a sense of belonging. According to Psalm 16, this sense of belonging reveals itself on two levels: in a feeling of security and in knowing that one's life has new direction. In the presence of the risen Christ, the believer can

therefore joyfully repeat: "Therefore my heart is glad, and my soul rejoices; my body also dwells secure" (v. 9, reflecting our security), and "Thou dost show me the path of life" (v. 11, acknowledging God's leading). This, in short, is the message of Psalm 16 in the light of Easter.

Exegetically, this is a very interesting psalm. There are indications of some very old material woven into the text, and there are also some striking differences among translations of this psalm. Verse 3 is an example of differences in translation: "As for the saints in the land, they are the noble, in whom is all my delight" (RSV); or "How excellent are the Lord's faithful people! My greatest pleasure is to be with them" (TEV).

However, it goes beyond our purpose here to examine these exegetical matters.

2. What follows is an outline of the psalm, with some brief remarks:

a. Verses 1-4: The psalm begins with a prayer and a confession. The prayer is: "Preserve me, O God, for in thee I take refuge" (v. 1). This prayer is possible because the supplicant also confesses: "Thou art my Lord; I have no good apart from thee" (v. 2). The privilege of belonging to the Lord and of living in his presence is in contrast to the condition depicted in verses 3-4: idolatry which causes increasing distress. The "good" that the believer in Yahweh experiences is contrasted with the multiplied afflictions of the idolater.

b. Verses 5-6: The trust expressed in verse 2 is elaborated upon in these verses. The "good" is described here as an inheritance: Yahweh is my inheritance. "The lines have fallen for me in pleasant places" (v. 6).

c. Verses 7-9: The contents of this inheritance is explained in more detail in what seems to be the heart of the psalm. Verses 7 and 9 contain similar elements: joy and praise, and an explanation of this joy.

Verse 7: "I bless the Lord who gives me counsel"—God has shown me the way of life.

Verse 9: "Therefore my heart is glad, and my soul rejoices; my body also dwells secure"—he has given me security.

Because of this parallel construction, verse 8, positioned between them, must be seen as a crucial statement: "I keep the Lord always before me; because he is at my right hand, I shall not be moved." This verse is particularly important for preaching. It speaks of an act of trust that believers must continually repeat.

These three verses can therefore be outlined as follows:

7: Praise for the path of life.
8: "I keep the Lord always before me."
9: Joy in our security.

d. Verses 10-11: The main ideas of the psalm are repeated in the conclusion: security (v. 10), the way of life (v. 11a), joy (v. 11b), and the goodly heritage (v. 11c).

e. Summary: Whoever trusts in the Lord's presence can rejoice in the assurance of both steadfast direction and security in life.

II. Hermeneutical

There are some important questions that should be considered here:

1. How can a psalm be used in proclaiming the Easter message? The foundation of Psalm 16 is the firm belief that Yahweh is alive and present in our lives. New Testament believers also confess this during Easter—through his resurrection, Christ is alive and present in his church. Psalm 16 focuses on especially one feature of Easter faith: in the presence of the living Lord believers experience a definite sense of belonging. And this presence of the Lord provides both their protection, and his guidance in the ways of righteousness.

2. How should verse 10 be understood by the church living in the light of Easter?

The main question is, of course, Does this verse refer only to protection in life, or does it also refer to protection from death?

It is immediately clear that the author of Psalm 16 prays for protection in this life. In part I we have seen the security the believer experiences in the presence of the Lord. Kraus considers the temple, a place of refuge, to be the background of this psalm. The suppliant of Psalm 16 fears for his life, so he prays for protection.

However, Acts 2:25-28 quotes this psalm (vv. 8-11) and applies it to the resurrection of Christ. Because of this, many exegetes believe that verse 10 must be interpreted with reference to Christ. The "real" meaning of this verse must, according to them, be sought in the resurrection of Christ.

The hermeneutical considerations concerning Old Testament quotations in the New Testament cannot be discussed here in detail. It is not necessary, however, to see a clash between these two interpretations. Psalm 16 does stress the protection of the believer in the presence of God. Through the New Testament events concerning Christ, the concept of God's presence was enhanced, so that not only did God's power make Christ's resurrection possible but it also promised resurrection and everlasting life to all believers. That, of course, is the message of the New Testament and not of Psalm 16 in its Old Testament context.

3. How can present-day believers experience the presence of the Lord? There is always a strong temptation to seek direct proof of God's presence in oneself. Many people and religious groups search for it by means of emotional experience. Often, however, when the feeling disappears, so does the conviction of God's nearness. An excessive emphasis on the *charismata* is often the twin brother of this subjectivism. Someone once admitted to me that if her special gift of the Spirit would stop, her faith would also cease. In her case, the special gift clearly functioned as proof of God's presence in her life. She therefore continuously and diligently had to seek for it and make sure it stayed with her.

The dangers of such an attitude are evident. According to Scripture, God's presence is meant for every believer. Certain charismata or gifts of the Spirit are not given to all believers and are also not necessarily given permanently to specific believers. For that reason one should never apply them as criteria of God's presence in the believer's life. God is a living God who makes himself known through his deeds, especially as they are described in the Bible, the climax being his revelation in Jesus Christ. Believers can only meet God and only experience his presence when they accept, through acts of faith and trust, the testimony of his deeds in the gospel.

III. Homiletical

1. Believers want continuing assurance that God is present in their lives. Like Moses we all say to God: "Please, show me your glory" (Ex. 33:18). We want to experience God's presence. That is the need of worshipers as well as of those who long for God's active involvement in their situations of fear, distress, misery, oppression, and hopelessness. A preacher ought to be able to identify specific areas in worshipers' lives where this need is most deeply felt.

Experiencing God's presence is not an impossible dream. It is within the reach of every believer and of groups of believers, because Jesus has risen from the dead. He arose to live with his church as Lord, the living Redeemer, the Resurrected One, present in history, present in suffering. That is the claim and the assurance of the Easter gospel.

2. A few situations in which Christians need Christ's protecting and liberating nearness can be mentioned, such as sickness, family problems, and political and economic distress. Believers can go to the Lord in these situations and say with the psalmist: "Preserve me, O God, for in thee I take refuge" (v. 1), and then declare with the same trust: "Therefore my heart is glad, and my soul rejoices; my body also dwells secure" (v. 9). This is the promise of the psalm, read in the light of Easter. Christ is a living Redeemer; he reveals himself to us in his divine power, the same power that made his resurrection possible (Eph. 1:19-20). In this power, he still meets those who go to him with their needs.

Kraus rightly points out that we should never spiritualize our crises, as though the redemption in which Psalm 16 rejoices were release from spiritual distress alone. Psalm 16 testifies of redemption from earthly suffering. God meets us in the despair that is part and parcel of our daily existence, filled as it is with affliction and trial. In all of life's troubles, we can feel safe with Christ. The background of this psalm, according to Kraus, can also be a good illustration: the supplicant flees from his enemies and looks for God's protection in the temple, where the right of asylum was in force.

3. But there is more to this. Living in Christ's presence, Christians not only experience safety, but also have direction in life (see part I). Verses 7b and 11a are relevant here. As our counselor, Christ penetrates even our deepest thoughts and our conscience with his words. The TEV translates this: "I praise the Lord because He guides me and in the night my conscience warns me" (v. 7b). As our living Redeemer, he addresses us and admonishes us. He teaches us and shows us the path of life. Because Christ has risen from the dead, he lives in relationship with us, in two-way communication with the church. Through his Spirit he leads us in the truth. Through this communication we come to know the "path of life" (v. 11a).

Of course, this instruction in the path of life is not mere subjective revelation to individuals. Throughout history, one can find many people who ruined themselves and others with so-called personal revelations of God. The only valid communication between God and his followers takes place under the normative guidance of his revealed Word, the Bible. This communication can, of course, be very personal with individual believers. When believers live in fellowship with the risen

Christ, they experience the Word of God and its implications for their lives very existentially, as a very personal reality. It must also be said that the role of the church here may never be neglected.

4. Whenever the presence of the Lord becomes real for believers, life becomes meaningful, and indeed "pleasant" and "goodly." Note the joy in verses 7 and 9. To live for the Lord brings joy. Life gains new meaning. The supplicant in Psalm 16 calls out joyfully: "The lines have fallen for me in pleasant places; yea, I have a goodly heritage" (v. 6). The secret of this optimistic outlook is that this believer is experiencing that the Lord is always near. He is our guarantor and protector, especially in negative circumstances. According to verse 5: "The Lord is my chosen portion and my cup; thou holdest my lot."

People seem to understand and experience the meaning of the cross more readily than they do the resurrection. They know how the cross functions as atonement for sin, and they often integrate this in their daily lives. Christ's resurrection, however, is a vague matter for many worshipers. Therefore it must be stressed that unless Christ's resurrection is part of our faith, we will never have the conviction of God's presence in our lives. Religion in such cases is religion without God; such people may be Christians, but they live without the power of Christ. Religion of this kind becomes shallow, often being only moralistic. All that is left of the Christian religion here is the law, a religion of rules and regulations. Such people cannot speak in the spirit of Psalm 16.

5. Therefore, Easter proclamation, according to Psalm 16, should aim at how we can experience Christ's presence. Psalm 16 can make an invaluable contribution here.

For example, the pastor can emphasize the trust in verses 2 and 5. Verse 8a is especially important: "I keep the Lord always before me." It suggests an act of faith on the part of the believer. The NEB shows this: "I have set the Lord continually before me." So does the TEV: "I am always aware of the Lord's presence." The believer should turn to God in faith, and live in the full conviction that God is real and that he acts. Van Ruler puts it this way: "I continually consider who the Lord God is, what thoughts are in his heart, what he plans for humanity and for the world, how he conducts himself in all his deeds."

This knowledge of God and of his ways is found in Scripture. The Lord reveals himself to us through his Word. Van Ruler says: "In the past he made himself known through his great deeds. We should remember those deeds constantly. Only in *that* way will we be keeping the Lord continually before us."

During Easter, we should especially keep in mind God's role in Christ's resurrection. The resurrection should form part of our life every day. Then we will be filled with the assurance of his presence in our lives. What God requires is trust in what he says about himself in his Word. Of course, this is at times very difficult, especially when because of our circumstances we find little evidence of God's nearness. The same thing happened to the psalmist. When he wrote this moving confession, he was in distress (v. 1). In such conditions, we should resist the temptation to "find" God through subjective experience (see II, 3). Here, too, we should set the Lord continually before us.

M. A. V. VAN DER MERWE

Fourth Sunday after Easter: Acts 2:22-36

Bibliography

Commentaries

Barclay, W. *The Acts of the Apostles.* Philadelphia: Westminster, 1976.

Bruce, F. F. *The Acts of the Apostles.* Chicago/Toronto: InterVarsity, 1952.

Calvin, J. *The Acts of the Apostles.* Vol. 1. Grand Rapids: Eerdmans, 1949.

Marshall, I. H. *The Acts of the Apostles.* Tyndale New Testament Commentaries. Grand Rapids: Eerdmans, 1980.

Munck, J. *The Acts of the Apostles.* The Anchor Bible. Garden City: Doubleday, 1967.

Homiletical

Ridderbos, H. N. *God is Liefde,* 44-53 (sermons on Acts 2:33). Kampen: Kok, 1979.

Additional

Bruce, F. F. "The Speeches in Acts: Thirty Years After," in *Reconciliation and Hope,* 53-75. Edited by Robert Banks. Exeter: Paternoster/Grand Rapids: Eerdmans, 1974.

Marshall, I. H. *Luke: Historian and Theologian.* Exeter: Paternoster, 1970.

Metzger, B. M. "The Meaning of Christ's Ascension," in *Search the Scriptures,* 118-28. Leiden: Brill, 1969.

Zehnle, R. F. *Peter's Pentecost Discourse.* Nashville/New York: Abingdon, 1971.

I. Exegetical

1. Much has been written about the sermons, or discourses, in Acts being very strategically placed. Many commentators believe that Acts 1:8 sets out the following structure for the book: (1) chapters 2-7; (2) chapters 8-11; (3) chapters 13-28. And, based on Acts 9:15, chapters 13-28 are further divided as follows: (1) 13-20 (among the Gentiles); (2) 24, 26 (before kings); and (3) 22, 28 (before the people of Israel). It does then seem clear that the discourses are placed according to this scheme.

It is also significant that these sermons have some common features. Peter's three speeches (2:14-36, 40; 3:12-26; and 10:34-43) can be divided as follows: the exordium (the direct provocation); the testimony concerning Jesus; and the paranesis (the summons to repentance and the promise of forgiveness). These three parts are also present, though in a different order, in Paul's three speeches in the second part of Acts.

This similar structure causes some, especially the school of form criticism (Dibelius *cum suis*) to regard these sermons as nonhistorical, yet ingenious, compositions by Luke. While many theologians accept this point of view with some minor variations, Ridderbos, like Dodd, holds that though, in accordance with the nature of the entire book of Acts, Luke did indeed compose them and that they do not contain the actual words Peter and Paul spoke on the specific occasions, they must nevertheless be regarded as reflecting "the original apostolic preaching." They are "typical examples or illustrations, carefully chosen, of the original apostolic witness" and, therefore, in that sense, "historical."

2. Peter's Pentecost speech can be divided as follows: introduction (direct provocation [vv. 14-16] and scriptural proof from Joel 3:1-5a LXX [vv. 17-21]), proclamation of the events concerning Jesus (vv. 22-36), and paranetic summons (vv. 37-39). The middle section is the pericope under discussion for this volume.

This middle section also consists of three parts: the early ministry, death, and resurrection of Jesus, with scriptural proofs (vv. 22-32); the exaltation of Jesus, with scriptural proofs (vv. 33-35); and the summary thesis of verse 36. Accordingly, more than half of Peter's sermon is devoted to the resurrection, because the Old Testament citation is so extensive here. The resurrection climaxes in Christ's exaltation, his position of honor and power that enables him to pour out the Holy Spirit.

Verse 36 is a résumé of this proclamation section as well as a bridge to the following paranesis. The chiastic structure of verse 36 (a-b-b-a) emphasizes that God has made Jesus *Lord* (on the basis of verse 34) and *Christ* (on the basis of verse 31). This is the final conclusion.

Haenchen rightly maintains that verses 22-36 contain the "actual kerygma." Schneider also speaks of an "actual kerygma" interrupted by the Scripture proofs in verses 24b-35 but then completed in verse 36: Jesus of Nazareth is the Lord and Messiah (v. 36), in whose name the hearers must be baptized (v. 38) in order to be saved (v. 40b). Bruce agrees that "the main theme is the proclamation of Jesus as Lord and Messiah."

3. Verses 22-36:

a. It is important to note the way in which Psalm 110:1 (LXX 109:1) functions here. No other text is quoted in the christological expressions of the New Testament more often (Mark 12:36; 16:19; Acts 2:32-35; 5:31; 7:55; Rom. 8:34; 1 Cor. 15:20ff.; Eph. 1:20; 2:5ff.; Col. 2:10, 15).

In his important study on the titles of Jesus, Hahn argues that all titles of honor in the early Christian church were aimed at describing Jesus' role in the end time, which they saw as imminent. He also sees the early church applying Psalm 110:1 to Jesus, and using the titles "Lord" and "Christ." According to him, in the early church attention was not focused on any activity of the living Lord in that time, but solely on the time of the end and on Jesus' role as Lord and Christ in *that* future, albeit imminent, time. When the church started to grow in the Hellenistic-Jewish communities and the second coming of Christ did not occur, new titles were formed and new meanings were attached to the old titles to elucidate Christ's role in that dispensation, the period of history *before* the second coming. According to Hahn, the idea with which the early Christians lived was of a temporary withdrawal of Jesus by means of the ascension, during which he was passive (and absent), until his glorious second coming as Lord and Christ.

In line with Hahn's ideas, several commentators have spoken of the "inactivity" of Jesus Christ according to Acts (Moule talks about "an absentee Christology"). Schweizer and Vielhauer, however, sharply criticize this theory. They maintain that, according to Acts, the exalted Christ did dwell with his church and that he was seen as actively present in many ways. (It is a controversial question whether, according to

Acts, this activity of Jesus as Lord extended to the world beyond the church.)

Vielhauer makes a useful distinction between "Erhöhtwerden," "Erhöhtsein," and "Wirksamkeit des Erhöhten" (the *act* of being exalted, the *position* of being exalted, and the *activity* of the exalted Lord). According to him, the book of Acts is not only concerned with the first two aspects, but it is also definitely concerned with the activity of Christ as exalted Lord. Expressions that are commonly used, for example, that the book of Acts is the proclamation concerning the *exalted* Jesus (P. G. R. de Villiers) and that "the exaltation of Jesus is the central point in the preaching of Acts" (Marshall), must be interpreted in the sense that the theme of the book of Acts is "the way in which the exalted Lord leads the history of his cause and through that effectuates the plan of God" (Stählin).

b. One should therefore distinguish between the expressions *resurrection, ascension,* and *exaltation* in Acts (though the relation between ascension and exaltation is very controversial). The resurrection has a confirming as well as an eschatological function. Through the resurrection Jesus is pronounced, ordained, "made" to be Messiah by God. (But not in an adoptive sense, because he had been the Messiah already during his earthly life—Schneider, Ridderbos.) The apostles are witnesses of that. At the same time, the resurrection also confirms that they are living in the end-times, hence the outpouring of the Holy Spirit, which is interpreted as eschatological fulfillment of Old Testament prophecies. Hence also the urgency of paranesis, calling for conversion and faith in his Name.

This resurrection (vv. 24-32) is followed by the new (and separate) act of exaltation (vv. 33-35). The exaltation *is* something more than the resurrection and the ascension. Consequently, verse 33 refers not only to the historical and visible events surrounding the ascension, as described in Acts 1:6-11, but also to the wider christological dimensions encompassing—but also surpassing—the resurrection and ascension. Apart from chapter 1 in Acts, the events surrounding the ascension are only mentioned indirectly within both this broader context and the more comprehensive meaning of the exaltation. In the speeches in Acts the ascension does not function independently. Although verses 33-36, therefore, refer indirectly to the events of the ascension (the first aspect of Vielhauer's threefold distinction), this passage obviously deals much more with the present heavenly position of power of Jesus (Vielhauer's second aspect) and with the activity of this exalted Jesus (Vielhauer's third aspect). For that reason the outpouring of the Spirit can be seen as empirical proof of Jesus' exaltation, and for that reason Jesus' titles become the climax of the argument.

It is in view of this that the *tē dexia* in verse 33 will have to be interpreted. While many exegetes view this as a dative of instrument ("exalted *by* the right hand"), others see it—and probably rightly—as a dative of place ("exalted *at* the right hand").

c. In an article on the history of traditions, which partly links up with Hahn's thesis concerning the origin of the titles, Loader judges that Psalm 110:1 was originally applied to Jesus in view of his expected lordship in the imminent eschatological future. Very soon, however not only because his parousia was delayed but also on account of their experience of his active presence and power, it became customary in the early church to confess his so-called interim heavenly activities. According to Loader's theory, however, the emphasis was still on Jesus' intercession in behalf of the church and on the sending of the Spirit (Acts 2:32-36; 5:31; 7:55ff.; Rom. 8:34, etc.), and less attention was paid to his active and present lordship in history. In yet a new phase, Jesus' activity was seen as a direct lordship in history (Eph. 1:20ff.; 2:5ff.; Col. 2:10, 15; 1 Peter 3:18ff.). During this period, the last part of Psalm 110:1, the enemies as "a footstool," was included when the verse was quoted.

Although I do not necessarily accept the correctness of such an analysis, Loader's conclusions are of interest. He situates Acts 2:22-36 in the second phase of the development of the tradition (Christ's intercession and the gift of the Spirit), but admits that although the primary interest might not have been the present lordship of Christ, that idea is not at all alien to the broader context of these verses, so that one may perhaps detect at least overtones of this.

d. In summary, one could say that the proclamation here, true to the rest of Acts, is that Jesus was exalted by God (which included more than merely the resurrection and ascension) to a position of lordship, as illustrated by the quotation of Psalm 110:1. The truth of this claim is proven by quotations from Scripture as well as the events of Pentecost, the occasion of this speech. Although this message obviously has other implications as well, it here focuses particularly on the fact that Jesus was thus made Lord and Christ. And this, in turn, made possible the forgiveness of sins in his name (v. 38), the gift of the Holy Spirit for those who repented (v. 38), and rescue from the crooked generation (v. 40).

4. Especially noticeable is that all of the speeches in Acts result in paranesis. Guillet quite rightly remarks that in Acts the "resurrection" (read: exaltation) implies first of all a "summons to conversion," an appeal for a complete transformation of life, for a radical decision and a change. That appeal takes on different forms throughout the book, but it is present everywhere. Ridderbos also underlines the fact that time and again paranesis is the "actual purpose" of the speeches. This repeated summons, he continues, elucidates the true nature of apostolic proclamation, which was not merely theological reflection, since it also demanded a response. For this reason, Luke presents the speeches of Peter and Paul as direct discourse. Every time, the content of the paranesis is the call to be "saved" (v. 40). Salvation, then, is the decisive factor in the book of Acts. Soteriology gives meaning to christology as well as to eschatology. It is precisely because salvation is given in fellowship with the person or "name" of Christ that so much emphasis is laid on him, his position, and his titles. It is precisely because of the fact that the time of salvation has entered its final phase that history has become filled with meaning, and that the witness of the apostles becomes so important and urgent. This appeal to conversion is, of course, accompanied by the important, but secondary, motif of the guilt of the inhabitants of Jerusalem. Jesus' exaltation, as God's deed of confirmation, reveals at the same time the ultimate depth of the sin of Israel: it rejected God's Messiah and Son!

5. For greater detail, for example, the way in which quotations from Scripture are used and how they function, as well as the important discussion on the meaning of the titles "Lord" and "Christ," commentaries can be consulted.

II. Hermeneutical

1. Preaching on this pericope requires some difficult hermeneutical decisions. Originally it was apostolic, missionary preaching addressed to unbelieving Jews. The argument is based on a visible, empirical event (the outpouring of the Holy Spirit). These events are interpreted by means of Old Testament quotations as proof that the same Jesus who has been crucified by them has been *made* (i.e. pronounced) Lord and Christ by God himself. The hearers are then sum-

moned to conversion: to acknowledge their guilt in the rejection of Christ, believe the apostles' preaching concerning his exaltation, receive forgiveness of sins through his faith, and be baptized.

Is it possible that this Pentecost sermon, with the same thrust, can be repeated today in a Christian congregation? Especially in the absence of an empirical phenomenon that has to be explained and without the worshipers' direct involvement in Jesus' rejection, that is, with members who already believe that Jesus is the Christ and Lord and who have already been baptized in his name? It is obviously impossible. A modern appeal to be converted and to accept forgiveness would differ radically from both the original logic of this argument and the original implications of this preaching.

2. But how then can it be preached? Perhaps the implications of some of the apostolic preaching can be pointed out for the present-day church. The reality of the resurrection from the bonds of death (vv. 24-32) could be the focus, as in the following section. One could perhaps also explain the meaning of the exaltation and of the expression "at the right hand." That could be done very concretely and existentially, perhaps also by means of the other texts in Scripture that quote Psalm 110:1. One could also follow the same procedure regarding the implications of the titles of Jesus given here, "Lord" and "Christ." One could also, in a sermon that would perhaps stay the closest to the argument of this speech, proclaim that, according to verse 36, the salvation is still to be found only in Jesus Christ. All other forms of human striving for salvation, life, glory, or deliverance must be rejected. The central position of the forgiveness of sins within salvation can also be pointed out, as opposed to approaches to salvation that give this little or no attention.

III. Homiletical

In verse 24 we find the remarkable comment that God raised Christ from the dead, "because it was not possible for him to be held by it." Death was not capable of holding Christ!

1. First, one could point out that we can understand the full meaning of this extraordinary claim only if we remember that in the Bible, and especially in the New Testament, death is often described as a power, the symbol *par excellence* of control and enslavement. Death is

almost a collective noun, denoting all the diverse powers that make us helpless.

First, death, of course, spells the end of our lives. It is the symbol of the finiteness of human life. It is the power that terminates all our work, plans, and dreams. Even while we are living, death causes emptiness and meaninglessness. Accordingly, the Bible describes death as the power that governs our lives (Rom. 8:20; Heb. 2:15). In the final analysis, deep down we know only too well that we are going to die, so we are often restless and worried about many things, so unfulfilled and frustrated.

In the New Testament, however, death is much more than merely this power of finiteness. It also stands for the power of sin. We are "dead" in sin (Eph. 2:1). This means that we are so paralyzed by the power of sin that we are incapable of doing any good or of truly serving God. Here, too, death reigns over us and keeps us in its grip.

In Romans 7 we read of someone of good will who is simply not capable of doing good, who is a captive of "the law"—literally, "the power"—of sin. And in 1 Corinthians 15 Paul describes death as our "last enemy" (v. 26).

We also use this word to describe our situations of hopelessness. We say: My life has no meaning . . . something inside me has died. Our marriage is ending . . . our love has died.

2. Second, one could remind the worshipers that in the Bible *God's* power is often manifested in a struggle against the power of death. Especially three areas of God's power are evident here: creating something out of nothing, enabling women to conceive, and giving life in a situation of death.

In the matter of conception, consider how often childbirth plays an important role in the Bible. It is especially noteworthy how many times children were born to infertile couples. Every time it is a situation of death, awaiting action from God; and every time God waits until it is almost too late, humanly speaking. Again and again, the question is: Is anything impossible for God?

In Hebrews 11:17ff. Abraham gave his only son, the son he had received according to God's promise, back to death, because he believed in the God who "was able to raise men even from the dead" (v. 19). That is faith! Faith that keeps looking to the God who is capable of transforming our situations of death and hopelessness into life!

3. Third, one could point out how the message of the resurrection

applies to verse 24. Death was not able to keep Christ because *God* raised him up. God loosened the bonds of death (*ōdines* in LXX for *heblê,* "bonds," "cords," "chains")! God finally and irrevocably won the struggle against our last enemy.

Christ was exalted out of death, to the Father's right hand. Now he has "the power"! The power to revive our dead hearts and our dead marriages, and to transform our political and economic crises into meaningful, life-sustaining human conditions.

4. Finally, one could call attention to the certainty with which Peter declares that it was impossible for death to hold Christ. It is almost as though he is incidentally mentioning an obvious fact. It is all the more remarkable when one compares this to the disciples' (including Peter) reaction when the women told them Jesus had risen. Luke 24:11 tells us the women's report seemed like an "idle tale" to them. This certainty with which Peter talks now, was missing then. Earlier he was without hope. He did not expect Jesus to rise. He had to experience it first. He had to meet the living Jesus and reflect on God's miraculous power before he would understand that everything is possible for God.

We are in the same position. It is not because we believe in God's omnipotence that we believe in the resurrection; it is because we believe in the resurrection that we can now believe that everything is possible for God and for Christ at his right hand. Christ's resurrection is the heart of the apostolic witness and the foundation of the church's faith. The empty grave in Joseph of Arimathea's garden two thousand years ago is the reason the church believes that all things are possible for God. And the church celebrates Christ's resurrection every Sunday. It is the day God conquered the powers that enslaved our lives, the day on which Jesus was exalted to the right hand of the Father. Christ is Lord, seated at the right hand of God. That is the Easter gospel!

D. J. SMIT

Ascension: Colossians 3:1-4

Bibliography

Commentaries

Beare, F. W. *Colossians*. The Interpreter's Bible. Vol. 11. New York/Nashville: Abingdon, 1955.

Martin, Ralph P. *Colossians*. Grand Rapids: Zondervan, 1972.

Moule, C. F. D. *The Epistles of Paul the Apostle to the Colossians and to Philemon*. Cambridge: Cambridge University Press, 1957.

Moule, H. C. G. *Colossian and Philemon Studies*. London: Pickering & Inglis, n.d.

Uitman, J. E. *De Brief van Paulus aan de Colossenzen*. Nijkerk: Callenbach, 1964.

Homiletical

Bannach, H. *Der Himmel is nicht mehr oben: Probleme des 20. Jahrhunderts im Spiegel des Kolosserbriefs*. Stuttgart: Quell, 1964.

Barclay, W. *The All-Sufficient Christ: Studies in Paul's Letter to the Colossians*. Philadelphia: Westminster, 1958.

Barth, K. *Fürchte Dich nicht!*, 119-26. Munich: Kaiser, 1949.

Barth, K., and Thurneysen, E. *Come Holy Spirit*, 183-93. Edinburgh: Clark, 1934.

I. Exegetical

This pericope does not present serious exegetical problems. Commentaries, therefore, generally do not give detailed explanations. The context, however, is crucial. The verses constitute the transition from the doctrinal part of the epistle (chs. 1 and 2) to the ethical part (chs. 3 and 4). The imperatives in verses 5ff. logically belong to this pericope, because they demonstrate some practical applications of the principles mentioned in verses 1-4.

At the same time the givens of chapters 1 and 2 are very important, because they form the presupposition of the present argument. Without them these verses will undoubtedly be misinterpreted. For the argument of the epistle, it is vitally important that the church be reminded of what is *already* true and is consequently applicable to them. This insight is the key to the interpretation of the epistle as a whole and of these verses.

This becomes evident from several features of the text. The author repeatedly juxtaposes "once" and "now" (Col. 1:21-22, 26; 3:7-8). Once this and that applied to them, but now such is no longer the case. It is also clear from the deliberate way the past and the present perfect tenses are used that all the aspects of Christ's work of redemption now apply to believers (cf., e.g., Col. 1:12, 14, 22; 2:6, 12, 13, 14, 20; 3:1, 3, 8, 12, 13). The "saints and faithful brethren" (1:2) were dead, but have been made alive; were buried with Christ and were also raised with him; have been forgiven; have been delivered; and have been reconciled.

This is splendidly summarized in 1:13-14, regarded by some exegetes as the heart of the epistle: "He has delivered us from the dominion of darkness and transferred us to the kingdom of his beloved Son, in whom we have redemption, the forgiveness of sins." He *has* delivered us. He *is* our Lord. That is the final truth about us.

The same certainty is also reflected by the fact that we have been baptized. In 2:11-13 the author once again mentions all the blessings that apply to them, starting with "baptism, in which you were also raised with him." The Heidelberg Catechism (Lord's Days 26 and 27) talks with this same assurance about baptism. And it is well known how Luther, in a moment of deep perplexity and doubt, scratched into his desk: "I was baptized!" Iwand considers this pericope as even more suitable for a baptism service than for Ascension Day.

The "if" (v. 1) should therefore not be seen as an expression of doubt. It rather means "since," "seeing that," "whereas," "because," "considering that," "in the light of." It is not conditional but causal. The imperatives to follow rest on the givens of the previous chapters. The fact that believers have to "seek" (v. 1) or "set your minds" (v. 2) on what is already true about them ("have been raised with Christ"; "have died, and your life is hid with Christ in God"; "when Christ who is our life appears, then you also will appear with him in glory"), simply means that they have to arrange their lives accordingly. They ought to let their lives be controlled by the truth and its implications. It is not a search for something they do not already have. The search only starts with those who have already found (Barth). The imperative is legitimized by this "tremendous fact" (Iwand).

Consequently, they have to seek after and live according to the truth of these givens. That which applies *to* them must now be applied *by* them. "Christians daily have to crawl back into their own baptism" (Luther). Sanctification belongs to salvation. The fact that Christ is above and that their life is "hid with Christ in God," so that they have to "set their minds on things that are above, not on things that are on earth" is therefore not an appeal for some kind of escapism, but the exact opposite. It is a summons to return to this life renewed!

The Christian concept of heaven is not meant to be "opium for the people" or a cause for passivity. On the contrary. The down-to-earth and everyday consequences of life with Christ, including its socioeconomic and political aspects, become clear in the admonitions of 3:5–4:6. This is how the epistle intends the words "seek" and "set your minds."

New Testament eschatology does not inhibit ethics but encourages it (cf. Moltmann). One could almost say that the difference between the false prophets of Colossae and Christians is that the former set their minds on earthly things (cf. the references to "human precepts and doctrines," and to "the elemental spirits of the universe" as well as the type of ascetism they advocate) to reach salvation/heaven, while the latter set their minds on salvation/heaven to get back to earth!

II. Hermeneutical

1. From a hermeneutical point of view, however, this is a very intricate pericope. Ridenour calls it one of those passages you put in a file labeled "Texts I'll have to ask the preacher about some day." According to Schweizer it is best—and in line with the intent of Colossians itself—not to involve oneself in cosmological or topographical speculations, but rather to concentrate on the existential or anthropological issues at stake. He asserts that, in the final analysis, the text is concerned with what a person really is, about the final definition of one's life. Eichholz claims that the issue at stake here is Christ's resurrection, but insofar as it redefines our lives. The same idea is expressed by Barth, who frequently discusses this text in detail. In one of these discussions

he coined his now well-known expression that we find here "the normative biblical definition of heaven." Heaven, like our lives, gets a christological definition. According to Iwand this means that the essence or final truth of the world is not immanent but eschatological, so that we should not try to derive our "Woher" and "Wohin" ("wherefrom" and "whereto," origin, goal, meaning, definition) from the cosmos but from the gospel, not from creation but from Christ.

The ethical relevance of these definitions is obvious. Precisely because their lives (their happiness, salvation, future) are safe and hidden above with Christ in God, Christians can now seek the real life. This new life means they need not seek themselves any more and they need not pursue their own profit, salvation, happiness "on earth," i.e. in the ways of this created cosmos. The qualification "with Christ" is consequently used throughout the admonitions from 3:1 onward. This expression relativizes all existing structures, orders, and relations in society and places them in a new light, the light from above.

It is therefore vital that the gospel, the given of salvation, gets through in the sermon. The congregation must understand what it means that its life is hidden with Christ in God. The exegesis already made clear that the given forms the presupposition of the imperative. Chapters 3 and 4 *follow* chapters 1 and 2. The ethics of "in God" (as it is found consistently throughout chapters 3 and 4) follows the gospel of "with Christ" or "in Christ" in chapters 1 and 2. In a certain sense the expressions "have been raised" (v. 1a), "things that are above" (v. 2), "your life is hid with Christ in God" (v. 3), and "Christ who is our life" (v. 4) are parallels, or synonyms, all expressing the same idea, namely the certainty, assurance, and reliability of (eschatological) salvation. This eschatology is the foundation of Christian ethics. What happened to Christ, also happened to us; and what will still happen to him, namely his appearance "in glory" (v. 4), will happen to us also. For that reason we are delivered from anxiously seeking after ourselves (Luther: *incurvatus in se*). We only have to think about, to consider, these given (though eschatological) realities to be delivered from all kinds of selfishness, anxiety, and jealousy (vv. 5ff.).

2. The expressions "seek" *(zēteite)* and "set your minds" *(phroneite)* imply much more than mere meditation or intellectual and mystical reflection. They also refer to the human will and aspirations, to the way people plan their lives and actions. It means to take something into account in such a way and to such a degree that it increas-

ingly dictates one's life. Put differently, it means to regard something as so real and important that it fundamentally influences one's daily reality.

Luther's entire theology, from his theological method right through to his doctrine of God, his christology, and his soteriology, was profoundly affected by this insight. He distinguished between visible reality, perceived by reason, and invisible reality perceived, pronounced into being, and thus created by God. This distinction is not the same as the distinction in dualism between material and spiritual realities, in the Greek sense of these terms. The invisible or imperceptible reality does not yet exist (as if somewhere beyond or above this earthly world). God, however, perceives this (as a possibility) because he "can perceive more than human reason" (Luther's exposition of Ps. 121:3). Through his word this possibility becomes a reality.

Faith focuses on (seeks! sets its mind on! is guided by!) this future reality, at present still invisible but already pronounced in God's Word (i.e. "in Christ"). Faith is simply the willingness to cling to this invisible reality, to trust in it and to live according to it, the willingness to take it as even more real than the visible reality of human experience. Thus faith can proclaim that we are just and holy in spite of our (still) sinful life *(simul iustus et peccator)*. Thus faith can state that the ungodly and the enemy are objects of God's love *(iustificatio impii)*. Thus faith can say that one's anxious seeking after oneself *(incurvatus in se)* is unnecessary, because one's life is already secure with Christ in God. God sees better, because his word is the final and decisive criterion. Real faith teaches us to see through his eyes and to take his word, capable of creating reality, into account.

One can find a moving example of Christians who lived according to these principles in the *Letter to Diognetos* (A.D. 150).

> They live, each in his native land—but as though they were not really at home there. They share in all duties like citizens and suffer all hardships like strangers. Every foreign land is for them a fatherland and every fatherland a foreign land. . . . They share a common board, but not a common bed. In the flesh as they are, they do not live according to the flesh. They dwell on earth, but they are citizens of heaven. They obey the laws that men make, but their lives are better than the laws. They love all men, but are persecuted by all. . . . They are paupers, but they make many rich. They lack all things, and yet in all things they abound. They are dishonored, yet glory in their dishonor. . . . They are reviled, and yet they bless. They suffer insult, yet they pay respect.

They do good, yet are punished with the wicked. When they are punished, they rejoice, as though they were getting more of life. They are attacked by the Jews as Gentiles and are persecuted by the Greeks, yet those who hate them can give no reason for their hatred.

3. Calvin spent much time with the so-called meditation of the future life *(meditatio futurae vitae)*. The entire chapter III/9 of the *Institutes* deals with this topic, but he also frequently raised the matter elsewhere. In a certain sense it forms a "substantial component of his theology and piety" (Exalto).

The position it occupies in Calvin's thought is important. It is part of his broader discussion of the Christian life. Chapter 6 deals with general admonitions on the Christian life. Chapters 7-9 deal with self-denial (7), the bearing of the cross (8), and the meditation on the future life (9) as three fundamental aspects of this Christian life. In chapter 10 are comments on how to use the present-day life.

This order is important. Meditation on the future life is essential for the sake of living present-day life. The object of the *meditatio futurae vitae* is the sinner's vivification, or coming to life. The new life of believers is strengthened and stimulated by this meditation. As opposed to nonbelievers, who live according to the principle that one should abide by the rules of nature (the perceptible!), Scripture (the Word of God!) teaches that a Christian should live according to Christ (the invisible but normative definition!). For this purpose, self-denial, the bearing of the cross, and meditation on the future life are essential. The accompanying disdain for earthly life is not contempt *per se,* but rather the result of the comparison with the future, true life as defined in Christ. Exalto therefore correctly asserts that Calvin was not concerned with pessimism, denial of the world, or neo-Platonic ideas, but with an expression "of a reality in which he believed, and which he deeply experienced himself."

4. The preacher will have to touch on the renunciation, or denial of the world. On the one hand it is clear that these verses do not teach a denial of the world in the strict sense of the term. The "things that are above" should not be interpreted as higher, eternal spiritual values that make the present life unimportant or even less important. On the other hand Steck quite rightly criticizes numerous modern exegetes who try to avoid, with a kind of "apologetic zeal," every hint of Christian renunciation of the world. If eschatological hope indeed fulfills a critical function with regard to our present-day existence, an aspect of aversion

to the sinful world cannot be excluded (Steck, Conzelmann, and, of course, Calvin).

This has nothing to do with utopian thought (contrary to numerous critics). From the new creation (cf. "the new nature," 3:10), better still, from reality "in Christ" (which means "in the Lord" [Col. 3]), a *critical* light is shed on the fallen creation. Obviously, this truth should not be absolutized in some extreme variation of the neo-Marxist critical theory, in which existing reality is totally negated and rejected ("That which is cannot be true"—Bloch). This also is a form of revolutionary denial of the world!

In his political ethics—as indeed throughout his entire ethics—Thielicke argues that a Christian lives within the field of tension between the "already" and the "not yet," between the "new aeon" and the "old aeon." This compels us to guard against two extremes, political radicalism and false conservatism. The same emphasis occurs in these verses. The Christian can never withdraw from down-to-earth reality to a heavenly sphere "above," but on the other hand neither should the wordly sphere "down below" be the decisive authority in the Christian's life. The Christian should, in a manner of speaking, pay frequent visits to heaven in order to return and start life on earth anew.

5. In the Lutheran pericope-series, this is a text for Ascension Day. Several exegetes warn that this may obscure the emphasis of the pericope. But that fear is unfounded. If the pericope is preached correctly, which means not cosmologically but existentially, proclaiming the given of the redemption that is "hid with Christ in God" and appealing for sanctification in the form of the imperatives, it is most suitable for Ascension Day.

III. Homiletical

1. One can perhaps begin by explaining that, on the basis of the assurance of redemption (cf., e.g., the argument and expressions of chs. 1-2; the use of the past tense; the logic of the "if" construction of v. 1; and the synonymous phrases in vv. 1-4), the epistle proceeds at this point to the more practical part. The first part of the sermon will determine whether the congregation will hear the message correctly, i.e. as gospel. Especially the meaning of "your life is hid with Christ in God" will have to become comprehensible in an existential manner.

2. One can then proclaim that we therefore no longer have to

"seek" ourselves, but that we can live relaxed and confident, and practice Christian self-denial because our lives (i.e. our thoughts, plans, values, dreams, actions, etc.) are directed by this reality above on which we set our minds.

It may also be helpful to warn against possible misunderstandings of this admonition. The purpose is not that we should no longer take this life seriously and that it is better to think about spiritual things and to occupy oneself with those rather than with everyday life. The epistle does not advocate a monastic mentality, an attempt to serve God "better" by living in seclusion, meditating all day and every day on heavenly matters.

The author does not mean that we should seek heavenly things and in so doing neglect or undervalue earthly things, but rather that we should seek the heavenly things and set our minds on them so that we can be occupied with the earthly things in a new, different way. He does not mean that we should live in another— spiritual—world, but that we should think about spiritual things so that we can live *differently*—spiritually—in this present world.

This insight is very important. Too often Christians create the impression that a really pious and devoted Christian neglects this world. It is as though the spiritual and earthly life were opposed to each other and as though the Lord God did not want to have anything to do with earthly things. Too often we confuse nonbelievers with this view and give rise to slogans like Marx's "Religion is the opium of the people" and Nietzsche's appeal, "Brethren, remain true to the earth." In this way we misrepresent the gospel.

In this chapter also, verses 1-4 only form the transition or key to 3:5–4:6, where all possible relationships in this world are mentioned concretely. It simply is not true that when one seeks the things that are above and sets one's mind on them that one has to dissociate oneself from life on earth. On the contrary, one is supposed to return to this life and live differently, having a new set of values, like Christians, like people who know that their lives are "hid with Christ in God." Christians know they need not seek themselves and maintain themselves at all costs. Van Ruler points out the same thing when he says that we are not humans so that we can become Christians, but that we are Christians so that we can become human: real, genuine people living according to God's intention and God's heart.

Even the church is not an end in itself. One should not live only for church activities and worship services. The church is the training school for life! The church is extremely important for life in the world, for life in the kingdom! Hence Calvin's emphasis on meditating on the future life: it should enable Christians to renounce themselves, seek themselves less fervently, and live a holy life of discipleship.

One often meets people who are so pious that they can hardly serve God! They have become so strange to the ways of the world, so different from everybody else and therefore so indifferent to the issues that fundamentally affect the lives of their neighbor and all other people that no one wants to be like them. Consequently they can hardly function as the salt of the earth and the light of the world. They are rather like the salt in the salt shaker: pure, but separate, and, for the present, worthless.

The gospel and the proclamation of Ascension Day do not ask us to abandon the earth for the sake of heaven, but rather to bring something of heaven on earth; to live on earth, but like people who continuously see and experience something of heaven, to be *in* this world, concretely and practically in all the activities and responsibilities, but not *of* this world. We are to be of heaven, which means not like the world but like Christ. We have to set our minds on Christ to such an extent that he will rule over our lives, change us, and guide us.

3. To conclude, one could repeat everything from a different angle. The gospel of Ascension Day aims to turn us into Christian realists. Realism means to take reality into account; it means not to live in a world of fantasy or dreams, but to take the facts into account and to deal with them as they are. The epistle to the Colossians tells us that there are two forms of realism: one that takes into account only the perceptible, earthly facts (an eye for an eye, a tooth for a tooth, business is business, politics is politics) and another kind, the Christian kind, which also takes into account the invisible, heavenly realities, that which is already true about us, namely that our lives and our happiness are already safe and "hid with Christ."

Christian realism also takes into account, in this present life, Christ's example and God's power, given to the One seated at his right hand. Christian realism is not blinded by the way things seem to be, by the status quo, by so-called sinful reality, by irreconcilabilities, by discord, by hopeless situations, as though these things have the last word and as though they are the final realities; Christian realism takes into account the presence and power of the living Christ.

Luther's views may be useful, as well as specific examples in chapter 3, where the expression "in the Lord" is used to rule out our type of realism. Our so-called realism often is nothing but a barely disguised lack of faith, and our arguments are often only earthly, superficial, and fleshly. Often our lives are much more the echoes or reflections of our environment and of the norms valid in those environments than the reflections of the reality above and the facts valid there, namely that our lives are safely "hid with Christ in God."

Of course, Christian realism will make us aliens and exiles, like immigrants or visitors who are easily recognizable by their strange habits, customs, values, and practices. The church has understood something of this through all ages. Just think about the popularity of John Bunyan's well-known *Pilgrim's Progress*. And still it is regrettable that the church, even today, often understands so little of this. We often show so little of this strangeness, this otherness, this heavenly spirituality, this "new nature" (v. 10). So often we are nothing more than ordinary realists who live according to an eye for an eye and a tooth for a tooth. The reason is that we do not seek the realities that are above earnestly enough and that we do not "set" our minds on them. We need more of the *meditatio futurae vitae*. We are too earthly.

D. J. SMIT

The Sunday after Ascension: Acts 1:1-8

Bibliography

Commentaries

Barclay, W. *The Acts of the Apostles*. Philadelphia: Westminster, 1976.

Bruce, F. F. *The Acts of the Apostles*. Chicago/Toronto: InterVarsity, 1952.

Calvin, J. *The Acts of the Apostles*. Vol. 1. Grand Rapids: Eerdmans, 1949.

Lindijer, C. H. *Handelingen van de Apostelen*. Vol. 1. Nijkerk: Callenbach, 1975.

Marshall, I. H. *The Acts of the Apostles*. Tyndale New Testament Commentaries. Grand Rapids: Eerdmans, 1980.

Munck, J. *The Acts of the Apostles*. The Anchor Bible. Garden City: Doubleday, 1967.

Homiletical

Luccock, H. E. *The Acts of the Apostles in Present-day Preaching*. New York: Harper, 1942.

Morgan, G. *The Acts of the Apostles*. New York/London: Revell, 1924.

Additional

Interpretation: A Journal of Bible & Theology 13 (April 1959). (The entire issue is devoted to the book of Acts.)

Oepke, A., on "Apokathistemi, Apokatastasis" in *Theological Dictionary of the New Testament*. Vol. 1, 387-93. Grand Rapids: Eerdmans, 1964.

Schweizer, A., on "Pneuma," in *Theological Dictionary of the New Testament*. Vol. 6, 396-455. Grand Rapids: Eerdmans, 1968.

I. Exegetical

1. In referring to his "former book" in the opening verse, Luke underlines the crucial transition brought about in the history of redemption by Christ's resurrection and ascension. In the first phase, his Gospel, Luke deals with the origins of faith, with the "precious gifts of the Christian faith" (Haenchen)—all those things that give the church its identity. In the book of Acts Luke describes the second phase: the church's evangelization of the world. The ecclesiological dimension is now added to the christological dimension.

Of course, these two realms are very closely related. Jesus Christ works in and through the church, and the church finds its identity and purpose in the person and work of Jesus Christ. Without the church, Christ does not fulfill history. Without the remembrance of Christ, as normative figure, the church ceases to be church. "Preservation and progress are not in opposition to each other; one is a condition and the other a result. The conservative and progressive approaches do not exclude each other. On the journey to the end of the world, the link with the Source *(erksato)* may not be broken, otherwise Christianity will lose its identity in the absence of the Lord" (Eisinger).

The church is not a substitute for the Lord; it is the place where he is found. The exalted Lord will build his kingdom through his Spirit, and that means through the church. A new phase is about to begin, progress is made after Pentecost when the missionary church carries on the triumphal procession of the Lord (see Lindijer's discussion of Theophilus).

There are no serious exegetical problems in this passage, so it may be summarized as follows:

2. A new phase is about to start in the history of redemption, so Christ equips his chosen assistants, the apostles, through the Holy Spirit (vv. 2-3). There is a difference of opinion on "through the Holy Spirit": does it refer to "giving instructions" or to "the apostles he had chosen"? It may be best to read it in conjunction with both expressions. The point is that the apostles did not enter into the service of the Lord by their own choice or on account of their zeal, or even because of their love, for the Lord, but because they were called by the Holy Spirit. This instruction was given by the living Lord, and it occurs over forty days. Many exegetes see this instruction as a deliberate attempt to parallel the instruction in the law that Moses received on Sinai. Jesus instructs the

apostles in "the kingdom of God." One commentator interprets this as: "Things they already knew, had heard, were reminded of, but which were now also being interpreted or explained anew by the risen Lord himself" (Iwand).

3. Next, Luke tells of a discussion during a meal (v. 4: *sunalizomenos,* "to eat salt with someone," i.e. "to eat with someone"). Jesus' meals play an all-important role in the gospel, both during his earthly ministry and in his postresurrection appearances. The sermons recorded in Acts quite often refer to the fact that those who ate with Jesus received the authority to proclaim his message. Through the disciples' fellowship with Jesus at meals, they were accepted, strengthened, and sent out. Jesus now commands them to wait for the baptism by the Holy Spirit. This promise was about to be fulfilled; things would start happening soon. "Thus [Luke] brings the action still closer to the reader; he works almost like a photographer, zooming in for a close-up" (Lindijer). "The apostles have to wait where they last saw Jesus, until the moment comes when they will first hear him through his Spirit. The sequence is: see, wait, hear" (Eisinger).

4. The most difficult exegetical problem in this pericope is the thrust of the disciples' question and Jesus' answer. Some exegetes think the question arose out of a one-sided Jewish particularism, the disciples hoping for the restoration of the Davidic kingdom. In this view, the disciples expected the kingdom in some way to be limited to Israel alone. A similar view sees the disciples' question as their limiting the *universal* scope of salvation, a misunderstanding corrected by Jesus with the command to spread the gospel to the ends of the earth. Many others, however, refute this view, saying that the disciples' question was about time, How *soon* is the kingdom going to come? They explain that the disciples are expectant. The resurrection of the first-born from the grave and the promise of the Comforter are clear signs that the Restorer of all things is at hand! The last days have begun! The baptism with the Holy Spirit is the point at which the end of the world breaks in (see Oepke: *apokathistemi* as *terminus technicus* for the restoration of the order according to God's purpose). It seems that both options, the timing and the cup of the kingdom, should be taken into account and that Jesus' answer can be understood as being threefold.

a. Only God knows the "times" (cf. Lindijer on *chronoi* and *kairoi*). Therefore, calculations have no meaning. The apostles do not receive an answer to their question. Those who are aware of the "not yet" of salvation history can only groan inwardly with all of creation and with the Spirit (Rom. 8:19ff.) and also cry "Come, Lord Jesus!" with the Spirit (Rev. 22:17).

b. The narrow-mindedness of Israel, so "foolish . . . and slow of heart to believe" (Luke 24:25), is broadened by Christ to encompass the whole world. Israel has a role in this program, but only as the first stage in a progression that will include the whole world. The book of Acts deals extensively with this slowness of heart and misunderstanding, showing how it is overcome step by step.

c. Jesus turns the faces, lifted expectantly toward him, to the Spirit, who will give them the power to proclaim the returning Christ. All that is recorded in the book of Acts is inconceivable without this twofold approach: "the Holy Spirit [will] come on you" and "you will be my witnesses." These words therefore have the character of both a promise and a command. In addition, "*my* witnesses" indicates the content of the message as well as the divine presence that accompanies its proclamation. Together these expressions underline the missionary character of the church. Evangelization is not just one of the charges given to the church. The whole structure of the church is determined by her missionary task.

5. Verse 8 is rightly seen as much more than merely Luke's parallel to the great commission in Matthew 28:18-20. This verse plays a crucial role in the structure of the book of Acts. It provides the key to Luke's understanding of all that will follow; so it must be read in conjunction with other passages in Acts. It serves as the announcement of a program for the future, an indication of the road ahead and therefore almost an index to the book.

a. Three stages (6:7: Jerusalem; 9:31: Judea, Galilee, and Samaria; 28:31: Rome—see also 19:21; 23:11) in the progression of the gospel are indicated here, and they will play an important role in the structure of the book. Whereas the three stages in Luke's Gospel (9:51; 10:33; 17:11ff.) end in Jerusalem, the book of Acts ends in Rome. The cultic capital is replaced by the ecumenical (in the original sense of the word) capital. Rome is a symbol representing the uttermost corners of the world. Nevertheless, Acts 1:8 goes even further than Rome. It, too, is merely "an important station on the way to all nations" (Lindijer).

b. The entire book tells of the struggle to make this command and this promise (see 4c above) come true. Time and again the disciples are slow to grasp the promise, and then they cannot obey the command!

Time and again they hold back, or are at least slow to approach God, so that he frequently has to push them into the full expression of the promise (e.g., 8:5ff.; 10:9ff.; 10:42; 11:19ff.; 15:12). Time and again the misunderstanding and the opposition, which border on spiritual "foolishness," block the progress of the gospel message. It seems as if their proclamation will be heard only in Jerusalem, will be limited to the Jews, and will be encumbered with all sorts of Jewish regulations. In such cases they must see new visions, and arrive at new horizons, on occasion even through persecution! When the book is read from this perspective, as a single narrative, it becomes a gripping tale of human failure, divine intervention, and growing expectation.

c. Although the church's vision frequently has to be broadened, sometimes even by force, that force is yet the power of the Holy Spirit. The final say belongs to the Spirit! The story ends "at the end of the earth," and, more than that, there they proclaim the message "boldly and without hindrance" (the last words of the book, 28:31). In spite of all the misunderstanding, disobedience, failure, and persecution, the Spirit achieves marvelous results! The commandment and promise of 1:8 come to fruition in 28:31 when (at last!) Paul proclaims the kingdom of God in Rome. Hallelujah! What a triumphant final comment on this pericope!

6. The prologue draws to a close (vv. 9-11). Jesus has departed. But no, the disciples learn that the departing Christ is also the returning Christ. In the meantime, the disciples continue to live on earth, amid persecution, but equipped by his Spirit. Thus his ascension into heaven is bound to our progress on earth, his journey into heaven becomes the church's journey into the world—the church's mission is propelled by the reality of the returning Christ. During our mission into the world, our journey to the end of the earth, we are comforted by him who has ascended into heaven. He accompanies us in Word and in Spirit—and in Person.

II. Hermeneutical

Some of the following approaches may be useful when studying this pericope:

1. Eisinger makes a valuable contribution in his homiletical meditation. He argues that Luke provides answers to two questions: the time and the place of the kingdom of God.

a. With Jesus no longer there and his return not imminent, the community is left with an urgent problem, a problem of time. How would the church conduct herself in the meantime? If one knows the "times" or "seasons," it is possible to make life meaningful and to give it direction. Without such knowledge, however, it is so easy to resort to awkward solutions, to adapt one's life-style to the uncertainties of the present. Then we so easily begin to make all sorts of compromises. There exists a real danger that believers may perish from thirst in the seemingly endless time that lies ahead, and that despair may drive them to rely on inadequate methods of self-preservation. That is why so often our priorities are shifted and our urgency is lost.

b. Christ's answer, however, shifts us to the question of place. Salvation does not depend on knowledge of the times! Christ's second coming is not a question of the duration or the termination of history, but of salvation for the entire world. In answering this question in 1:8, the book of Acts describes the progress of events from Jerusalem to Rome! God's kingdom is not an object for nor the result of human planning and ingenious endeavors, but of being "positioned" by God (*etheto,* v. 7), through the power of his Spirit, and then to stay obedient and faithful. In our asking about God, it is not the "when" that matters but the "where to" and "for whom." Through his Word and his presence, God gives dynamic form to his church as mission church. Thus the church and all believers are not looking backward, nor restlessly round about, nor vainly upward—they are looking forward!

2. Roloff argues in a similar way:

a. Time, with all its changes, may often seem "omnipotent" to Christian believers. We all experience the inescapable power of these changes and the finality of time's effects on our lives. We may so easily feel powerless in the face of all these events. So often new situations arise, whether in our personal or our public lives, that we experience as crises, as terrible threats to our lives and happiness, and we feel totally incompetent to deal with them. However, for believers, this is not necessary. Time is not omnipotent, crises are never final. They rather provide opportunities for the coming of the kingdom! Christ is also Lord of time. So there is no need for us to make Christ up-to-date, relevant, and acceptable. All we need to do is witness in the power of the Spirit, who will unlock opportunities for faith, hope, and love within these seemingly difficult changes.

b. These witnesses, he continues, need not be "substitutes" or "executors" for Christ, keeping alive memories of his grave. Acts 1:1-22 is not a farewell scene for the crucified and resurrected Lord, but instead an advertisement of a new task in a new era! By making Christ's business our own, we are called, like the disciples, to testify far beyond our own (and their) limited horizons. We are also called to witness in new realms of human thought and action. Whatever changes may occur in history, whatever new situations may arise, the church is called to be there with the self-same message! After Ascension and Pentecost, time itself has also been changed and is now being renewed and prepared with a view to God's new heaven and new earth!

3. Voigt points out that the book of Acts is the beginning of the era of the church and in this era the gospel is spread to all nations. Much has changed since these events and much has disappeared since then, but the gospel remains, because the history of the church is the work of Christ. This Jesus is:

a. *The exalted Lord.* The church does not live in memories of the past, but in the present, in the presence of the risen Christ. This is the innermost secret of the life of the church.

b. *The proclaimed Lord.* The disciples feel anxious, now that the Lord has ascended into heaven. People may well say "Where is your God?" (Ps. 42:3). Where is he to whom "all authority in heaven and on earth has been given"? Why doesn't he react to tyranny, hunger, and crime? That is why verse 6 is really everyone's question. What is he going to do now that he has become Lord of heaven? Has this Lord forgotten his "ground staff"? However, it is precisely this situation into which the church is being pressed, a situation of conflict and hostility, of doubt and criticism. The church is left as his witness, with only his Word, not with "silver and gold" (Acts 3:6), nor with economic nor political power.

In this way their confession falls in line with the despised and rejected figure of the crucified Christ. It almost seems as if Jesus has condemned them to disaster and frustration. "One may almost say that the history of the church is the continuous attempt to achieve the impossible, with only the Word, and their own readiness to suffer." But before they can tackle the "impossible," they have to wait for the power of the Spirit—not for new plans, methods, or strategies. The Spirit is to be their only weapon.

c. *The coming Lord.* He is coming to meet us, to assemble his people. The history of the church is not, as it may seem, one long chain of unnecessary and painful persecutions, but rather a progression from miracle to miracle! This progress does not depend on what the church possesses or has attained, but on the One who "draws" the church ever forward!

4. A useful sermon on the mission of the church is contained in Andersen's scheme:

a. Before being sent forth, the disciples must gather around Jesus (v. 4). They are drawn into fellowship with him, elected by him, taught by him, and equipped by his Spirit.

b. The apostles' centeredness on Israel-and-self was broken down by sending them forth. In this way the missionary function of the church is established. The power of the Spirit lies in mission.

c. Through mission, the church and the world are oriented to the ultimate goal (cf. Matt. 24:14). This eschatological aspect may under no circumstances be neglected. Time is filled with meaning by the church's mission, when people devote their lives to the service of the gospel.

III. Homiletical

I recommend the following framework for a sermon, assuming that Acts 1:8 presents a structure for the entire book. Illustrations for each of the motifs will easily be found throughout the book of Acts.

In the introduction to the sermon, the pastor could point out that the role of the church is presently the focal point of many heated discussions. Because it often seems as if the church has become irrelevant, there exists a grave and continuing temptation to make all sorts of adjustments in order to "sell" the message more effectively, and to make the church more "relevant" (cf. Eisinger's framework in II, 1). To bear witness, however, does not mean to sell the gospel, or to do business in the Word of God, or to mark the price down with a view to a bargain sale.

Ultimately it is salvation that is important, the *quality* of the church's life, role, and witness, and not so much the impression she makes and the degree of acceptance she receives in all circles. Even in times when the church has been most faithful to her calling and has indeed been playing the role she is destined to play, she has not always been relevant, acceptable, or influential. On the contrary! This fact is borne out by the life and destiny of Jesus and by the actions of the apostles!

The church must therefore strive to preserve her identity throughout history and amid all changes of culture and politics, and must abide by what the Lord "taught from the beginning." Of course, she has not always succeeded in that! Not even in the very beginning! It is also a fact that this pericope, like the rest of the book of Acts, illustrates the reluctance of the disciples. The progress of the gospel "to the end of the earth" is not a smooth development. It is characterized by manifold undulations, or labor pains, which are accompanied by both reluctance and persecution, before each new stage is reached. That is why the following must occur time and time again:

1. The church's vision must constantly be enlarged and broadened. The Holy Spirit wants to broaden our vision, to have us see what has not been seen, to dream what has not been dreamed, to tackle what has never been tried before. The Spirit has plans and dreams of vast dimensions. We, however, are so narrow-minded and so self-satisfied. We soon feel complacent, we think that we have done what could be done, that we ourselves are saved, that we have done our share for the mission, etc. The Spirit, however, sees far beyond what we are able to see, and wants us to see further, so that we see the distress of the world, the immense need, the suffering.

The Spirit is constantly trying to give us enthusiasm and strength for the task, trying to open our eyes and in the process trying to break open our small and often too comfortable worlds so that we see the distress and needs of others. Our piety, our churches, our sound traditions, our Christian habits, our efficient church organization, can all too easily become havens, safe bunkers where we live in comfort.

There is a story about a terrible disaster off the inhospitable coast of Canada. In the aftermath, the fishermen of the surrounding area decided to build a rescue station with emergency equipment available and to man it, especially in bad weather. For many years it functioned as a rescue station, but gradually more and more comforts were added: television sets, innerspring mattresses, central heating. Then one night there was another shipwreck, but the men at the station slept right through the disaster and no one was saved. The rescue station had become a club. It is all too easy for the church, which should be a rescue station, to become a comfortable, air-conditioned club!

2. Resistance within the church must continually be broken down

(cf. 10:14; 11:1-3; 15:1-2). In spite of Pentecost and the Lord's clear command to us, there is still so much resistance, misunderstanding, unwillingness, prejudice, and selfishness. In spite of our sincerity and our good Christian intentions, so often our attitudes, our shortcomings, and our lack of insight (Luke 24:25) keep people out of the church. There are so many misunderstandings which we must be relieved of before we can really become and remain a true Pentecost church. It may even be that sometimes only persecution will liberate us to see what we must see and do what we must do (cf. 8:1-3).

3. Our crises must be seen as opportunities for the Holy Spirit (e.g., 8:4ff.; 11:19). Time and again, persecutions intended to destroy the disciples became important turning points on the road to salvation for the whole world! And this knowledge should comfort us and encourage us not to give in to pressures and influences.

The fervor of the Holy Spirit seeks to make us *restless* and enthusiastic. The church has not yet achieved its goals, but it is moving along on its way "to the end of the earth," continuously searching for new territory to bear witness. She should look neither to the right nor the left, but forward.

The church is also *restful* and secure in knowing that the future—as well as the present!—is in God's hands. Jesus meets us in our crises, troubles, questions, and distress. He also meets us in the crises of our country and our world. Through this assurance he will strengthen our faith and enrich our lives, but also use us in his service: in our neighborhood and in our country. Though we may at times feel frustrated and depressed, and sometimes be attacked and humiliated, we should always realize that Christ can turn difficult circumstances into opportunities for victory, in which the gospel is able to move forward to new horizons (28:31). Preachers should apply this truth concretely and prophetically in their own local situation.

B. A. MÜLLER

Pentecost: Acts 2:1-13

Bibliography

Commentaries

Barclay, W. *The Acts of the Apostles*. Philadelphia: Westminster, 1976.

Bruce, F. F. *The Acts of the Apostles*. Chicago/Toronto: InterVarsity, 1952.

Calvin, J. *The Acts of the Apostles*. Vol. 1. Grand Rapids: Eerdmans, 1949.

Marshall, I. H. *The Acts of the Apostles*. Tyndale New Testament Commentaries. Grand Rapids: Eerdmans, 1980.

Munck, J. *The Acts of the Apostles*. The Anchor Bible. Garden City: Doubleday, 1967.

Homiletical

Barth, K., and Thurneysen, E. *Come Holy Spirit*. Edinburgh: Clark, 1934.

Eichholz, G. *Herr Tue Meine Lippen auf*. Vol. 2, 319-31. Wuppertal/Barmen: Müller, 1959.

Additional

Marshall, I. H. *Luke: Historian and Theologian*. Exeter: Paternoster, 1970.

Noordegraaf, A. *Creatura Verbi: De groei van de gemeente volgens de Handelingen der Apostelen*. The Hague: Boekencentrum, 1984. (On church growth in Acts.)

Noordmans, O. *Verzamelde Werken*. Vol. 8, 351-73. Kampen: Kok, 1980. (Meditations on Acts.)

I. Exegetical

1. This passage is the only suitable historical material for a sermon on Pentecost, because Luke's rendering of the pouring out of the Spirit is unique. The only other reference to this event is the short and cryptic account in John 20:22. The Acts account is the basis for the Chris-

tian celebration of this festival, which is ten days after Ascension Day and fifty days after Passover (Good Friday).

2. In homiletics and exegesis, the passage is usually treated from a historical point of view. When taken as a journalistic report, however, the text offers puzzling questions. How could Peter have made himself heard to 3,000 people? Which "one space" (2:1) was large enough for at least 3,000 people? This already shows the exegete that Luke does not try to answer such questions. The exegesis must therefore sail between the Scylla of faulty reconstruction that has no basis in the text, and the Charybdis of an explanation according to which this text is simply a pious invention of Luke, with hardly any historical grounds (Haenchen). When preparing a sermon, important exegetical decisions must be made concerning three issues that are often misunderstood.

a. The Feast of Pentecost:

(i) Pentecost ("the fiftieth" in Greek) was the fiftieth day after Passover. Until the destruction of the temple in A.D. 70, this was the day on which the harvest festival was celebrated. Festival-goers took their harvest offerings to the temple and handed them to the priests, as a token of thanksgiving. It was not one of the most important feasts of the Jewish believers, as is shown by the fact that it was later called Pentecost.

As time passed, Pentecost was important only as the closing celebration of the much more important Feast of the Passover. After the destruction of Jerusalem, Pentecost could not take place any longer, because the temple was destroyed. As a result, the feast gradually changed to become the commemoration of the day Moses received the law. However, it was only much later, in the second century A.D. and especially in the third century, that it took on this form.

Lutheran exegetes explain the story of Pentecost in Acts 2:1-13 against what they regard as a religious-historical background: according to them it celebrates "the new revelation of God by the Spirit," in contrast with the Jewish feast that commemorated the revelation of God on Sinai through the law (e.g., Bohren). This is wrong. There is no proof that Luke could have interpreted the Feast of Pentecost in this way. Nor does his story in Acts 2 refer to the law. Indeed, such an explanation would be in contrast to what Luke writes about the law in the rest of the book.

Although the law was not a necessary condition for salvation anymore, it was still valid for the believers, and not in opposition to the gospel. That is why Paul, in Acts 21, obeys the law (vv. 25-26) and even prescribes certain obligations for the Gentile believers in the congregational gathering in Acts 15:28-29.

This contrast between law and gospel should not therefore be used as a framework in the exegesis of this pericope. The idea of Pentecost as "the feast of harvest gathering" should also not be spiritualized too strongly, especially because Luke does not include any harvest-gathering motifs or allegories in his rendering.

(ii) The question now arises, Why does Luke mention the Feast of Pentecost? In this connection, the preacher must be aware of Luke's literary style. One finds an excellent example of his gripping style in the healing of the lame man in Acts 3:1-10. See how elaborately, concretely, and dramatically Luke describes the healed man's actions (vv. 8-9): after his feet and ankles had ("immediately," v. 7) become strong, he leaped up, stood up straight, he could walk, and entered the temple with the disciples, walking and leaping and praising God. All the people saw him walking there and praising God. Luke uses a contrast to this scene in verse 10, where he depicts the amazement of the people who were used to seeing him sitting at the Beautiful Gate, begging for alms.

When the story of Pentecost is compared to this healing, it is just as realistic. There is a sudden sound from heaven, like a mighty wind; and the onlookers are amazed and bewildered, or speak mockingly about what happened.

This literary style is not merely a technique that could be expected from an ancient storyteller; it is not merely a device for attracting the readers' attention. He is retelling a mighty event that witnesses and his readers will not soon forget. In comparison with the Pentecost "narrative" in John 20:20-22, Luke is quite clearly successful!

It is, however, even more important to understand Luke's theological intention with this story: he tells how God himself is the Instigator of what happens at Pentecost. What makes this idea more probable is the usage of the motifs of a mighty wind and fire, which are regarded in the Old Testament as signs of God's appearances. Luke tells the Pentecost story in a very realistic and detailed manner because he wants to emphasize the reality of God's intervention and his presence.

Luke's naming a specific day for these events is part of this realistic style, and he is consistent in this style, for Acts 3:1 is another example of how he puts his narrative in a specific framework of place and time ("at the hour of prayer, the ninth hour").

Still, it is clear that the first words of Acts 2:1 are important for a different reason. The Greek expression *egeneto de en tō sumplērous-thai* also appears in Luke 9:51, where it indicates an important turning point in the Gospel. It indicates that the time appointed by God has dawned and has now become reality. The word *sumplērousthai* is used in the same way in Acts 2:1.

(iii) Luke has concluded the introductory chapter of his story (Acts 1) and now, in Acts 2:1, he starts to sketch an important new development. This narrative is consequently the first episode and by placing it first, as the beginning of the "period of the church" (Conzelmann), which is filled with the Holy Spirit, he emphasizes the importance of what is happening for the rest of the book of Acts.

But Pentecost is important not only because of where it is placed in the book of Acts. The word *sumplērousthai* gives it even more importance. At the beginning of the church's task of proclaiming the gospel, God himself is directly involved in this work. Luke tells in Acts 1:5 how, during his forty days with his disciples, shortly after his resurrection, Jesus has promised them that they would be baptized with the Spirit "before many days." This promise is fulfilled literally on the fiftieth day. It could hardly have been sooner! But at the same time it is the fulfillment of the prophecy by John the Baptist when he said (Luke 3:16) that they would be baptized with the Holy Spirit and with fire. The heart of the matter is that it really is an event the Father has "fixed by his own authority" (Acts 1:7).

The reference to the Feast of Pentecost therefore serves both to depict a realistic situation and an actual realization. This realization occurs on the Jewish feast day, when the Spirit is visibly poured out shortly after Jesus himself has made his disciples such a promise. John had already promised it earlier, and the Father has also made this promise (Acts 1:4)! Nothing here is accidental. These are events that could be seen and experienced by everyone, like the healing of the lame man (Acts 3:16: "in the presence of you all").

(iv) From these thoughts it is clear that the reference to the Feast of Pentecost is not nearly as important as the word *sumplērousthai* in verse 1. The day of Pentecost as the day of the Spirit does not dawn like any other day, but is "fulfilled." In addition, by placing this word at the beginning of the sentence, Luke underlines the importance of this idea of fulfillment. Here are obviously thoughts for further discussion: the day of the pouring out of the Spirit is not important because it coincides with the Feast of Pentecost, but rather because it is a day ordained by God (Sauter).

The fact that God rules and guides events in history is a very important motif in Luke's works. Some commentaries give more details on this issue (e.g., Marshall and Conzelmann). The first part of Peter's Pentecost sermon is very important here. One should pay special attention to the fact that God has not only fixed this day and held its events in his hand, but that, moreover, it forms a part of the final era of history. This becomes clear when Peter's sermon puts the events of Pentecost "in the last days" (Acts 2:17). The final phase in history is dawning here: God has started balancing the books for the day of reckoning.

The events of Pentecost, as the starting point of a new phase and as the conclusion of the previous "period of Jesus," which closed with his departure, are an important focal point in Luke's overall picture of history. After the period of Israel come the periods of Jesus and the church. Although the eras of the church and of Jesus are very closely connected, there is yet a difference. The era of the church, which starts at Pentecost, is distinguished by the pouring out and workings of the Spirit. (See also II, 2.)

The era of the Spirit is an era of new life, new courage, of fearless witness, of fire and languages, and the unity of all people. There are no limits to the power of this life breaking loose on the day of Pentecost. It engulfs everything and everybody.

b. Glossolalia:

Luke's mention of the apostles speaking in other tongues after they are filled with the Holy Spirit also causes a number of problems.

(i) First, there is the question of the function of this event. Contrary to what some exegetes say, speaking in tongues plays a limited role in the events of Pentecost. In Peter's sermon, it is ignored almost completely. Its limited function is further underlined when Peter addresses the crowd. The Word is preached to them in one language, and it is only after the sermon that the people are willing to be baptized while earlier, after the speaking in tongues, they were only amazed— or scornful! Speaking in tongues, therefore, does not have the same salutary effects as does Peter's sermon.

In addition, there is no speaking in tongues among the crowd. This forms a strong contrast to Acts 10:44-46, where the Gentile crowds also speak in tongues after hearing the Word. The limited function of speaking in tongues shows that exegetically it would not be correct to single this out as the most significant aspect of Acts 2:1-13.

(ii) Second, it is noteworthy that the Holy Spirit gives the gift of tongues to the apostles (v. 4). Thus the emphasis is on the Spirit's presence and the Spirit's taking care of the church. Peter begins his sermon (Acts 2:17-21) by quoting Joel's prophecy, and the fulfillment of this prophecy is the outpouring of the Spirit, and not merely the giving of one gift of the Spirit, namely glossolalia. After his sermon Peter promises that everyone who believes will receive the gift of the Holy Spirit, so once again it is not glossolalia that is promised. In a similar vein, at the end of his sermon, Peter refers to the exalted Jesus who has received the Holy Spirit from God and who pours out the Spirit (v. 33).

This section thus presents the glossolalia in a hierarchical way. The Spirit is the giver of the glossolalia (2:4), but can also be the gift. But even the Spirit is, to a certain extent, subordinated to Jesus, who pours out the Spirit (v. 33), and to God, as the giver of the Spirit to Jesus.

(iii) Finally, it is important that the Spirit proclaims the deeds of God in the speaking in tongues. The content is much more important than the medium of glossolalia.

Thus, speaking in tongues does not function as an autonomous phenomenon in the story of Pentecost. Through his Spirit, God enables people to preach the Word of God. They can now openly and powerfully speak about the things they have experienced with Jesus. The Spirit now lives in the church, with the result that they are strong. One sign of this new, dynamic life is glossolalia.

c. The list of nations:

(i) The main part of the introduction to the Pentecost narrative is a description of the reaction of witnesses other than the disciples to this pouring out of the Spirit (vv. 5-13). Preachers often see the tower of Babel as the context for this part of Luke's Pentecost story. According to them, with Pentecost God once again unites all the nations who were cursed during the events at Babel. Thus the confusion of tongues was brought to an end. One should, however, avoid this view, because there is no indication in the text, and it severs the meaning of this event from its context.

Even more problematical is the further attempt to explain the events of Pentecost as God's act of reuniting the nations of the world, without them losing their separate identities. Note that speaking in tongues does not lead to the conversion of the crowd (and thus it cannot be equated with preaching the Word). Peter's sermon in one language to all the gathered people results in conversions. It is, moreover, especially important to note that the crowds do not represent heathen nations, but the Jewish nation, believers from all parts of the world.

(ii) To understand this fully, one must look carefully at the division of the book of Acts. In the first part, Peter and the apostles in Jerusalem are presented as preachers of the Word to all Jews. This is not only clear from the context (Acts 2–6), but also from the way Peter addresses the people in his sermon (Acts 2:14, 22, 36) and from the reaction of the crowd (2:37: "*Brethren,* what shall we do?"—compare this with the question of the jailer in Philippi in 16:30: "*Men,* what must I do to be saved?"). The words of Paul and Barnabas in Acts 13:46 also make this very clear: "It was necessary that the word of God should be spoken *first* to you. Since you thrust it from you, and judge yourselves unworthy of eternal life, behold, we turn to the Gentiles." The turning point in Acts is in the Cornelius story in chapter 10 (especially vv. 44-48). Only then do the Gentile nations come into focus and is the gospel preached to them, as we can read in the second part of Acts.

There are no Gentiles in the list of nations in Acts 2. The response of the Jewish people is emphasized: on Pentecost 3,000 become believers. According to Acts 6:7, "The number of the disciples multiplied greatly in Jerusalem, and a great many of the priests were obedient to the faith." And in Acts 21:20 the elders in Jerusalem told Paul: "Many thousands there are among the Jews of those who have believed."

All this goes to show the important place of Jerusalem and the Jewish nation in the gospel. Nowhere does Luke tell of such massive numbers of Gentiles becoming believers. Acts 2:1-13 consequently does not deal with the task of the church's missionary work among the heathen nations and with possible methods for the proclamation of the Word and the structures of churches in mission fields.

(iii) In the list of the nations, the focal point is that God's people of the covenant are now confronted by the deeds of God. This covenant people must now come to a decision. The sermon can fruitfully refer to Acts 3:25-26 (cf. especially the "you first" in v. 26).

Many exegetes have commented on the significance of the list of nations. A few points are of special interest: some understand verses 9-11 as the crowd talking among themselves. However, this is impossible. It must therefore be taken as Luke's comments on the crowd. This list is really only an explanation of verse 5, namely that religious Jews from all nations under the sun were present at the outpouring of the Spirit. Luke thus wants to compile a list of Jews from nations all over the world. What is also important is that these people are not pilgrims, but inhabitants of Jerusalem (cf. also 2:14!). This is important to Luke, because the congregation of Jews who become believers stay in Jerusalem and cannot return to their cities. Only after Stephen's death are the believers dispersed (cf. Acts 8:4: "those who were scattered went about preaching the word").

(iv) The onlookers on the day of Pentecost consequently are faithful Jews and Jewish proselytes who have returned to Jerusalem from the diaspora and are present in the city in great numbers on the day of the Feast of Pentecost. By means of this list, Luke underscores that the Jewish people as a whole are the object of God's patient intervention. This fits in well with the first part of Acts, where the Word is brought especially to the Jewish people. When God himself restores the fallen house of David, builds up and repairs the ruins (Acts 15:16), he starts with the people with whom he originally made the covenant (Acts 3:24, 25).

No one is denied the privilege of the gift of the Spirit. This is also the meaning of the Joel citation, according to which the Spirit will be poured on *all* persons. And that is why Peter closes his sermon with a warning: "Let all the house of Israel therefore know assuredly that God has made him both Lord and Christ, this Jesus whom you crucified" (Acts 2:36).

Yet it is clear that the emphasis of the story of Pentecost is on *one* group of people who have together seen great things happen. They are witnesses of the first Christian sermon in one language. For precisely this reason, this rendering can never be explained in terms of separate groups and various languages.

II. Hermeneutical

1. The passage ends with a question: "What does this mean?" This demonstrates its introductory nature and confirms how necessary it is to expound it in the light of what follows. It is vital that Peter's sermon and also the account of the course of events on Pentecost (2:37-41) are taken into consideration when interpreting verses 1-13.

The Pentecost sermon, with its christological thrust, sheds light on the relationship between Christ and the Holy Spirit. This is characterized strikingly by Luther: "The Holy Spirit can only proclaim Christ; the poor Holy Spirit cannot do anything more." And after completing his sermon, Peter gives an important description of his contemporaries: "Save yourselves from this crooked generation" (v. 40). One can find a similar description of the Jews in Acts 7:51 ("You stiff-necked people, uncircumcised in heart and ears, you always resist the Holy Spirit"). (Although these two aspects, the crooked listeners and the christological sermon, are not used as the theme for these guidelines, they form an essential part of the basis for interpreting Acts 2:1-13 correctly.)

2. A few aspects of Luke's theological message are important for preaching correctly on this passage. It is very important that one read the commentaries critically, because it is a common hypothesis in later research that Luke presents the account of salvation in a threefold scheme, a scheme in which the story of Pentecost inaugurates the final era, that of the church and the Spirit.

In this view, Luke considers the church to be in the center in this era, as intermediary between God and the believers. For the present, the Spirit is given to believers as a pledge until the end. The story of Jesus is then preached by the church as an event in the distant past, which becomes in itself the promise of the consummation of all things. But in the time between Jesus' earthly life and the last days, we find the period of the church. Until believers receive salvation in the end, they have to be satisfied with the Spirit as substitute. The Spirit is therefore not a sign of the last days.

In opposition to this view, it must be emphasized that the outpouring of the Spirit is already of an eschatological nature, according to Luke (2:17). The Spirit is a sign of the end, the last days. It is not the task of the church to act as intermediary for salvation. The opposite, rather, is true: the exalted Jesus is the giver of salvation, precisely because he has sent the Spirit to the church so that the Word could be proclaimed (Acts 2:33). Through the Spirit the exalted Jesus is the active custodian and shepherd of his church. Throughout Acts the church is conscious of its dependence on Jesus (e.g., Acts 4:23-31).

Pentecost introduces a new era, the era of the Spirit. In this respect we may safely say that Luke divides history into eras. But the time of Jesus and the time of the church belong very closely together and as such they are opposed to the old dispensation of Israel.

3. It is indeed possible to construe a theology of the relationship between the Holy Spirit and Christ, or about the character of the Spirit.

But it is important that preachers not discuss these issues in a speculative, abstract way. One should ask, How can the hearers become aware of the working of the Spirit today? The congregation must become enthusiastic about the gift of the Holy Spirit to the church at Pentecost.

The exegesis, however, which shows that the outpouring of the Spirit and Peter's message about Jesus are very closely connected, makes it impossible to preach about the Spirit as if it brings a revelation other than Jesus. Speaking about Jesus cannot be omitted or neglected when speaking about the active fulfillment of the Spirit! To preach on the Spirit is to proclaim Jesus! Even today, the Spirit does not bring new truths apart from Jesus, though it is true that the Spirit helps us time and again to explain Jesus in new situations, and enables us to live for him. The challenge for the preacher is to bring home to the listener something of the new life that the Spirit can bring to us today.

4. As we have already seen in the exegetical remarks, it is wrong to read the story of Pentecost as though it were a journalistic report. This only causes difficulties. A more important question is to inquire after Luke's theological intention with this report. Especially the book of Acts, which is often used for preaching only during Pentecost, is frequently misused in this respect, because Luke's theological intention is ignored or forgotten.

III. Homiletical

Two models for a sermon are suggested:

Model 1:

a. The Holy Spirit comes from *God.* Here we have a miracle that cannot be ascribed to people's imaginations, Furthermore, Pentecost shows how faithfully God fulfills his promises.

b. The heart of the matter: The Holy Spirit tells of the great deeds of God in Jesus. Here one can describe the limited role of the speaking in tongues. What really moves people is not so much the miracle of the languages, but Peter's message about Jesus.

c. The Holy Spirit transforms and unites people. One can discuss the way the apostles fearlessly began witnessing and how the Spirit was given by God to all Jewish believers. The theme will consequently be the work of the Holy Spirit.

Model 2:

a. One could ask an introductory question, How do present-day Christians experience the events of Pentecost? Our experiences here can vary from an interest in the strangeness of the events to desperation at being unable to experience the power of Pentecost. Our experiences of Pentecost often result in one of two popular attitudes. Some people look to Pentecost for a repetition of the supernatural events, while others explain away the events as remains from ancient mystery religions.

b. The question is, of course, whether these two attitudes do justice to Scripture. With Jesus' departure, God gives the great gift of the Spirit to believers. We need not live on memories of what Jesus was like. In a concrete way God intervenes in our lives: He is present at all times, through his Spirit. What he has promised in Acts 1 is now being realized in Acts 2! Futhermore, the Spirit is not a gift confined to the ancient past. From the course of the book of Acts one can clearly demonstrate that not only was he poured out "again" (Acts 8 and 10) but also that he constantly guided the lives of believers in the early church (e.g., Acts 13:4). Scripture shows us that the Spirit should still be a reality to all believers.

c. By means of Acts 2:40 one can demonstrate the desperation that results from our powerlessness to experience the workings of the Spirit. In Acts 2:40, Peter speaks of "this crooked generation" (cf. the mockery of the crowd in v. 13). The sermon may expand upon this theme and demonstrate the crookedness of every generation and their inability to understand God and his deeds.

d. *Two things* underlie the miracle of Pentecost: on the one hand we must acknowledge that there was supernatural intervention. The essence of Pentecost is the total contrast between our human experience and God's coming from heaven with his fire and making everything new. The signs on the day of Pentecost symbolize that, and the change in the disciples confirms this working from above. The Spirit transforms common, uneducated people into bold witnesses who minister fearlessly to the world and even to Caesar (27:24). Our wretchedness, happily, does not keep God from creating dynamic new life. On the other hand we must recognize the simplicity of Pentecost. The signs are accompanied by an understandable message, explaining what God has done in Jesus. Only after having seen Jesus are the people clearly sorry for their sin (v. 37) and then repentance becomes possible (vv. 37-38).

We must understand Christ in order to experience Pentecost. Here the preacher may emphasize the christological aspect of the Pentecost event.

> Wherever it happens that human beings realize that they become children of God just as they are, when they understand that they are taken into eternal arms in spite of and still in their transitoriness, so that they do not fear the grave and judgment any longer, and now have faith amidst the most bewildering times, when people therefore understand Jesus Christ, then it is not any more their own petty human spirits which help them to understand, but it is already the Spirit of God who empowers them. (Barth)

This not only brings out the fact that the Spirit can become a reality to people today but also the way in which this can happen. It will not happen in the same spectacular way. But it will produce spectacular results.

P. G. R. DE VILLIERS

Pericopes from
the Old Testament and
the Pauline Letters

Easter Sunday:
1 Corinthians 15:12-20

Bibliography

Commentaries

Barrett, C. K. *A Commentary on the First Epistle to the Corinthians*. New York and Evanston: Harper & Row, 1968.

Bruce, F. F. *1 and 2 Corinthians*. New Century Bible. London: Marshall, Morgan & Scott, 1971; Grand Rapids: Eerdmans, 1980.

Calvin, J. *The Corinthians*. Vol. 2. Grand Rapids: Eerdmans, 1948.

Conzelmann, H. *A Commentary on the First Epistle to the Corinthians*. Philadelphia: Fortress, 1975.

Fee, G. D. *Commentary on the First Epistle to the Corinthians*. The New International Commentary on the New Testament. Grand Rapids: Eerdmans, 1987.

McCaughey, J. D. "The Death of Death," in *Reconciliation and Hope*, 246-61. Edited by Robert Banks. Grand Rapids: Eerdmans, 1974.

Pop, F. J. *De Erste Brief van Paulus aan de Corinthiers*. De prediking van het Nieuwe Testament. Nijkerk: Callenbach, 1965.

Homiletical

Barth, K., and Thurneysen, E. *Come Holy Spirit*, 158-70. Edinburgh: Clark, 1934.

Noordmans, O. *Verzamelde Werken*. Vol. 8, 94, 95, 138-40. Kampen: Kok, 1980.

Ridderbos, H. N. *God is Liefde*, 109-17. Kampen: Kok, 1979.

Stedman, R. C. *The Deep Things of God: Expository Studies in I Corinthians*, 294-309. Waco: Word, 1981.

Van Ruler, A. A. *De dood wordt overwonnen*. Nijkerk: Callenbach, n.d.

Zodhiates, S. *Conquering the Fear of Death,* 176-269. Grand Rapids: Eerdmans, 1970.

Additional

Barth, K. *The Resurrection of the Dead.* New York: Revell, 1933.

Berkhof, H. *Christ and the Powers.* Scottdale: Herald, 1977.

Versteeg, J. P. *Christus en de Geest,* 4-96. Kampen: Kok, 1971.

I. Exegetical

The broader context of the pericope (i.e. within the argument of the epistle) is very important. It is well known how much value Barth attaches to chapter 15. According to him it must be regarded as the key to the epistle, because it deals not merely with one problem among others, but forms the crux and climax of the epistle, the "critical presupposition," the "pinnacle and crown," the "key pronouncement" of everything. (It is, of course, equally well known how Bultmann and his followers, including Fuchs, regard chapter 13 as the key to the epistle, and see the kind of eschatology expounded in chapter 15 as a rather unfortunate deviation, an attempt to present existential truth as objective and historical-apocalyptic reality!)

1. There is near unanimity regarding the subdivisions of chapter 15. Verses 1-11 deal with the resurrection as the heart of the apostolic tradition. It is the basis of the church's own existence, and it rests on the testimony of a large number of reliable witnesses. In these opening remarks Paul therefore appeals to common convictions held by himself as well as his opponents.

In verses 12-20 he mentions for the first time their denial of the resurrection of the dead and explains that it is not in agreement with their own confession (v. 1-11). He points out that such a denial would fundamentally affect the confession they share with him and with all Christians. Preaching and faith would then be empty, the apostles would be false witnesses, all Christians, including the Corinthians, would still be lost in sin, and death would still be a final terror. Should they be right, Christians, in spite of their faith and hope, would be "of all men most to be pitied."

In verse 20 he in effect interrupts his own argument and implies that all these conclusions are fortunately absurd, as there is absolutely no doubt that Christ has indeed been raised from the dead. His opponents of course agree with him on this! Differences arise, however, over the meaning of this confession.

Paul therefore explains his own interpretation in verses 21-28. With the aid of the parallel Adam-Christ (vv. 21-22) and then with apocalyptic metaphors and terminology (vv. 23-28), he shows that the resurrection of Christ should not be regarded as an isolated incident or miracle. His resurrection is the breakthrough of God's all-embracing reign; it therefore includes the victory over all powers, including death, and consequently the resurrection of those who belong to him. He has been raised as the first fruits of the perfect kingdom that still lies in the future but will certainly appear. This positive exposition is the key to chapter 15.

In verses 29-34 he once more takes up the negative way of reasoning followed in verses 12-19, and points again to the absurd consequences of their interpretation. While verses 12-19 deal with the absurdity of faith in view of their position, this section deals with the absurdity of the Christian way of life in view of their position.

In verses 35-49 he discusses how the dead can or will be raised, and the exposition concludes in verses 50-58 with a discussion of how the resurrection will take place and the implications of this resurrection for those still living at the time. The pericope ends with a jubilant doxology and a final practical exhortation.

There is some difference of opinion about the precise division between verses 12-20 and 19-28. The ambivalence in Lutheran exposition demonstrates this. There are those who divide this section after verse 19 because the nihilistic conclusions end there (Bruce, Klappert, Van Ruler, Conzelmann). Others, especially some German guidelines adhering to the prescribed division, add verse 20 to the first section (G. Barth). Then there are also those who include verses 21-22 in the preceding pericope and divide the section into verses 12-22 and 23-28 (McCaughey, Delling, Barrett). Others, and once more mainly German exegetes, take verse 19 as the summary conclusion of the preceding pericope, together with the part that follows.

It is virtually impossible to do justice to all the ideas from verses 12 to 28 in a single sermon. Almost without exception, however, verse 19 (as a summary of the preceding) and verse 20 (as the introduction to what follows) will play an important part. In this guideline therefore we shall focus on these two verses and on the way they are related to the preceding verses, 12ff.

2. There is much discussion on the precise viewpoint of those opponents against whom Paul was writing. In verse 12 it is clearly stated that they deny the resurrection of the dead, but from the argument it appears that they did not disavow Christ's resurrection. The question therefore is, What did they understand by Christ's resurrection? And, Why did they deny the resurrection of the dead? As this is not explained, the only possibility is to try to construe their position by deduction from Paul's argument. Of course, some exegetes are of the opinion that Paul misunderstood his opponents and that some of his arguments were therefore aimed at a misrepresentation (Bultmann, Schmithals, Becker, Conzelmann)!

There are those who believe that the opponents were supporters of a type of popular platonic doctrine of immortality that scorned material existence and consequently regarded the resurrection of the body or the flesh as impossible or superfluous, since the soul continued to exist anyway (Lietzmann, Moffatt, Meyer, Grosheide, Horsley, Pop). Others are of the opinion that the opposition were supporters of Paul's original preaching in Corinth, when he believed that all people would be alive at the second coming and that there was therefore no need to think of a resurrection of the dead (cf. 1 Thess. 4:13-18). According to this view, Paul had to change his viewpoint, due to the deaths that occurred in the churches (Héring, Hurd).

Others think that these were ultraconservative Jewish Christians with a strong earthly expectation of the future (Schlatter, A. Schweizer, Büchsel), a type of Christian Sadducee. Another view is that they were consistent realists who regarded death as the only final reality and were therefore almost rationalists in the modern sense of the word. This viewpoint, however, looks doubtful, since they had no problem regarding Christ's resurrection.

Others see Paul's opponents as "enthusiastic pneumatics," or spiritualists, who already experienced eschatology as real or present either in baptism or in a form of Spirit-filled life (Ridderbos, Thiselton, Weber, Von Soden, and cf. 2 Tim. 2:18). According to them, the resurrection has already taken place for them. Most exegetes presume that this "presentistic-enthusiastic eschatology" (Klappert) shows gnostic influence of some kind (Schniewind, Wendland, Brandenburger, Bartsch, Schmithals, Bultmann, Güttgemans, Blank, Versteeg).

Finally, others assume that Paul's opposition were people who expected a transformation of believers still alive at the second coming, but without any hope of a resurrection of those already dead (Spörlein, Conzelmann).

Obviously, many of these theories overlap. One cannot find a final answer to the question. It is more important to realize that Paul is trying to "explain the credo or confession of faith" (Conzelmann). This means that chapter 15 is not so much an apologetic directed against one point of view and only to be understood in relation to this, but is rather a positive theology that also applies in other situations and with respect to other forms of doubt and denial. The cardinal point therefore, in the words of Ridderbos, is the denial, for whatever reason, of the bodily resurrection of the believers. Christ's future victory over the powers, including death as the final enemy, is at stake.

3. The argument of verses 12-20, in spite of the above-mentioned obscurities and the many conflicting viewpoints, is in a certain sense quite plain. Verse 12 addresses the opponents' denial of the resurrection and states that it is irreconcilable with their confession. From verse 13 onward, Paul draws two (Rupprecht), three (Ridderbos, Weber), or five (Van Ruler) nihilistic conclusions from his opponents' viewpoint.

If the dead are not raised, Christ has not been raised either (v. 13). The logic behind this is not the principle that if the dead cannot be raised, Christ could not have been raised either, because he cannot be an exception to the general rule. It is rather that, according to Paul, it is impossible to confess that Christ has been raised without at the same time confessing that the dead will also be raised. The resurrection of the dead is included in the very *nature* of Christ's resurrection.

"The essential clue to Paul's mind, as appears later from verses 20-22, is that Christ's resurrection is no isolated event" (McCaughey). "If the resurrection of Christ is isolated to a single instance, it is no longer the Christ event" (H. Braun).

The denial of the future resurrection isolates Christ's resurrection in such a way that it is robbed of all meaning. In this way one would deny everything that resulted from his resurrection and was preached among them (v. 14), believed by them (v. 14b), on which the churches were based (vv. 1ff.), and that was professed by the apostles everywhere (v. 15). It would make no sense to believe in such a resurrection of Christ, such faith would be "futile" (v. 17). They would be "most to be pitied" (v. 19).

Paul does not ask them to believe, with a decision that is a kind of *sacrificium intellectus,* in the theoretical possibility of the resurrection of the dead so that they can then believe in Christ's resurrection (v. 16 could be misunderstood in this way), but rather the reverse: that they fully consider the implications of confessing that Christ has been raised. By doing this they would avoid a faith—in Christ's resurrection!—that is an illusion and a hopeless contradiction. He therefore unfolds here, though in a negative and antithetical way, the implications of the Christ-event. In verses 23-28 he will do this in a positive and thetical exposition.

Paul's purpose is to explain that Christians should consider and accept these implications, otherwise their confession becomes meaningless and even foolish. Faith in Christ without the prospect of a future resurrection and glory is still subject to sin (v. 17), death (v. 18), and the meaninglessness of life (v. 19). Verse 19 is the summary judgment on a faith that has given up hope for the future.

In verse 20 he interrupts this nihilistic argument by explaining that—fortunately!—this is not necessary. Their confession excludes such nihilistic conclusions. "This fact of salvation destroys all human opinions regarding death" (Pop). And it thereby gives meaning to preaching and faith.

4. For minor details, commentaries can be used. Two matters, however, are important:

a. The expression *monon* ("only") in verse 19 poses translation problems. Those who think it refers to the verb read, "If we only hope in Christ." Others claim that it refers to the phrase "for (in) this life." They read, "If for this life only we have hoped in Christ" (Luther, Weber, Van Ruler, Conzelmann, Kümmel, Héring, Riesenfeld, RSV). Others say that it refers to the whole sentence. They paraphrase the sentence, "If in this life we have hoped in Christ—that and nothing more . . ." (Barrett, Bachmann, Harris), or, "If we build our hope in this life on Christ and there is only that hope, we are . . ." (Pop).

b. The precise background and thrust of the metaphor "first fruits" (v. 20) are uncertain. *Aparchē* is used here. Elsewhere Paul uses *archē* (Col. 1:18) or *prōtotokos* (Rom. 8:29). Although Conzelmann is of the opinion that neither the history of this concept nor its usage in the Old Testament cast much light on its meaning in this context, many others differ with him. Ridderbos points out that it is not so much the sequence ("first") that is important, but rather the dignity and especially the inseparable connection with the rest of the brethren in the future resurrection.

The term shows Christ as a pioneer, or inaugurator. The whole harvest is already represented and visible in the first fruits. Grosheide maintains that this metaphor is derived from the Mosaic cult and that the offering of the first ripe fruits represents the whole crop. Barrett says: "The first installment of the crop . . . foreshadows and pledges the ultimate offering of the whole." He also calls attention to the theory that the first sheaves of the harvest were offered on the day after the Sabbath of the Passover (Lev. 23:10ff.)—the day Christ was raised, but he admits that these contexts do not necessarily play a part in Paul's view.

With this metaphor Paul is therefore alluding to an inseparable connection between Christ's resurrection and that of believers. He expounds this view in a more thetical way by means of the Adam-Christ parallel (vv. 21-22) and apocalyptic terminology (vv. 23-28). The first fruits bear the guarantee and assurance of the eventual fulfillment.

II. Hermeneutical

1. Many exegetes draw attention to the radical nature of Paul's resistance and conclusions. With the denial of the resurrection of the dead, everything is lost (vv. 13-18). These believers are then "of all men most to be pitied" (v. 19). The preacher should grasp Paul's seriousness here.

In the convictions of Paul's opponents, says De Quervain, the gospel itself is being rejected. "The church becomes a mere religious community, and this is a terrible development! Proclamation becomes null and void, faith becomes null and void. . . . One lives from illusions and wishes. One does not live from the Word of God and is therefore far removed from God, without true comfort or real help. Faith is changed into religious compassion."

Barth is equally harsh: "This kind of Christian life, this hope in Christ which is limited only to this life, without a divine horizon, without the certainty of the resurrection . . . what else is this than utter nonsense, the most dreadful, yes double, self-deceit?"

The Christian hope, writes Van Ruler, remains hope in Christ, even in death. If salvation is not equal to death in all its intense reality, it is no salvation at all. Death is the great power that rules life and makes it what it is, namely a "gradual death."

Over against this power Christians cling to the "only comfort" of the gospel. This means, according to Lord's Day 1 in the Heidelberg Catechism, that we belong to Christ in life *and in death*. If this is not true, Christian proclamation becomes "a lie placed where it is likely to do most damage; in a statement about God" (Barrett, referring to v. 15). In that case the gospel is indeed "projection," "illusion," "wishful thinking," "opium for the people," "to no avail and empty," "mere morality" (and more than that, foolish morality!), "ordinary civil religiosity."

That is why Weber calls the Easter message an "intrusion into our everyday churchly life." And that is why Barth says that in the debate concerning the resurrection "two worlds clash with each other: that of the gospel . . . and that of religiosity and morality. The one world is built on living realities, no, on *the* Living Reality and on firm promises . . . the other one is constructed from below on human convictions, ideologies, values, philosophies and is, in actual fact, illusion and projection."

On the one hand, this means that the Christian hope does not rest on any kind of continuity within human nature, for example, the immortality of the soul. The Christian hope rests entirely on the surprising, almost unbelievable message of Christ's resurrection. Here christology should determine anthropology and eschatology, and not vice versa. Anthropological viewpoints come and go, they vary from time to time and from community to community. If we build our hope on these, we may become disillusioned, because the view we are holding may begin sounding implausible or we may start doubting. Ultimately the onslaught of death and the grave, of suffering and meaningless is powerful enough and real enough to expose all man-made philosophies and worldviews for what they are, namely illusions and mere wishes. The more sharply the power of death is taken into account, however, the more wonderful the sound of the Easter message. The preacher will therefore do well to take into account the radical nature and the finality of death and the somber shadow it casts over everything that may look good in this life.

On the other hand, the Christian hope likewise means that any "hope" that denies the future bodily resurrection, because one is too impressed by the reality, power, and finality of death and the grave, should also be rejected. It is not without reason that various writers discover many modern theological viewpoints in the false doctrine of Corinth.

Iwand writes about some theologians of the nineteenth century (including W. Herrmann and Schleiermacher) and concludes that they advocate the same kind of gnosis as do those in Corinth. He warns against attempts to demythologize faith and to make it more understandable and acceptable to the point where the Easter message gets lost.

Scheffczyk also writes in this vein against Christians (e.g., Sölle) who are occupied in "thoughts and hopes of such an immanent nature" that the heart of the gospel itself is lacking! He warns that these thoughts can only stir up illusions that are even worse than an immanent realism trying to cope without such false dreams and hopes. Referring to verse 19, he points to the "hard fact" that "when we only see Jesus, in the modern sense of the word, as the example of true humanity, the inspirer of freedom, or as the initiator of a political transformation . . . *then* we are of all men most to be pitied."

He sees the problem here as that Christ's resurrection is indispensable also for the Christian hope "in (for) this world," i.e. for the relevance of Christianity in this world. Christianity without the resurrection is ultimately void and empty. One could say that the so-called eschatological reserve, the "critical distance" toward all internal worldly hope, expectations, and happiness should never be lost.

All immanent kingdoms, of blood and language, of "volk," race and identity, of "many possessions" (the rich fool), and political transformations and utopias are finite, and therefore "penultimate" (Bonhoeffer). If these values in themselves are seen as the ultimate, such aspirations and dreams become wishful thinking, and their followers become "of all people most to be pitied."

The severity of Paul's resistance and conclusions is a clear reminder that we are here faced with a radical "Entweder-Oder," a final Either-Or (Barth). "Here Paul speaks as a witness, not as a pastor" (Iwand). This is not a theory that can be easily softened for the sake of those who have problems with it. Everything stands or falls here. At the same time Paul does not "excommunicate" (Pop) his opponents. On the contrary, he reminds them of their own confession and wishes only to expound its wonderful implications in such a way that they too will be convinced and inspired.

The preacher must first of all try to understand the similar choice—immanent civil religion or eschatological Easter faith?— that faces the present-day congregation. Next, one must have clearly in mind the mode (reproachful? critical? pastoral? apologetic?) for presenting the message. And the preacher must be equally clear about the effect to be achieved (change of viewpoint? joy? hope?).

2. It will be important to reckon fully with the shadow that the power of sin and death casts on human life and the utter hopelessness of life without forgiveness and without future life. Such meaningless-

ness and nihilism have been put into words by the existentialists, such as Camus and Sartre. The theater of the absurd (Beckett, Adamov, Ionesco, Genet) can help one understand something of the radical hopelessness that exists where the more things are changed, the more things remain the same.

One can, however, obtain even more important illustrative material in exposing the hopelessness, albeit unconscious, of all civil morality and religion, striving only after penultimate values and ideals. If death really has the final word, how much of what fills our lives every day is complete vanity and transitoriness? How much of our fervor, for hearth and home, for success in our jobs, for prosperity, for showing off our children, for the preservation of our identity and our civilization is wasted on what is temporary and insignificant?

Is it not too often true that our deepest "comfort," yes, the meaning in our lives, what we dream and hope about, is insignificant, brittle, and—if only we are honest with ourselves—no real and lasting comfort? It is against such a dismal background that the Easter gospel resounds.

3. The Easter message means that Christ's resurrection includes our resurrection, and this fills our lives with a future, with hope, and with meaning. He was raised from the dead *non sibi sed nobis* (Calvin), "not for his own sake, but for ours." The most important aspect of his resurrection is not the *that* or the *how* of it, but the fact that it was "for our sake" (Luther).

In Sartre's well-known "Discourse of the Dead Christ" he says: "We are all orphans, without a Father. Everyone is alone. Everyone is his own creator and his own angel of death. There is no tomorrow. There is no healing hand." Fortunately, however, according to 1 Corinthians 15, this is only a dream, a nightmare, an illusion! The truth is, Christ has been raised, as first fruits, *for us!*

The purpose of Easter proclamation is consequently not to argue and to proclaim the isolated, historical fact of Christ's resurrection, but to think about its redemptive, comforting, meaningful, and creative implications. Noordmans writes of verse 21: "The reference is not to an appearance but to an awakening. The resurrection is here caught, as it were, in its first stirrings, when the new life began to extricate itself from death's grip. This is a human being who is awakening here . . . and we are related to this human being as the harvest to the first fruits. The first fruits are dedicated to God, later to be followed by the whole harvest. The same sequence applies to us."

These are words pregnant with meaning: "This is *a human being who is awakening here.*" Whoever has stood alongside an open grave and experienced death's finality, whoever has been tormented about the utter meaninglessness of life, will understand something of the wonderful—almost unbelievable!— message of these words.

III. Homiletical

1. In a sermon, one can initially explain that it is possible to live as though Christ has not been raised from the dead. This does not of course mean that one explicitly or consciously denies Christ's resurrection. The false disciples in Corinth did not do that either. It rather means that one does not live with an awareness of the implications of his resurrection.

The immediate effect of such an attitude toward life is that one only hopes in Christ "for this life." Although this attitude can take shape in many different lifestyles, one can mention some of the most obvious and important of these within the context of the specific congregation.

Without resurrection faith religion becomes completely subservient to our earthly dreams and expectations. Our deepest comfort then lies in the empires and kingdoms of our own desires and aspirations. We absolutize the penultimate and very often identify it with Christianity itself, thus sounding very pious.

Our prayers then become lists of requests. We love the gifts of life more than we love the One who gives them; we love the bestower of gifts for the sake of his gifts. We then seek our deepest security, our highest ecstasy, the ultimate meaning of our lives in earthly things. These things in themselves may indeed be worthwhile and noble, our children, our careers, our recreation, our health, our treasures, our political plans, our moral activism, but Christ may then become nothing more than the great Guarantor, the One responsible for all these dreams being crowned with success. We become kings, and God becomes our servant.

2. Second, one can indicate that such an attitude toward life will make us "of all men most to be pitied." This is so because death will still have the final word. Death eventually dashes all our hopes and comforts. Death casts its dismal shadow over every moment of happi-

ness—and deep inside us we are only too aware of this. This brings an element of sadness to even our happiest moments. Isn't this why we often cry with joy? We feel intuitively that happiness is too wonderful to be true. It cannot last.

Death relativizes everything, makes a bitter joke of life, demonstrates that life is nothing but foolishness and absurdity. Whoever looks for ultimate meaning in something under the sun, the Preacher of Ecclesiastes reminds us, will finally have to admit that everything is meaningless. In the end we are all subjected to futility, in bondage to transience, slaves of meaninglessness. We *have* a final enemy.

Sometimes—and with many of us, most of the time!—we succeed in suppressing this knowledge. Sometimes we are prosperous and experience life as very meaningful. Sometimes we taste happiness and success and believe that it will last forever. This, however, can change in a single moment. A crisis can overturn the very foundation of our certainty, and rob us of our comfort. What is most terrible, says Paul, is that it can even happen to our religion, our hope.

If our faith functions only as an insurance policy, meant to protect, guarantee, and bless our earthly joys, or as an extra incentive for our political ideas, they will all be exposed as worthless and empty in those moments when we fall victim to transience. Then it will become clear that our optimistic attitude toward life was only an illusion, a projection, yes, a form of self-delusion. And that it was therefore worse than nihilistic realism. We will be "of all men most to be pitied."

3. Third, one can proclaim the Easter gospel in all its power and wonder. Death, of course, does *not* have the last word! Christ *has* been raised from the dead! On Easter morning a human being was awakened, the first fruits, and we with him. The last remaining enemy has been destroyed. Our yoke of subjection, of being slaves to transience and futility, has been taken off our shoulders. We have reason to hope.

This message has many practical, down-to-earth implications. Life is not without meaning. Even our crises, which so often seem to destroy our security and rob us of our comfort, do not really have the final word. We need not be frivolous or depressed, cynical or afraid. Even when we meet face to face with the last remaining enemy, we can still do it with trust and without fear. Our hopelessness has been changed into meaning, our sadness has been transformed into great joy.

Of course this hope does not in the least take away from the seriousness and zeal with which we live for Christ in this life, and with which we put our hope in him. It is simply our deepest comfort that even when all our seriousness and zeal in this life have crumbled to pieces, even when we face our last enemy, we may still hope and rejoice. Bonhoeffer, who gave his life for despised fellow human beings, said to other prisoners when he was taken away to die: "This is the end. For me the beginning of life."

D. J. SMIT

First Sunday after Easter: 1 Corinthians 15:29-34

Bibliography

Commentaries

Barrett, C. K. *A Commentary on the First Epistle to the Corinthians.* New York and Evanston: Harper & Row, 1968.

Bruce, F. F. *1 and 2 Corinthians.* New Century Bible. London: Marshall, Morgan & Scott, 1971; Grand Rapids: Eerdmans, 1980.

Calvin, J. *The Corinthians.* Vol. 2. Grand Rapids: Eerdmans, 1948.

Conzelmann, H. *A Commentary on the First Epistle to the Corinthians.* Philadelphia: Fortress, 1975.

Fee, G. D. *Commentary on the First Epistle to the Corinthians.* The New International Commentary on the New Testament. Grand Rapids: Eerdmans, 1987.

Pop, F. J. *De Eerste Brief van Paulus aan de Corinthiers.* De prediking van het Nieuwe Testament. Nijkerk: Callenbach, 1965.

Additional

Barth, K. *The Resurrection of the Dead.* New York: Revell, 1933.

Bonhoeffer, D. *Letters and Papers from Prison.* Edited by Eberhard Bethge. New York: Macmillan, 1971.

McCaughey, J. D. "The Death of Death (1 Cor. 15:26)," in *Reconciliation and Hope,* 246-61. Edited by Robert Banks. Grand Rapids: Eerdmans, 1974.

Van Ruler, A. A. *De dood wordt overwonnen,* 84-106. Nijkerk: Callenbach, n.d.

Van Ruler, A. A. *Het leven een feest,* 64-66, 74-78. Nijkerk: Callenbach, 1972.

Versteeg, J. P. *Christus en de Geest,* 18ff. Kampen: Kok, 1971.

I. Exegetical

The guidelines on 1 Corinthians 15:12-20 (see pp. 131-43) discuss the broader context. Verses 29-34 contain some very practical comments added between the more theoretical expositions (vv. 21-28 and 35-49). The purpose of this section is to reiterate, in a more negative way, the foolish implications of the denial of the resurrection of the dead by Paul's opponents. While verses 12-20 deal with the nihilistic shadow that such a viewpoint casts on the Christian message and faith, the subject here is the nihilistic shadow cast on Christian conduct.

1. As for the structure of the pericope, some exegetes (Rissi, Barrett) recognize three arguments, while others (Wendland, Conzelmann, Güttgemanns, Versteeg) opt for two, in verses 29-32, together with an admonition in verses 33-34. Barrett says that Paul's arguments are based on Christian customs (vicarious baptism, v. 29), Christian suffering (vv. 30-32a) and Christian ethics (v. 32b). All three arguments derive their meaning from the fact that the resurrection of the dead is assumed. Those exegetes who accept only two arguments regard Barrett's second and third arguments as one. The crux of the matter, therefore, is that "the Christian existence can be fully understood only in terms of the future" (Barrett). Or, "[Only] the resurrection gives meaning to the life of the church" (Pop).

2. Paul's style is clearly polemical and *ad hominem*. He argues his case by means of rhetorical questions, which have only one answer— an answer moreover that will expose the untenability of his opponents' position.

3. Although virtually every commentary gives the same basic information, some general comments may be helpful.

a. The baptism "on behalf of the dead" in verse 29 is completely unintelligible. Throughout the ages numerous theories have been presented to explain it. Van Ruler mentions more than thirty, but since then many more have been added. While some are of the opinion that it is precisely at this point that Paul misunderstood his opponents (Bultmann, Schmithals, et al.), the majority of expositors are prepared to admit their ignorance on this point.

This difficulty, however, does not hamper one's understanding of the line of thought. Paul is obviously referring to some unknown baptismal practice, exercised by people who were either the opponents themselves or some of the other Corinthian church members. He neither approves nor condemns it, but simply takes it for granted and uses it in his rhetorical argument. The logic here is that at least one Christian practice becomes totally meaningless if there is no future resurrection.

b. Verses 30-32a likewise present a problem in that it is not clear what he means by the expression "fought with beasts at Ephesus." Once more, however, this need not affect the preaching, as the line of thought is clear. His own apostolic and Christian conduct in life, and more specifically the suffering he had to bear for the sake of the gospel, all become totally meaningless if there is no future resurrection.

c. One can understand the quotation from Isaiah 22:13 in verse 32b ("If the dead are not raised, 'Let us eat and drink, for tomorrow we die'") in two ways. It can be taken as the conclusion of the immediately preceding point, in that Paul regards it as a much better choice, and as a matter of fact the only consistent choice, if his opponents are correct. It can, however, also be seen as another argument.

In any case Paul does not so much want to accuse his opponents of having such a philosophy of life, but is rather saying that they might just as well adopt such a philosophy, as it would indeed be more logical and consistent if they are right! According to him, there is absolutely no reason for not choosing such a lifestyle if one supports their viewpoint. To choose the Christian way of suffering, and, says Van Ruler, thus to be made the "lightning rod of the world's problems," but without any real and valid hope, would indeed make them "of all men most to be pitied" (v. 19).

There are, of course, many people who do not choose such a hedonistic way of life, though they have no hope for a future life. But Paul argues that ultimately this is inconsistent. "Surely, there are also many motives and reasons that could be advanced as to why one would restrain oneself without having this hope, e.g., evil consequences for body and soul, the necessity of socially accepted behavior, the state's intolerance toward and punishment of unlawful conduct, fear of God or the gods, etc. But all these and similar motives are unequal to the awareness that one can only live once" (Pop).

d. Verse 33 is a quotation from the classical author Menander, but because these words most likely had become a popular proverb, Paul is not necessarily quoting him consciously. Although the quote expresses a generally accepted truth, it seems as though, in this context, Paul's intention is quite specific: evil discussions and viewpoints concerning the resurrection will have a negative influence on good Christian manners in the long run.

The reason is obvious. The deepest motivation and ultimate power behind Christian ethics is, at least according to Paul, precisely this faith in the resurrection. Therefore, without this hope, Christian ethics must collapse in the end. "The Christian behavior of the Corinthians will be ruined if they mix much with those who, not sharing the resurrection hope, live as they please" says Barrett. He continues by explaining that, bearing in mind the preceding chapters dealing with meat sacrificed to idols, Paul would never warn against ordinary mixing with unbelievers. But "mixing deliberately to cultivate bad company and taking pleasure in it was another matter."

What is even more dangerous, of course, is "that the bad company was *inside* the church" (Barrett, Héring). It involves people who indeed have hope in Christ "for this life" (v. 19), people who are moreover unaware of their mistake and of the fact that, in spite of their enthusiastic piety, they do not fully appreciate the implications of the resurrection faith and therefore of their own confession. The admonition "Do not be deceived" is written in the passive voice, and Pop therefore would rather translate it with "Do not be misled" or "Do not allow yourselves to be led astray."

e. In verse 34 Paul says that the reverse should rather happen, they should "come to [their] right mind." They should meditate on and comprehend the implications of their own confession, they should pull themselves together and turn from their foolish and inconsistent way of living, and they should "sin no more." Possibly alluding to Jesus' answer regarding the resurrection in Matthew 22:29-33, Paul declares that "some have no knowledge of God."

The implicit assumption is that the reason for their denial of the resurrection is their lack of knowledge of God. The word *agnōsia* "is an actively pursued way of life . . . [as is] shown by the connection of thought between ignorance and sin" (Conzelmann). Barrett says that the "no knowledge" is related to the Corinthian's boasting of knowledge (ch. 8). If such "knowledge" leads to moral indifference, these people are misled. *Agnōsia* with regard to God is therefore speculation that can only have "regrettable moral consequences."

Pop explains that ignorance of God is something other than "no idea of God." Because "some" are of the opinion that they have in fact a very good knowledge of God, even better than Paul himself, they are much more dangerous for the church than people who obviously have no knowledge of God at all! Grosheide writes of Paul's reproach: "The entire congregation must seriously take to heart the fact that there are some people amongst them with a wrong relationship to God."

II. Hermeneutical

Here are several starting points for a sermon on this passage:

1. A first possibility would be to use the same arguments that Paul uses, i.e. by reasoning that at least some Christian customs, that all Christian suffering and sacrifice, and, finally, that even Christian ethics all become meaningless, without ground or motivation, if the hope for the resurrection and the future are false. Such an argument would have to be *ad hominem*, i.e. concrete and practical, addressing specific issues in the life of the present-day church.

The preacher will therefore have to take pains to sort out thoroughly which customs, which types of suffering and sacrifice, and which ethical choices of the congregation would become meaningless if the resurrection were to be denied or underestimated. This way of preaching will, of course, only be relevant if the preacher believes that some of the members of the congregation do indeed deny the future hope in some way or another, whether explicitly or unconsciously, or have at least lost it as the primary comfort and basic motivation of their lives.

2. A second possibility would perhaps be easier. One could—by reversing Paul's own logic!—argue that church members, in view of their hope for the future and the faith in the resurrection that they so often confess, ought to think about Christian customs more seriously, and practice the Christian spirit of self-denial and sacrifice as well as the Christian lifestyle and ethics more faithfully and consistently.

One can find something of this in Van Ruler's two meditations called "Accepting the High-Risk Calling" and "The Willingness to Die." He writes that it is no easy task to be called by God. One is called from safe hideouts into a dangerous life. In a revolution it is better not to be seen on the streets! God calls us to serve in the very heart of a revolution, and often it ends on a cross. It happened with his own Son, and it is still the case with everyone who fully accepts this dangerous calling. Christians are like soldiers sent to the frontline.

It is simply not worthwhile, Van Ruler continues, if there were not resurrection of the dead. It would be better to live life to its full, to take no risks but to try to enjoy every moment, to have, to possess, to eat, and to drink. Then the dangerous Christian lifestyle could only seem meaningless and futile. Only Easter can save us from such spiritual paralysis. Only Easter can give us the inner freedom to be available and willing to serve God in the midst of the struggle, the revolt, the danger. Because of that, risking one's life becomes an essential part of the new life of the resurrection. Eternal life is no lighthearted picnic in the sun, but rather a walk through the valley of death.

The description of the resurrection gospel, with all its implications, becomes an indirect appeal to a life free from desperation and free to be called, free from spiritual paralysis and full of willingness to risk one's own life continually.

3. A very topical starting point would be to expose the attitude of "eat and drink, for tomorrow we die" present, though perhaps unconsciously, in the lives of many ordinary Christians. This attitude, of course, does not become visible only in a hedonistic lifestyle, but also, and indeed very often, in a bourgeois parochialism. It aptly characterizes people who are content with the good life of everyday. It could even refer to decent, respected church members, honorable and reliable citizens—those whose lives are perfectly ordinary, filled simply with the bitter and sweet of every day's successes and troubles, who find sufficient enjoyment in a "good standard of living" and are not moved in any way by deeper questions.

An eat-and-drink attitude toward life can also go to extremes: for example, that of excessive revelry and extravagance, of worldly enjoyment, of empty frivolity; or—less extravagant, but equally futile—the blind chase after an increasingly higher standard of living, the keen but senseless competition of the rat race for better jobs, bigger refrigerators, and faster cars than those of neighbors and friends.

This attitude, however, can even take on the seemingly innocent form of bourgeois religion, of a pious Christianity as the mask behind which a life with transient aspirations hides. The Christian faith is then changed into a form of idolatry: we expect blessings and help from above to supply our daily needs—but nothing more. God must then answer our call, instead of the other way around. He becomes our servant, instead of the opposite. The decisive question becomes, What can the Lord do for me/us in this life? rather than, What can I/we do for the Lord?

The irony for the preacher, of course, is that we are often not free from this attitude ourselves. We, too, easily loose the willingness and freedom to serve the Lord. In that case our Christianity also becomes mundane and material. We will therefore have to examine ourselves to gain some understanding of the radical choices that are at stake. The argument of verses 29-32 can be used for illustration here.

One can also find inspiring material in a meditation by Van Ruler, "The Fear of Death and Zest for Life." He states that often when we seem to be acting out of love of life, we are actually motivated by death! Many of us suffer the "only-so-many-days-to-live" syndrome! Because we are aware that life is fleeting and that nothing really lasts, we easily lose ourselves in the small occurrences of every day and we try to deceive and to give these things the appearance of being eternal and having ultimate meaning.

Van Ruler explains that death not only becomes the boundary but also the very basis of human life! "The zest for life thrives on a deeply hidden sorrow. . . . The certainty of death makes us very depressed in the innermost corners of our heart. But in order to camouflage this depression, to hide it from ourselves and from others, we put on a thick layer of exuberant pleasure. Eating and drinking becomes a veil drawn to cover death."

The gospel, he continues, creates a completely different motivation. The keynote is no longer struck by sorrow and depression, but by joy! Thus life—ordinary, daily human life—obtains a new, wonderful, and happy character. Now we can indeed enjoy it, but for a different reason: not because of the certainty of death, but because we have been made aware of the certainty of life!

4. One could find another starting point for a sermon in the admonition of verse 33: "Bad company ruins good morals." In an introduction one could underscore the truth of this proverb. We are social beings. Our thinking and rationality are greatly affected by our environment and background. The norms and convictions and ideologies of the world in which we grow up and move about influence and shape our lives. We come to know reality by means of the world of language and thought in which we live. We find ourselves at home in a socially constructed reality (P. Berger).

No one should underestimate the importance of these factors in our development. These influences are visible everywhere, from fashions to the general spirit of the time, from propaganda to cultural trends.

Propaganda, for example, is based on the assumption that when people hear a message over and over again, they will start to believe it and then respond to it.

Bad company does ruin good morals. And good company ruins bad morals. For both of these reasons, the church has the duty to watch over its own standards and over the environment in which its members live and learn to think. When we live as if there is no resurrection, as if eating and drinking and making merry is the final word, it becomes all the more difficult to believe and act differently. Van Ruler writes: "The Christian church is therefore rightfully concerned when it becomes clear how rapidly the dechristianization of society proceeds." (One can mention matters such as secularization and the influence of the mass media and literature in this regard.)

5. Verse 34 also offers a possible point of departure. Paul reproaches some for having "no knowledge of God." In this regard one can make use of the biblical theme of "foolishness," which always includes an element of moral guilt. Foolishness, according to the Bible, has nothing to do with intellectual insufficiency, but rather with a moral defect. Because of this moral defect, one is found guilty.

In Bonhoeffer's "Of Folly"—which can almost be read as a commentary on these verses!—one finds a most extraordinary discussion. He states that folly is a more dangerous enemy to the good than evil or outright malice could ever be. One can protest against, unmask, and even prevent evil. Moreover, evil contains in itself the seeds of its own destruction, since it always makes people feel uneasy, if not guilty.

Against folly, however, there is no defense. And this is precisely because the fool is so insensitive and self-assured. When reality contradicts the fool's personal prejudices, this person will simply claim that there is no need to face this. And when reality cannot be denied, the fool ignores the facts at hand as being exceptions. The fool, in contrast to the scoundrel, is totally complacent. Moreover, the fool can easily become aggressive. One needs to be more cautious when dealing with folly than when dealing with evil. To argue with a fool is both useless and dangerous.

In order to deal adequately with folly, Bonhoeffer continues, one should recognize it for what it is, a moral rather than an intellectual defect. There are people of great intellect who are fools and people of low intellect who are anything but fools. Folly is acquired rather than congenital. In addition, it is more common with people who live and think in a group context. In a way, folly is more a sociological than a psychological problem. (Cf. the proverb in verse 33!)

External factors, such as political or religious convictions, tend to blind people *en masse*. More than that, people in positions of power need the folly of others, because they need followers. The upsurge of communal power can become so powerful that it deprives people of independent judgment, and then, more or less unconsciously, they give up trying to analyze and judge matters for themselves. Although the fool can often be very stubborn, one should not be misled into thinking that this person is therefore an independent thinker. On the contrary,

> one feels somehow, especially in conversation with him, that it is impossible to talk with the man himself, to talk with him personally. Instead, one is confronted with a series of slogans, watchwords, and the like, which have acquired power over him. He is under a spell, he is blinded, his very humanity is being prostituted and exploited. Once he has surrendered his will and become a mere tool, there are no lengths of evil to which the fool will not go, yet all the time he is unable to see that it is evil. Here lies the danger of a diabolical exploitation of humanity, which can do irreparable damage to the human character.

For these very reasons the fool cannot be saved by education, but only by redemption. Not by rational argument, but by spiritual renewal.

Folly, says Gerhard von Rad, is "practical atheism." It does not so much deny God's existence verbally or theoretically, but rather in the daily practice of life. The everyday activities of the fool deny the implications of one's sound confession. This is what makes folly so very dangerous. It is unconscious and self-deceiving. The fool is not aware of being foolish! On the contrary, because folly always includes an element of truth, it easily creates the appearance of wisdom. It becomes tempting and persuasive.

This is the folly of those who miss the relationship between the knowledge of God and belief in the resurrection. Van Ruler says:

> There will always be people who are troubled by the message of the resurrection. . . . But *that* is actually the most typical and the most characteristic aspect of God, *that* is precisely the fidelity and the power of God, *that* is God's being in its purest nature, namely the fact that he is Lord over life and death. . . . Just about everything is at stake here, all of the knowledge of God. Whoever stumbles here must fall into heathendom. . . . (*Het leven een feest,* 64-66; see also 74-78)

III. Homiletical

The five above-mentioned approaches are all quite legitimate. A final possibility would be to combine them, but proceeding from the last to the first. One could start by saying that the resurrection message is concerned with the final issues at stake in the gospel, especially the questions, Who is God? What do we think of him? What do we expect from him? One can then discuss the danger of folly (the failure to acknowledge God), as well as its allurement (v. 34), its logical implication (v. 33), and its practical forms (vv. 29-32—our practices and lifestyle become hollow and false).

D. J. SMIT

Second Sunday after Easter:
1 Corinthians 15:50-58

Bibliography

Commentaries

Barrett, C. K. *A Commentary on the First Epistle to the Corinthians.* New York and Evanston: Harper & Row, 1968.

Bruce, F. F. *1 and 2 Corinthians.* New Century Bible. London: Marshall, Morgan & Scott, 1971; Grand Rapids: Eerdmans, 1980.

Calvin, J. *The Corinthians.* Vol. 2. Grand Rapids: Eerdmans, 1948.

Conzelmann, H. *A Commentary on the First Epistle to the Corinthians.* Philadelphia: Fortress, 1975.

Fee, G. D. *Commentary on the First Epistle to the Corinthians.* The New International Commentary on the New Testament. Grand Rapids: Eerdmans, 1987.

Pop, F. J. *De Erste Brief van Paulus aan de Corinthiers.* De prediking van het Nieuwe Testament. Nijkerk: Callenbach, 1965.

Homiletical

In addition to the works listed in the two preceding bibliographies, see: Moltmann, J. *The Power of the Powerless,* 122-35. San Fransisco: Harper & Row, 1983.

I. Exegetical

The broader context is discussed in the guidelines on verses 12-20 (see pp. 131-43). It is extremely difficult to describe in a few words the theme or thrust of this pericope, because these verses include several clear transitions. Diverse subjects are presented in equally diverse styles in order to conclude the argument of chapter 15.

    1. In verse 50, Paul once again summarizes and rejects the op-

ponents' thesis that the resurrection of the dead is not necessary in order to experience salvation. Weber quite rightly extends Paul's criticism to include all views that regard life after death as simply a linear and natural continuation of some element of human nature itself. Flesh and blood, Paul is convinced, cannot inherit the kingdom in any way, except by passing through death and being resurrected into a new life! This makes Christ's resurrection so "impossible to coordinate, impossible to categorize" (Weber). Without familiar coordinates or points of reference, it is beyond all known human categories. The eschaton, the kingdom of God, lies beyond all our linear expectations.

Paul is dealing with perhaps the most critical question his opponents could ask of his resurrection message, What about those still alive when the kingdom comes? After his discussion of the reality (vv. 1-11), the necessity (vv. 12-20, 29-34), the hope (vv. 21-28), and the nature (vv. 35-49) of the resurrection, he now concludes by examining whether those still alive will not perhaps be exceptions to the rule. Or, phrased differently, whether flesh and blood cannot after all inherit the kingdom "unchanged." Or, said in still another way, questioning whether the message of the resurrection is indeed so wonderful, so strange, and so necessary. He rejects this possibility, no matter how it is stated, very emphatically in verse 50.

In verses 51-52 he elaborates on this conviction, saying that all those still alive will also be "changed," "transformed," "clothed." Flesh and blood definitely cannot avoid the complete break with transitoriness, perishability, and mortality. There will be *no* exceptions to the rule. The mere restoration or continuation of that which already constitutes human life is not salvation (Weber).

Paul's gospel of the resurrection of the dead therefore does not become absurd, though some will still be alive. "The absurdity indeed lies in the other way; religion and morality alike make no sense if there is no resurrection" (Barrett).

2. In verses 51ff. he uses apocalyptic language once again (the *dei,* "must," of verse 53; the metaphor of the last trumpet, etc.) to make exactly the same point. McCaughey agrees with Becker's assertion that as far as this apocalyptic imagery is concerned, one must be careful in the conclusion drawn. The use of this imagery is in itself no proof that Paul understands it literally. One should always ask how it is used and for what purpose, and McCaughey then comes to the conclusion that Paul only wants to reinforce his preceding statement with language

"which has perhaps greater imaginative power, which certainly has its peculiar eloquence."

3. Paul now changes into a hymnlike style, because "one can only talk about the victory over death in a doxological way" (Klein). He uses two quotations from the Old Testament, Isaiah 25:8 and Hosea 13:14, to boast about the fact that death has been conquered and swallowed up in victory. (Cf. Conzelmann, 292ff.; Pop, 401ff. for the tradition behind his use of these texts and the nature of his own amendments. Noordmans calls it "a liturgical, rather than a homiletical quotation.") The exact meaning of the *kentron* in verses 55 and 56 is uncertain. It can either be the "prick" or "stick" used to drive animals along, or the poisonous sting with which a dangerous animal wounds and kills.

4. In verse 56 Paul suddenly returns to his well-known terminology of death and sin and law. Because of the abruptness of the change, some are of the opinion that these words represent a later addition (Weiss, Moffatt, et al.). Barrett, however, is convinced that they "completely misunderstand" the verse, and Klein says that it is "stupid" to regard this as an addition. He sees it as an essential counteranswer to ward off any metaphysical speculation from the argument and to bring the argument back down to earth. He therefore grants it a key position in the pericope and builds his entire sermon on it! Conzelmann asserts that the verse fits too well into the context to take it as an addition. He calls it a kind of exegetical remark that has already been prepared for in verses 3-5 and 17.

5. Verse 57 brings the pericope to an end with a thanksgiving and a song of praise. Weber quite rightly draws attention to the fact that the doxology in verses 55-57 is actually a hymn on Christ. Just as he has done throughout the chapter, Paul once again does not build the Christian expectation of the future on all kinds of speculation or anthropological probabilities, but solely on what God did in Christ (his resurrection) and just as assuredly will do in the future. This chapter concludes in similar fashion to Paul's argument in Romans 7:7ff., which also ends in triumph (v. 25) and the boast in the *nikos,* the "victory," in Christ.

6. Verse 58 then presents a final and summary paranesis. Paul draws some practical, ethical conclusions in the light of the preceding argument. The introductory "therefore" can refer either to verse 57 or to the whole chapter. Although Schmithals wants to separate verse 58 from the context on grounds of literary criticism, his effort is uncon-

vincing because this verse dovetails very well with the entire line of thought in this chapter. Paul thus concludes with the promise that, in view of the resurrection, Christian labor in the Lord is not in vain.

II. Hermeneutical

There are quite a few possibilities to explore with a view to a sermon.

1. Like Van Ruler in his meditation "Communism Is More Bourgeois than Christianity" (in *De dood wordt overwonnen,* 145), one could start off with the necessity of those still alive being changed, because flesh and blood cannot inherit the kingdom (vv. 50-53). He then examines the relation between history and eschaton, concluding that the communist revolutions are child's play compared to the changes that, according to Christianity, the world really requires. The communists, therefore, still have "something narrow-minded and bourgeois" in their approach. The Christian eschatology criticizes a too-immediate and a too-earthly expectation of salvation.

2. As a second possibility, one could try to make something of the scorn of verses 54-55 and the boasting in verses 55-57. In the church's ancient Easter songs there was indeed often an element of laughter and scorn. During the Middle Ages it was still customary to start each Easter sermon with a joke. The people made fun of the powers and of death, which had been stripped and ridiculed in Christ's resurrection. Moltmann also does it when he preaches on "Easter: The Festal Protest against Death." He proceeds from the meaninglessness and the living death that many people in both the West and the Third World experience. He asserts that judging from these experiences and from the suffering of humanity it looks as though Jesus' resurrection is absolutely absurd and without any evidence. Conversely, however, violence and death are absurd if seen in the light of Christ's resurrection. God proves himself as the one with whom the impossible is possible, who calls into existence the things that do not exist (Rom. 4:17). In this way Easter faith becomes faith in God's protest against death, and faith in God's willingness to suffer out of love. Easter becomes the festival of joy, the laughter of the redeemed, the dance of the liberated, the creative game of fantasy.

In another of Van Ruler's meditations entitled "A Matter of Surprise, Astonishment, and Scorn" (*De dood wordt,* 156), he points out the irony and humor of the Easter gospel, which really turns everything upside down! It seems as though in spite of all human abilities and achievements there is only one victory this side of the grave, the victory of death. We are all subjected to "the grim logic of the grave" (Dijk). We seem helpless and overpowered. But, in imitation of the prophets of old, the apostle suddenly mocks death with a cheerful, jeering laugh. This change, however, can best be proclaimed in "proverb and song."

In another meditation, "Doxology As the Interruption of Human Logic" (ibid., 164), Van Ruler says that the gospel does bring a triumphant tone into the Christian life, but that this should not be exaggerated. It is never a permanently joyful frame of mind, but always a triumph born out of affliction.

Buskes, as a result of his brother Gijs' illness, also writes very touchingly about his own deep trust in the resurrection, but coupled with his "deep mistrust of the Hallelujah-Christianity" that superficially tries to ignore or forget the harsh reality of death. The joy of Easter never forgets! The joy of Easter is a joy in spite of. . . .

3. A third starting point would be to use, as Klein did, the very "Pauline" ideas of verse 56, where death, sin, and the law are related to each other in kinds of "concentric circles," to describe the scope of the powers that have been conquered in the resurrection. When combined with the praise of verse 57, this becomes a doxology on the scope of our redemption. To treat the pericope in this way, however, would mean that its specific features would probably be lost and that everything would be reduced to a more traditional exposition of Paul's theology as it is presented in far greater detail in other parts of his writings.

4. The paranesis of verse 58 can also be a starting point. Van Ruler treats it as "Expectation Makes Us Free for Action" (ibid., 167). He points out how Paul undermines the opposition by including his opponents in the Christian family with his greeting "my beloved brethren." Van Ruler maintains that Paul arrives at three conclusions.

First, Christians should remain steadfast in this faith and in their hope. Christ's resurrection puts "a gigantic and firm foundation" under the feet of Christians! Christians can "stand, sit and even lie down" on this foundation! Paul wants us always to remember this reality and continuously to confirm it with our thoughts and actions.

Second, Christians should be steadfast. This steadfastness is fiercely and persistently attacked and shaken, pulled and tugged at from all sides. Christians should practice steadfastness against these attacks, by following a "training program" that makes them immune. "We have to harden ourselves in the faith we have heard." Christians must learn to withstand temptation by steadfastly clinging to this message.

Paul's third conclusion, Van Ruler argues, is that this attitude toward life is never only a matter of thinking and reasoning, but also a matter of doing. That is, everyone is faced with an either-or choice. One can either say that there is purpose, destiny, future, and consequently meaning in life, because God is alive and involved with people and the world. In this case we can then get involved as a co-operator in God's work. Or we can deny the resurrection and eternal life, but then we also deny all real meaning in life. In that case one may keep on working and striving—everyone is always busy anyway!—yet then such toil is actually in vain.

This is the basic choice everyone faces daily, not in theory, but in practice. We answer this question with our actions. No one has any guarantees on earth. Everyone is active, everyone is continuously busy, but in the final analysis everyone lives either in hope or in despair. Christians should allow themselves to be liberated in order to tackle life in a steadfast and unfaltering way, believing that they have been called to do the work of God on this earth. One's entire life is encompassed by this calling. There is no more time to worry or fret. There is always more work than can be done. Christians should excel in that.

Yet it is not "desperate activism." Christians do not plunge themselves into busyness to escape being smothered in despair; on the contrary, they know that their work, trouble, and exertion are not in vain because it is done "in the Lord." Through Christ's resurrection the entire life of obedience is sheltered in and directed toward eternal life. "Every transient effort contains the fruit of eternity. . . . The faith in the apostolic gospel is the permanent presupposition of all our endeavors in this world" (Van Ruler).

Pop makes a somewhat forced division: "steadfast in faith, unfaltering in hope, abundant in love—that is what the apostle wants them to be." He explains that this steadfastness should be seen against the background of the Old Testament, in that one stands with both feet on the firm ground of God's promises, and not merely as an ethical exhortation to a personal moral effort. In this context Paul deals specifically with steadfastness "in faith." Because of *that,* the Christian's work is not "in vain," an expression that describes the most characteristic and widespread of all human frustrations surrounding work, says Pop.

III. Homiletical

1. If one wants to take the whole pericope into account in a single sermon, one could perhaps devote a first argument to the point made in verses 50-55, namely that this life (flesh and blood, with all this entails) must first pass through the grave, like a kind of "transformer," before entering the kingdom. As a starting point, one could refer to the moving question written on a wall in Londonderry, Northern Ireland: "Is there a life this side of the grave?"

A Christian should first experience something of this bitterness, cynicism, and loathing of life—in spite of all its blessings—before being able to hear the gospel. A Christian should know that the bitter bonds of death, sin, and law (v. 56) smother this life in their grip and stretch their somber shadow over all of life, including its highest and happiest moments. Christians should therefore be liberated from the bourgeois mentality (cf. Van Ruler regarding communism), from all cheap equations of something in this life with the kingdom of God. Christians should be able to laugh at those who think too optimistically about this life and who underestimate the seriousness of the unholy covenant of death.

2. One can then proclaim the resurrection gospel in a second argument. This gospel is the only message that can make one laugh at the somber bonds and powers themselves! Laughter, ridicule, festivity, and thanksgiving (vv. 54-57) should be proposed as being the most authentic style for celebrating Easter. Cynicism and somberness should be driven away with anecdotes, singing, proverbs, and laughter.

3. In a third part one could show that this joyful laughter of Easter will eventually become the happy laughter of every day. In a way the Lord gives Christians everyday life—snatched from them by the powers of sin, law, and death and in the process made futile and empty—back from the grave. We can now take new delight in life. Now Christians enjoy life anew, no longer because they underestimate the powers, but because they have (already) sensed the ridiculousness of these powers vis-à-vis Christ's victorious resurrection. Thus the laughter of festivity becomes laughter amid daily life and work. It therefore remains laughter amid temptation, not the exaggerated and artificial happiness of someone trying to ignore reality, but the deep thankfulness and joy of someone for whom life, true life, has become reality and for whom work will therefore ultimately prove to be meaningful.

D. J. SMIT

Third Sunday after Easter: Ecclesiastes 9:7-10

Bibliography

Commentaries

Eaton, M. *Ecclesiastes: An Introduction and Commentary.* Tyndale Old Testament Commentaries. London/Downers Grove: InterVarsity, 1983.

Gordis, R. *Koheleth: The Man and His World.* 3d ed. New York: Schocken, 1968.

Kidner, D. *A Time to Mourn and a Time to Dance.* London/Downers Grove: InterVarsity, 1976.

Loader, J. A. *Ecclesiastes.* Text and Interpretation. Grand Rapids: Eerdmans, 1986.

Homiletical

Hubbard, D. A. *Beyond Futility: Messages of Hope from the Book of Ecclesiastes.* Grand Rapids: Eerdmans, 1976.

Van Reyendam-Beek, L. W. *Postille,* 172-75. Vol. 26. The Hague: Boekencentrum.

Van Ruler, A. A. *Dwaasheden in het leven.* Vol. 2, 14-17 (Eccl. 9-12). Nijkerk: Callenbach.

Additional

Johnston, R. K. "Confessions of a Workaholic: A Reappraisal of Qoheleth." *Catholic Biblical Quarterly* 38 (1976): 14-28.

Scott, R. B. Y. *The Way of Wisdom in the Old Testament.* New York: Macmillan, 1971.

I. Exegetical

1. Does a book that begins with the verdict "All is vanity" (1:2) have a place in the history of redemption? Could one, during Easter, possibly preach from a book that apparently struggles with a problem already solved by the Easter events?

The book of Ecclesiastes is difficult to interpret. Some Jewish scholars are of the opinion that the book was written by a plagiarist. They judge it a mediocre work that, because of its low standard, hardly deserves a place in the canon. Orthodox Jews viewed verses such as 11:9b and 12:7b as later insertions saving the "honor" of the book.

It is all the more remarkable that Ecclesiastes was read in the synagogue during the Feast of Tabernacles. The feasts of Israel were never somber; they were extremely joyful. The Hebrew word for "feast," *ḥag,* is usually connected with a verb whose stem may mean "dancing." The Feast of Tabernacles is also called the Feast of Harvest. Except for the fact that this feast coincided with the reaping of the harvest, the Israelites had to live in huts for seven days (Lev. 23:43). This practice was meant to remind them of their homeless wandering in the desert and of the fact that Yahweh's care took the form of very practical, concrete acts of salvation: the exodus from Egypt and God's gracious provision in the desert. Throughout the Bible the hut is a symbol of protection (Ps. 27:5). During the Feast of Tabernacles the faithful Israelite rejoices in the protection the Lord guarantees.

To a certain extent the problems of insignificance, transitoriness, and homelessness, with which Ecclesiastes is concerned, form a sharp contrast with such a feast; security is contrasted with wandering and insignificance. The contrast, however, fits in neatly with the method used by the author of this book. Basically the book consists of two main contrasting sections. In order to understand the message of this book better, we have to take a closer look at the nature of this contrast.

2. According to Ecclesiastes, life has two sides, like a coin. Everything depends on the way one approaches it. The contrast is very clear. Does one prefer to live from an armful of troubles, or from God's open hand?

At first the author of Ecclesiastes has the attitude of people who want to stand on their own two feet and have their own way. The final result, however, is that everything is turned upside down. The coin is flipped. Heads become tails. Ecclesiastes views life from the viewpoint of a person who wishes to create meaning and purpose in life without God, through one's own achievement and material security. How successful can one be without God in life? Where do these efforts lead?

This search for meaning first leads the author of Ecclesiastes to wisdom. Wisdom—human knowledge and rational insight—however, brings no lasting peace. On the contrary, it increases sorrow (1:18; cf. also 2:15-16).

Next, he tries pleasure (2:1), wealth and prosperity (all of ch. 2). Culture, with all its progress, recreation, and comfort, however, does not bring lasting happiness. Engineering ingenuity, design, planning, and technique (vv. 4-6); possessions (v. 7-8); the arts (v. 8), and splendid achievements (v. 9)—all these things cannot fill the vacuum in our existence.

Third, even by working hard and throwing all one's energy into work and career one cannot shake off the feeling of discontent and meaninglessness (2:11; 4:4). When we honestly analyze all our toil, we discover with a shock that much of it comes down to a superficial rat-race in which selfishness is the deepest motivation behind everything. When we look at our seemingly noble activities through a microscope, we often discover the bacteria that threaten life from the inside: jealousy and enviousness. "Then I saw that all toil and all skill in work come from a man's envy of his neighbor" (4:4).

According to Ecclesiastes, we can come to the following conclusion: If the most important things in life are those we can grasp with our own hands and clasp in our fist, to enjoy and to use on our own, life is meaningless and a striving after wind. Human works, successes, and pleasures are transitory and ultimately do not guarantee anything.

In contrast to these dismal deductions, the book of Ecclesiastes also sketches life as a gift from God's hand. Describing human beings as unique creations who are able to grasp the idea of eternity (3:11) already shows that there is another perspective on life. God is presented as Creator of it all (3:11-14). In his divine wisdom, he is in command. "God meets us in this book in three main aspects: as Creator, as Sovereign, and as Unsearchable Wisdom" (Kidner).

Wisdom, prosperity, pleasure, and toil do not present any answer to the question of the meaning of life. Life only becomes meaningful when one gets the following perspective: "This also, I saw, is from the hand of God; for apart from him who can eat or who can have enjoyment?" (2:24-25).

The book of Ecclesiastes proclaims to us the following truth: sin (godlessness) = meaninglessness; faith in Yahweh (the creative God who fulfills all needs) = meaning. With this perspective Ecclesiastes puts life, the gift of God, in the light of thankfulness to him.

This viewpoint coincides with the thrust of wisdom literature in general (cf. also the book of Proverbs). Wisdom seeks to make religion practical. It does not aim at justification by works, but rather at sanctification, as an answer to and as thankfulness for the revelation and the law. To a certain extent wisdom literature sings the same song as the Torah, but composed in a key of gratitude and joy.

3. The author of Ecclesiastes has often been wrongly described as a pessimist. The verdict "All is in vain" is not to be regarded as a philosophy of life, applicable in general and therefore reason for pessimism. "All is in vain" is rather a polemical statement, meant to describe the most extreme consequence of a life in which one takes one's point of departure in transitoriness. The Hebrew expression here is a superlative for insignificance or vanity. Futility or vanity is the state into which one declines when life becomes an absolute zero, total emptiness—nonsense. The expression "under the sun" (1:3) refers to the perceptible, sensory world. In this earthly reality there are no windows open to an extramundane reality.

Ecclesiastes does not maintain that life is meaningless *per se*. The author differs from Schopenhauer, who wrote, "Life is something that should not have been." The nihilism and pessimism of Ecclesiastes illustrates the extreme consequence of one choice in life. Nor is the Preacher an optimist or opportunist. He does not come to Leibnitz's conclusion that this world must be seen as the best of all possibilities.

The truth is: "He looked about him and saw the human enterprise—busy, busy man (a human anthill), in mad pursuit of many things, trying now this, now that, laboring away as if he could master the world, lay bare its secrets, change its fundamental structures, somehow burst through the bounds of human limitations, build for himself enduring monuments, master his destiny, achieve a state of secure and lasting happiness—laboring at life with an overblown conception of the powers of man, vainly pursuing unrealistic hopes and expectations. From this perspective all is vanity and a striving after wind" (Stek). The author of Ecclesiastes is a realist who respects the fundamental tension between sin and grace, between creation and the fall (insignificance), between human destiny and the human condition. At the end of the book, therefore, he raises the topic of judgment (8:11-13; 11:9; 12:14). The prosperity of the godless person ends in disaster (Ps. 73:3, 17). The side of life that seemed to be "heads" is unmasked as "tails" in the end.

Ecclesiastes shows us a life that possesses everything under the sun. Unfortunately, however, it is a life underneath a closed heaven, cut off from the Provider of life. This is in contrast to the book of Job, where we find an afflicted person, with only a minimum of possessions, living on a rubbish heap. Fortunately, however, Job sits under an open heaven. He hurls out his complaints to the Giver of life.

Another aspect of the realism of the book of Ecclesiastes is that a life built with a golden dome under the sun is handicapped by the bare facts of sin (3:16-17), death (3:20), and the passing of time (9:11-12).

This book contains a hidden element of holy mockery. When one looks toward heaven through the glasses of human skill and human achievement, heaven seems to be empty. When one looks at nature through the glasses of revelation and grace, all our works are child's play—mud pies! But, in fact, they *are* meaningful, because we make them under the watchful eyes of our heavenly Father.

4. Against this background, Ecclesiastes 9:7-10 can now be studied. Verses 7-9 deal with genuine joy in life. Life is described in its festiveness and is contrasted with the dreariness of the grave (v. 5). For the people of the Old Testament, life could be festive because they lived under the blessing of the Lord of the Covenant. Life was more important than death because life meant the chance to praise God and to live by God's blessing. The practical meaning of this blessing was that God saves and that he is merciful. Within the cult and liturgy, as well as through the feasts, the Israelites were reminded that by saving his people out of Egypt, God had triumphed over the powers of darkness, death, insignificance, idols. Faith in God's conquering omnipotence changed life into an overflowing joy, in spite of suffering and misery.

Life as a gracious gift from God's hand is suggested here with the expressions "bread" and "wine" (v. 7). Bread and wine were the basic daily foods of the people. The laborer who harvests under the open sky may indeed enjoy the fruit of his labor. Thus, when the Israelites entered Canaan, this fulfillment of God's promise made life a feast. A person living in God's Canaan *has* to be cheerful (Deut. 12:7, 12). Abundance exists so that humanity can serve God with joy (Deut. 28:47).

White clothes (v. 8) are in sharp contrast to mourning dress. When Israelites wore white clothes, they were either feasting or very wealthy.

White garments serve here as a symbol of abundance and festivity. They do not refer to spiritual purity, and the preacher should not spiritualize this. The "oil" used as perfume had a sweet odor. This is a further indication of festiveness. "Always to wear white garments and to have one's head perfumed, therefore, means to be constantly cheerful and happy, to regard life as if it were a holiday" (Gindsburg).

Verse 9 tells us, first, that our enjoyment in love, especially the relationship between husband and wife, are part of God's gracious gift. Sexual enjoyment, therefore is not excluded from the luminous circle of religion (cf. Adam's exclamation in Gen. 2:23). The context of marriage is important in this verse.

II. Hermeneutical

The connection between this passage and the New Testament proclamation of the resurrection can be found in the following:

1. Joy means gratitude for the life received from the hand of the God of the Covenant, who conquered the powers of destruction. The resurrection proclaims to the church that all destructive powers are conquered in principle by Christ's resurrection. Even death, which threatens to devour life and to equalize "the sons of men and . . . beasts" (Eccl. 3:19-20), has been robbed of its power. Humans, in their transitoriness, are not equal to death. God, however, is more than equal to it. Death has been swallowed up in victory (1 Cor. 15:54).

Without the resurrection of Jesus Christ the vision of Ecclesiastes would be very limited, and the contrast it draws between the frenzy of the wicked and the joy of the pious would be robbed of its deepest meaning. "If the dead are not raised, 'Let us eat and drink, for tomorrow we die'" (1 Cor. 15:32).

2. Sheer enjoyment, however, without obedience and responsibility to God, puts one under God's judgment. According to Ecclesiastes 12:14, every act is put under God's magnifying glass. God is concerned with every aspect of our lives. That is why life is meaningful. But, then, we must fear God and keep his commandments (Eccl. 12:13).

With Christ's resurrection, death (as retribution for sin and the symbol of God's judgment) has been finally destroyed by the triumph of grace. The resurrection focuses all of creation on eschatology, the second coming of Christ and the final judgment. Those who persist in fearing God, who do not live according to an "under the sun" mentality, will be resurrected to life eternal, sharing in never-ending happiness.

3. The life of resurrection is a life full of joy and thankfulness. This must be demonstrated every day in the way we eat and drink, in the way we live in marriage, and in our work. Question 90 of the Heidelberg Catechism is relevant here. "What is the resurrection of the new man?" Answer: "It is a cordial joy in God through Christ and a longing and love to live according to God's will in all good works" (cf. also 1 Cor. 10:31).

III. Homiletical

1. A sermon from this book can be very topical and timely. One can perhaps start by referring to the many ways we, too, are still trying to give meaning to an often hollow and empty lifestyle ("under the sun," cf. I, 3). Specific illustrations will, of course, depend on the needs and problems in each congregation. One may perhaps think of the greed of our society, or our obsession with achievement and success. The extravagance that accompanies our prosperity is ruthlessly unmasked in Ecclesiastes 1:3: "What does man gain by all [his] toil?" This is the judgment on a world that strives after only profit, gain, growth, development, expansion. "Bigger and better"—to what end? All is in vain, says Ecclesiastes! What a sentence on all of our lives!

2. This leads to some questions. Are we only concerned with getting as much as possible out of this life? Or do we discover that there is more to life, namely the gracious gifts of God? Do we discover that life is loaded with blessings from the One who is above the sun, blessings which make life a continuous feast?

The author of Ecclesiastes knows about vanity and death. As a matter of fact, he is deeply impressed by these realities (cf. 2:16). But he knows more than that: he knows about the providence and fidelity of God, the God we have to fear and whose commandments we have to keep (12:13). Through his assurance of God's fidelity and through his fear of the Lord, the Preacher finds a sure foundation. This explains his steadfast joy even under changing circumstances, suffering, and vanity.

3. The resurrection, of course, gives this unwavering joy a new depth and a new sincerity, because it conquers all destructive powers— yes, even death, which threatens to devour life (9:10). Without Christ's resurrection the pious Christian's faith might seesaw (II, 1).

4. Because of the resurrection, the believer is called to fear God and live in obedience (12:13). But this is a call then to lead an insurrectionary life, not to accept life "under the sun" as it is, but to transform it, to subject all aspects of life to God's sovereignty; to lead a victorious and joyful life in marriage and family, in work and recreation, in all one's relationships. "For God will bring every deed into judgment" (12:14). This is not intended to spoil our fun or to cut the wings of our joy, but to protect us from destruction and to distinguish joy from frenzy. Christ's resurrection allows us to rise to joy and to enjoy life. Christ guarantees life! Because he is alive! The sting of death has been removed! Life *must* be enjoyed!

D. J. LOUW

Fourth Sunday after Easter:
1 Thessalonians 4:13-18

Bibliography

Commentaries

Best, E. *A Commentary on the First and Second Epistles to the Thessalonians*. New York/Evanston: Harper & Row, 1972.

Bolkestein, M. H. *De Brieven aan de Tessalonizensen*. Nijkerk: Callenbach, 1970.

De Boor, W. *Die Briefe des Paulus An Die Thessalonicher*. Wuppertal: Brockhaus, 1960.

Hendriksen, W. *I and II Thessalonians*. Grand Rapids: Baker, 1955.

Hiebert, D. E. *The Thessalonian Epistles*. Chicago: Moody, 1971.

Marshall, I. H. *1 and 2 Thessalonians*. New Century Bible. London: Marshall, Morgan & Scott; Grand Rapids: Eerdmans, 1983.

Marxsen, W. *Der erste Brief an die Thessalonicher*. Zürich: Theologischer, 1979.

Morris, L. *The First and Second Epistles to the Thessalonians*. Tyndale New Testament Commentaries. Grand Rapids: Eerdmans, 1984.

Homiletical

Ogilvie, L. J. *Life As It Was Meant To Be*. Ventura, Calif.: Regal, 1980.

Additional

Berkhof, H. *Well-Founded Hope*. Richmond: Knox, 1969.

Berkouwer, G. C. *Man: The Image of God*. Grand Rapids: Eerdmans, 1962.

Berkouwer, G. C. *The Return of Christ*. Grand Rapids: Eerdmans, 1972.

Minear, P. S. *Christian Hope and the Second Coming*. Philadelphia: Westminster, 1954.

Moltmann, J. *Theology of Hope*. New York/Evanston: Harper & Row, 1965.

I. Exegetical

In First Thessalonians, Paul responds to various questions of the Thessalonian church, especially concerning the second coming of Christ. Apparently there were some members of the church who could no longer see any need for daily work, because they expected the Lord to return soon. Those "apocalyptic fanatics" and "pneumatic agitators" (Bolkestein) are admonished to "live quietly" and to "work" (4:11). At the same time they had to be alert and vigilant for the second coming (5:1-11). In between these two sections lies the pericope we study here.

First Thessalonians 4:13-18 deals with two matters: the believers' grieving "as others do who have no hope," and whether those still alive at the second coming will precede those who have "fallen asleep." In the Jewish apocalyptic writings those who did not live to experience the dawning of the messianic era were pitied. The fact that some believers died after being converted (perhaps under Paul's own ministry?) caused the question to arise: Is this not contradictory to the Easter gospel and/or their expectations of the second coming? Did not this shake the very foundations of their faith?

Paul replies to these queries with his well-known expression "we would not have you ignorant" (cf. Rom. 1:13; 11:25; 1 Cor. 10:1, 12). Ignorance, i.e. lack of the right knowledge of the great truths concerning faith, not only impedes a clear vision of the case in point, but also influences our whole way of life. Knowledge concerning one's faith and putting that faith into practice are always correlated. That is why Paul takes the trouble to answer these questions.

1. At the outset he offers a pastoral injunction not to "grieve as others do who have no hope." Here "grieve" surely refers to an inner mourning that cannot be overcome, a sorrow born of hopelessness. Hiebert translates and explains the expression as: "to experience pain, to grieve, to be distressed: it is not merely natural sorrow and the sense of loss we feel at the death of loved ones." Paul tells them that the manner in which they grieve must not be like that of unbelievers (= "others"; cf. 5:6; Rom. 11:7; 1 Cor. 7:12); i.e. people who "do not yet live by faith in Christ and therefore cannot die with their hope in Christ" (Du Preez).

Without hope there is no glorious life, no glorious death, no glorious resurrection, and no glorious future in heaven. This is exactly what Paul warns against: do not grieve as though you have not been "born anew to a living hope through the resurrection of Jesus Christ

from the dead" (1 Peter 1:3). "The contrast does not lie in the degree or
nature of sorrow . . . but lies between Christian hope and pagan sorrow"
(Best).

The content of true Christian consolation in times of death can be
explained in a threefold manner:

a. Paul does not justify death or try to give it meaning by soften-
ing the blow. He shows that death is destroyed by Christ's victory on
the cross and in his resurrection (14a; 1 Cor. 15:54b). The finished nature (perfect tense) of this history, i.e. the single powerful reality of salvation through the cross and resurrection, guarantees the hope of personal resurrection. Jesus' death and resurrection are closely connected
with the death and resurrection of the believer (cf. Rom. 6:5; 8:11; 14:7-
9; 1 Cor. 6:14; 15:20; 2 Cor. 4:14; etc.). He takes them with him in his
death, through the gateways of his resurrection (cf. Moltmann).

b. Christians who have already died in Thessalonica are described
as "those who are asleep"; literally, "are asleep in him." (Cf. Hendriksen, et al., concerning the position of *dia tou Iēsou,* whether in conjunction with the verb "are asleep" or with the expression "will bring with
him [Jesus]." It does make a difference in the way it is translated—cf.
the KJV and the RSV!—but the implications remain clear.) Thus the
faithful die "faithfully": the way they die is related to the way they have
lived. In the same way that their lives on earth with Christ are hidden
in God, so they will be hidden when they die in Christ (16b). As they
have lived, so will they also end their lives "in Christ," i.e. enfolded in
his power, his closeness, and his shelter. Many questions concerning
life and death may remain unanswered, but the faithful are absolutely
certain of Christ's closeness in death.

c. In passing from life to death, it is God who acts. Through Jesus,
God will bring with him those who have fallen asleep. Not only does
God guarantee the resurrection of the faithful through the resurrection
of Christ, but God will also bring them out of death into his glory. The
word that is used for this action is a powerful military term (*axei*—leading a military parade). The Lord God makes the resurrection a festive
military parade: "Here, with his victory, Christ will act like a mighty
conqueror entering a city with tambourines, banners, drums and a
band" (Luther *WA 36,* 268).

2. Next (vv. 15b-17), Paul explains that at the second coming the
living will not precede those who have already fallen asleep. It is not
clear if this is something the Lord himself said, perhaps during his

earthly ministry (e.g., in Matt. 26:30-31)? Or is it an *agraphon,* an orally transmitted pronouncement by Jesus? Or is it a summary and paraphrase of several of Jesus' teachings? Or is it a truth revealed to Paul himself? (For an exhaustive discussion of this issue, cf. De Boor, Bolkestein.) Once again, however, the thrust is clear. God's Word here assures us that the living will not precede the dead. The image used here is that of an athlete who takes the lead and is first to reach the finish line; it will not be like this at the second coming. To substantiate this, Paul once again presents three arguments:

a. The parousia of the Lord ushers in the parousia of the dead. The word *parousia* (lit., "presence," "appearance," "arrival," "advent") has a festive note. It was used for the arrival of the emperor, bringing peace and order to a city after his conquest. In the same way, Christ's parousia is the coming of the Conqueror of the world to put everything in order again. All this is announced with military fanfare; the trumpet call signals that the parade is about to begin; it is the cry of command of the conqueror (Schmidt: "shout of command"). Bolkestein speaks of the trumpet call as a sign of judgment and hope. Minear says: "The trumpet calls men into the life of a New Day, a new Sabbath, a New Year, a new Jubilee Year." Thus the coming is made visible and audible, though all these things are merely signs of the tremendous event, which is the coming of Christ himself. "So after all, Pauline eschatology is less concerned with the trumpet blast and the clouds of heaven, than with the crowning experience of rejoining Him that they may be 'forever with the Lord'" (Howard).

b. In this tremendous procession the faithful who have died in Christ will rise first (v. 16b). The dominion of death, the headquarters of the prison, is the first to be attacked! The dead will certainly not be "left." To the contrary. The descending Conqueror will lead the living parade out of the dark prison of death. The first fruits of the dead (1 Cor. 15:20ff.), the great holder of the keys of death and Hades (Rev. 1:18), will lead the procession himself.

c. The description of the triumphal parade continues. The dead and the living go out to meet the Lord "in the clouds" as triumphal vehicles. They are going to welcome him (*apantēsis* is used for the festive reception of an emperor or other personage). Thus Christ is brought into the city, not as the lonely one, but surrounded by his church, "which is his body, the fulness of him" (Eph. 1:23). Like the storm troopers of the new world (Berkhof), the dead and the living are drawn together into the mighty, victorious procession of Christ into the world. They will be "with" each other; the living will certainly not precede the dead.

3. The believers can now "comfort" (v. 18) each other with these words, a comfort based on the completed resurrection and the expected second coming of Christ. That is why, when preaching on this section, Augustine is able to say, "Let sorrow cease where there is so much comfort." They must comfort "each other" with these words. People need other people to be comforted. True comfort only comes into its own within the congregation. In our time this is a truth we must learn anew!

II. Hermeneutical

1. By way of introduction, one should point out that here, once again, Paul is answering urgent questions concerning life and death. He is involved in intensive pastoral work (v. 18, *parakaleō*) and not with doctrine (Best: "pastor, not theologian"; Bolkestein, De Boor). For this reason one should not expect a complete eschatology here. Besides, Paul is describing this comforting reality in the idiom of his time, with the exciting images of Jewish apocalyptic writings (for a detailed discussion, cf. Bolkestein). Bohren rightly asserts that in our proclamation we should never lose the imaginative power, yes, the fantasy that is evoked by this apocalyptic imagery, especially not when preaching about the second coming. When preaching on this pericope, the powerful military images are also very important.

2. Christ's resurrection is a central theme in Paul's teachings (cf. Rom. 1:4; 5:10; 6:9; 1 Cor. 15:1-12; Col. 1:18; 2 Tim. 1:10; etc.). Between his resurrection and the resurrection of believers there exists a very important link, a bond that cannot be broken (2 Cor. 4:14; Eph. 2:5; Col. 3:4, etc.; this is extensively discussed in Berkouwer). It is precisely this link that differentiates Paul's message clearly from the pagan philosophy of those times (cf. Acts 17:18, 31-32). Hiebert states: "Among the common people of the pagan world hopelessness and despair prevailed in the face of death." It is true that pagan philosophers had a doctrine concerning the immortality of the soul, but the belief in resurrection throughout the New Testament is radically different from this vague hope that can so easily degenerate into depression or into a superficial "eat, drink, and be merry" attitude.

J. du Preez refers to a letter of condolence written by a certain Irene to the parents of a boy who had recently died. She concludes by saying,

"Well, there is nothing one can do about such things. So console each other. Farewell." How far removed these empty words are from Paul's message of comfort! No wonder it is one of the central aspects of his teaching: "Christ Jesus, who abolished death and brought life and immortality to light through the gospel. For this gospel I was appointed a preacher and apostle and teacher" (2 Tim. 1:10-11). As teacher Paul has to preach this message of resurrection in a world where there were slogans such as "Hopes are among the living; the dead are without hope" (Theocritus); "No one awakes and arises who has once been overtaken by the chilling end of life" (Lucretius).

3. Death is a reality that brings the sorrow of a life ending and of parting. The Bible not only acknowledges the universality of death as an unavoidable power (Josh. 23:14; Ps. 49:9; Song of Sol. 8:6), but also of death as an enemy (1 Cor. 15:26), a destroyer of life and happiness (Job 16:22; Ps. 39:13; cf. Berkouwer; K. Barth, *CD* III/2, speaks of this radical one-way street onto which death propels one). That is why the Bible also acknowledges the right to sorrow (Rom. 12:15). But faith in the resurrection prevents believers from slipping down into unending sorrow; instead, it provides a fundamental and radical hope. Faith in the resurrection prevents the scale from tipping totally toward grief. It "relativizes" our sorrow, however heartfelt and bitter it may be, because it places sorrow in relation to Christ, who has taken death's sting away and borne our suffering for us. His death is the death of our death and his resurrection the gateway to our resurrection. (Luther, *WA 26,* 243, rightly says, "One must learn to see Christ's death as though it has 'strangled' our death.")

4. Did Paul expect that he and most of the readers of this Epistle (cf. v. 15) would live to see the second coming? Although one cannot make such a deduction from this section, there is no doubt that Paul and early Christians believed that the second coming of Christ was imminent. (One can find more on this subject, especially in Best, Bolkestein, De Boor, and Berkouwer.)

III. Homiletical

A sermon based on this pericope would do well to begin with the hypothesis that death is a painful reality for all people, a reality that many try to cope with through some form of escape. Deep down we know that death has the final word. It is the unwelcome "thief in the night" in every home! And it is also true that Christians experience death as terror—the termination of life and parting from those we love is so final. It is indeed part of God's mercy that we are able somehow to cope with death through our weeping and tears!

But God in his mercy and grace wants to achieve much more; he wants to break the bonds of death and thus destroy it (2 Tim. 1:9b-10). And it is precisely because we so seldom experience the bonds of death being broken that our funerals are often without consolation and our hope too powerless to wipe the tears from our eyes. All too frequently the power of death around us seems far more real than the power of hope within us. A sermon on this pericope can present the comfort of the resurrection.

1. Human life is inexorably hedged in by death. Death is a hurdle no one can bypass. Nor are we spared the grief that it brings. But in the midst of this grief and suffering, Christ descends! Through his resurrection he prepares a "way" for us to pass through death and the grave and its sorrow. Death cannot be avoided in this "way," but it has been robbed of its power. That is why believers may now "long to put on our heavenly dwelling" (2 Cor. 5:2). Christian hope, founded on our faith in the resurrection, enables us not to "grieve as others do who have no hope" (cf. I, 1). This message should form the central theme of an Easter sermon on this pericope.

2. The second coming of Christ will be the triumphal seal, set by God on our faith in the resurrection. All the faithful may therefore rejoice and console each other with this hope at the graveside, time and again! Nevertheless, one should not interpret the second coming simply in an individualistic way, as the gathering of the faithful. It announces the coming of the King and the advent of the new creation (cf. Berkouwer). If only we could have a vision of the new heaven and the new earth and the future union of the church out of all tribes and tongues and nations, would that not cure us of much of our self-centeredness? If only our hearts could once again be filled with the triumph of the kingdom, could that not make us less concerned about our own heartaches and "incurable" illnesses? Could that not make us more joyful, more victorious? But also more prepared for suffering and more willing to live lives prepared for death?

3. Should we not learn what it means to comfort one another in the communion of the saints, and for that very reason as the church living in hope? We must not leave people comfortless, nor leave them to await

death in their loneliness. We should comfort one another in life and in death, and thus support one another in life and in death—in living and in dying. We should be able to die comforted in Christ (cf. Heidelberg Catechism, Lord's Day 1). That is why God places us in a church during our life on earth. Such a sermon could also do much to summon the congregation to this mutual pastoral responsibility.

B. A. MÜLLER

Ascension: Ephesians 1:20-23

Bibliography

Commentaries

Barth, M. *Ephesians.* 2 vols. The Anchor Bible. Garden City: Doubleday, 1974.

Beare, F. W. *Ephesians.* The Interpreter's Bible. Vol. 10. New York/Nashville: Abingdon-Cokesbury, 1953.

Foulkes, F. *Ephesians.* Tyndale New Testament Commentaries. Grand Rapids: Eerdmans, 1956.

Moule, H. C. G. *Ephesian Studies.* London: Pickering & Inglis, n.d.

Bruce, F. F. *Commentary on the Epistles to the Colossians, to Philemon, and to the Ephesians.* The New International Commentary on the New Testament. Grand Rapids: Eerdmans, 1984.

Stott, J. R. W. *God's New Society: The Message of Ephesians.* Downers Grove: InterVarsity, 1980.

Homiletical

Putnam, R. C. *Getting It All Together.* Nashville: Abingdon, 1977.

Additional

Barth, K. *Dogmatics in Outline,* 124-28. New York: Philosophical Library, 1947.

Chesterton, G. K. *As I Was Saying: A Chesterton Reader,* 206-8. Grand Rapids: Eerdmans, 1985.

Ridderbos, H. *Paul: An Outline of His Theology.* Grand Rapids: Eerdmans, 1975.

Van Ruler, A. A. *Het leven een feest,* 66-68. Nijkerk: Callenbach, 1972.

I. Exegetical

1. One can divide Ephesians 1 into two parts. In verses 3-14 Paul praises God for the blessings the Ephesian church received in Christ and in verses 15-23 he prays that God may open the eyes of the church to know the full riches of these blessings. Verses 20-23 therefore function as "thanksgiving and intercession" (Gnilka), "a great intercession" (Stott), or at least "jubilation and radiation of joy" (Barth).

The prayer in verses 15-23, according to Stott, can be subdivided into "the hope of God's call" (i.e. the beginning or origin of the blessings), "the glory of the inheritance" (i.e. the future of the blessings), and the "greatness of His power" (i.e. the interim experience of the blessings). Verses 20-23, then, tell of the riches of the blessings in the present. Gnilka, who does not adhere to such a strict division, views verses 20-23 as a Christian credo, or confession of faith, while Barth calls it "a resurrection psalm."

2. Stott further subdivides verses 20-23. He see "the immeasurable greatness of his power" (v. 19) demonstrated in three stages—namely Jesus' being raised from the dead (v. 20a), his reign over evil (vv. 20b-22a), and his position as head of the church (vv. 22b-23). Barth and Gnilka point out that the four almost synonymous uses of *power* in verse 19 *(dunamis, energeia, kratos, ischus),* especially in such a doxological section, should not be differentiated, but should rather be seen as a comprehensive designation of God's power. In verses 20-23 the proof of this power is derived from God's acting in power. "The author wants to point out the absolutely unique and superior power exerted by God in the resurrection of Christ. He will speak of other 'powers' soon enough, and he is far from underestimating their potential, their actuality, their energy. But these 'powers' are outdone by the Power demonstrated in the resurrection" (Barth).

The syntax of verses 20-23 is important. The subject of verses 20-22 is God, but in verse 23 the church is the subject. Because sentences, according to Greek syntax, often end in a climax, Gaugler argues that this is a hymn of praise to the church and not to Christ. In opposition to this, however, Barth maintains that it is impossible to consider the ecclesiology of verse 23 more important than the triumphant theology and christology of verses 19-22. According to him, the church only reaches the center of attention in chapter 2:1, while this section is clearly a hymn to Christ.

There are two sets of parallel constructions. Two aorist participles read: "he raised him . . . [he] made him sit at his right hand." Two aorist indicatives follow: "he has put all things under his feet . . . [he] has made him the head." All four expressions describe what God did to Christ. The raising (instead of resurrection) and the "made him sit" (instead of "he went to sit") at the right hand are purposely formulated in the active voice to underscore that they are acts of *God*. Three different qualifications are put between these parallel expressions and once again all three explicitly and deliberately interpret God's saving acts to Christ as demonstrations of his unique power. First, his power itself is described in a series of synonyms (v. 19). Second, the "powers" conquered by this act of power are enumerated in such a way that the meaning becomes, "whichever power there still may be" (v. 21). Finally, Paul states that everything was made subservient to him and given to him (vv. 22-23). Two Old Testament quotations, from the enthronement psalms, are given (Ps. 110:1 in v. 20, and Ps. 8:6 in v. 22), enhancing the associations of power and authority.

3. Verse 23 presents extremely problematical questions of detail, concerning the translation as well as the grammatical construction. The translation problem is centered in *plērōma* ("fulfilling"? "fulfilled"? "fullness"?). The construction problem has to do with the nature of Christ's reign over the cosmos. It is clear that Christ's lordship over the church is confessed here. "Among the effects of God's power shown in Christ's resurrection, the church is outstanding" (Barth). The question arises, however, whether his reign over the church is the only way his authority, on the grounds of his resurrection, is manifested. Many exegetes discover some traces here of the cosmic lordship of Christ, in addition to his more direct lordship over the church.

Barth maintains that this section is indeed concerned with Christ's lordship over all things and that one has to say that the Lord of the church is also Lord of the world. "Christ's omnipotent rule over all powers is described as the presupposition of his rule by love over the church" (Barth). This problem of course cannot be solved by interpreting this intricate verse alone, as becomes clear from commentaries, but preachers will have to take this problem into account to guard against unwarranted conclusions. Perhaps Gnilka understands the obviously pastoral implications well when he says that this song of praise was to prevent the church in Asia Minor, sociologically insignificant and small in number, from becoming defeatist, and to help them understand and experience their unique position in the cosmos! Their Head is also Head of the cosmos, their Lord is Lord over all things!

II. Hermeneutical

1. It is crucial to understand the real meaning behind the question concerning God's power. Barth remarks that the later books of the Old Testament, as well as the Apocrypha containing the confession of the resurrection from the dead, were not primarily interested in the question of what will happen to human beings after death. "Rather it is a response to the outcry, Will God's righteousness ever be triumphant over the present slaughter of his servants and the seeming defeat of God's cause?" It is primarily a theological problem and not an anthropological one. This is also the case in these verses. We are concerned with the "suffocating problem" (Zahrnt) of who actually has the power in the world.

When the church starts to succumb in the face of the questions, Why does everything seems to go wrong? and Why does it seem as if evil and the "powers" reign and as if God's cause and his church come off second best?, then this prayer asks that the congregation receive insight into who actually has the power in his hands and who actually reigns over all powers. The foundation, the only visible proof in the midst of all the obvious and contradictory realities, is the raising of Jesus Christ. To underscore this comforting message, his resurrection is described in various metaphors and associations dealing with the display of power and the taking over of power.

2. This invokes a second problem, the nature of Christ's present rule. Two dangers lurk: proclaiming the cross without the resurrection, and proclaiming the resurrection without the cross.

a. Gollwitzer reminds us of Bonhoeffer's remark that God allows the world to oust him onto the cross. In view of this, he wants to know what "Jesus Christ's lordship" means in reality. It is of course true, as these verses also proclaim, that the cross was not God's final act, but that the resurrection followed. That means that Jesus Christ is now present in a different mode, as the resurrected and living One, and that he reigns. One has to keep in mind, however, that it is none other than Jesus of Nazareth, the Crucified One, who has been raised and legitimated by God. In this sense Marxsen *cum suis* are correct in saying that the resurrection means that "Jesus' cause" is continuing in the world. Barth also has this continuity in mind when he refers to Philippians 2:5ff., reminding us that Jesus sits in heaven and reigns from there as the Crucified Lord. The *theologia crucis* should therefore not be emphasized in such a one-sided way that a kind of ethical martyrdom without the consolation of victory is proclaimed, but neither should it be replaced by a triumphalist *theologia resurrectionis* or a *theologia gloriae* in which the cross of the Lord (with that of his disciples!) becomes forgotten.

b. This brings to mind Van Ruler's words on the lordship of Christ. He remarks, in words typical of his theology, that it means that "all the world is run Christianly" ("het gaat christelijk toe op de aarde"). He does not mean to say that people consistently act like Christians, but rather that Christ reigns as king over everything. At present God rules over all things through Jesus Christ. "His sacrifice is the great transformer through which the whole reign of God passes. God reigns over all things through his grace and his salvation. . . . That is the way in which 'all the world is run Christianly.' God is full of mercy and extremely patient. . . . Never say: we see nothing of his reign. Of course Paul himself says: I only see its very *opposite*. . . . Nevertheless, the promise is not that He will only reign over the earth *after* 'having put all things in subjection under his feet,' but '*until* he has put all his enemies under his feet'! He reigns in the midst of his enemies in the very darkness of world history."

In addition to the final enemy, death, Paul is thinking of other powers that have invaded God's fine creation and now seem to rule over it: corruption, futility, meaninglessness, suffering, hunger. In the midst of all these, Christ reigns. Van Ruler says,

> When we consider human beings in general and our own lives in particular, the same truth applies. Deep within ourselves we are in revolt against Christ. That is our basic problem. . . . And yet, God is present amongst us and establishes his kingdom, He reigns as King and supports us and saves us. It is utterly incomprehensible: we reject God and yet He stays with us; we nail Christ to the cross and precisely there he bears and reconciles our sins! You may want to retort that that is very unsatisfactory and in the long run intolerable. Indeed. It is unsatisfactory. And it will come to a conclusion. "In the end Christ will deliver the kingdom to God the Father after destroying every rule and every authority and power . . . that God may be all in all!" Then the world puzzle will be solved. Then the enormous dissonance of human hostility will be resolved into concord. But we are not there yet. We still live

in the unsatisfactory contradiction of God's wholesome rule through Christ in the hostility of humanity and the powers.

The fact that God reigns at present in a Christian and therefore salutary manner should warn us against premature and impatient efforts to end this unbearable situation and to solve these problems on our own, thereby yielding to the temptation to reign "in his Name." It is important to remember that it is Christ who reigns over the church *and* over the world and not the church reigning over the world! Christ's cause can be served only through his Spirit and not through power or violence. It is always extremely dangerous when Christians and the church identify their causes and their struggles with Jesus' cause, and then take on these struggles, in his name, by means of crusades, religious wars, revolution, etc.

Christians are of course allowed (and called!) to involve themselves in civil struggles, but then they have to remember that it concerns "penultimate" matters (Bonhoeffer), relative matters such as overthrowing discrimination and injustice, and not the kingdom of Christ itself. His lordship is exercised and served in another way. Even if many of these penultimate realities, on which we rightly spend our energy, should perhaps one day be ruined, his kingdom will still come. We do not believe in the power of internal worldly forces, but in the "working of his great might which he accomplished in Christ when he raised him from the dead" (vv. 19-20).

c. In the well-known detective story by Chesterton, "The Hammer of God," Father Brown investigates the murder of a rascal whose skull was crushed by a hammer. Although everyone suspects the village blacksmith, because he had more than enough reason to commit the crime, Father Brown finds out that the brother of the victim, a clergyman, is guilty. This priest, Wilfred, had the habit of retreating to the tallest tower of the cathedral, where he could watch everyone. He became so angry at his brother's criminality that he threw a hammer at him.

In a very dramatic scene Father Brown tells the pastor: "I think there is something rather dangerous about standing on these high places even to pray. . . . Heights were made to be looked at, not to be looked from."

"Do you mean that one may fall over?" asked Wilfred.

"I mean that one's soul may fall if one's body doesn't," said Father Brown. After a moment he resumed, "I knew a man," he said, "who began by worshiping with others before the altar, but who grew fond of high and lonely places to pray from. . . . And once in one of those dizzy places, where the whole world seemed to turn under him like a wheel, his brain turned also, and he fancied he was God. So that though he was a good man, he committed a great crime. . . . He thought that it was given to *him* to judge the world and strike down a sinner. He would never have had such a thought if he had been kneeling with other men upon a floor. But he saw all men walking about like insects."

d. The truth is, God reigns in the world in a Christian manner—not by force or violence, but through his Spirit. His reign is invisible. He reigns in the role of a servant, *sub contrario,* "hidden under its opposite." It can only be appropriated by faith. The church may at times catch a glimpse of it breaking through, only to realize that it was indeed only a glimpse. The powers still hold sway and individual experiences as well as collective history always remain ambiguous. Human experience can always be interpreted and experienced in various ways. The fact that Christ reigns is therefore not derived from experience, it is not a logical conclusion from a neutral analysis of events; it is a confession of faith proclaimed and believed in spite of all affliction and the seeming contradictions.

3. One could use these verses to explain the Heidelberg Catechism, Lord's Day 19, which deals with Christ's sitting "at the right hand of God" and its "benefits."

III. Homiletical

What does it mean that Jesus sits "at the right hand of God"?

1. It is metaphorical language, of course. One could say that God is spirit, that he neither sits somewhere on a throne nor has a right (or a left) hand, and that we should not talk in such a naive, anthropomorphic way. But what else can we do? We are not capable of talking about God other than from our human perspective. And that means in a stammering, searching, metaphorical way. (We cannot talk about transcendence in adequate, i.e. transcendent terms, *contra* Bultmann *cum suis.*)

Imagine a child describing a nuclear explosion as a huge mushroom rising from the sea. An expert physicist may well smile at that image and think, "May the child and the poet in us never die. Without that our world would become too small and our lives too poor." When our world and experience are reduced to the scientifically perceptible and measurable, one does not live fully any more. God is there even though we cannot see him or measure him or represent him adequately, even though we can only stammer about him. In view of this, "at the right hand of God" is not such a bad expression. It says exactly what it wants to say!

2. It says that Jesus assumed the position of authority. In the Old Testament God's right hand is the symbol of his power. Exodus 15:6, Psalm 18:35, Isaiah 51:5, 9 and 63:5 are excellent illustrations. God's right hand (or his "extended arm" or "hand") is his ability to accomplish mighty deeds on earth. When in the New Testament believers say that, according to Psalm 110:1, Jesus went to sit at the right hand of God, they mean that *he* now exercises this authority or power of God. This is the position from which Jesus helps them and cares for them and from which he reigns and conquers. It is identical in meaning with: "All authority in heaven and on earth has been given to me." The disciples confess this truth by saying, This Jesus whom we have known, with whom we have lived for a few years, now sits at the right hand of God. He now reigns over heaven and earth.

3. At the same time it means, of course, that if Jesus received all authority and if he reigns, there is no other power we have to fear. Every time the church confesses that Christ is at the right hand of God, more and more "powers" are added to the list of those that no longer have power over us. In Ephesians 1:21 Christ's power is "above every name that is named." It is as though the Epistle is proclaiming, "Name the powers. Let them come. We are not afraid!" (See also Rom. 8:34-35; 38-39; Phil. 2:10; Col. 1:16, 20b, with the all-embracing "nor anything else in all creation"; and 1 Peter 3:22.)

This is the issue at stake. It is also the reason Paul in his prayer asks that our insight may gradually deepen. The sociological threat under which the church lives is not the final word on our place in history. Jesus is our Head; He controls the world, history, and our personal woe. Nothing can separate us from his love. We can be "more than conquerors" under all circumstances.

"More than conquerors" is from Romans 8:37 (KJV), a chapter that resembles these verses in Ephesians 1 in several ways. It is also the name of W. Hendriksen's well-known exposition of Revelation, and one can indeed view this book of the Bible as a commentary on this pericope. The church suffers under persecution, it poses questions, it calls for help. Then John sees several perspectives on world history. In all these scenes, the Lamb that has been slain but now sits at the right hand of God holds the trump card. He has the last say! He gives final deliverance!

4. The Heidelberg Catechism asks how we benefit from this glory of Christ. The answer is, in part, that he "defends us and keeps us safe from all enemies." He is not far away from us, waiting for us. No, he is *with* us; but in a new way. Not as one of us any more, but as the mighty One who decides and rules. That is our comfort.

Barth wrote about this very movingly in his lectures on the Apostles' Creed. In his preface he explains that these lectures were given just after the Second World War, in a city that had been reduced to rubble. Every morning, before the bulldozers started cleaning up, a group of people gathered for these lectures. It was a somber period, a period according to Barth in which people had to learn to laugh anew. He pointed out that in this article the Creed suddenly changes from the past to the present tense. It is as though we have climbed a steep mountain and have reached the top, where we enjoy a marvelous view. Christ sitting at the right hand of God, wrote Barth, is "the first and last thing one can and should say about our lives and about the world." It is the most important thing one can say. Jesus reigns!

How do we know that? We know it through faith, not through experience. It is not always possible for the eye to see it. On the contrary, when we look at our personal experience and world history with the naked eye, the last conclusion that we often come to is that Jesus reigns. We do not see Jesus reigning in the world. Most of the time we don't even see that Jesus rules his church! (Many examples could be given here, from the history of the world and the church and from the present: schism, mutual persecution, condemnation, confusion and doubt, suffering.)

5. So Christians "walk by faith, therefore, not by sight." Sometimes, of course, faith does lead to sight, to glimpses of God's power! In Christ's resurrection the church clearly saw this demonstrated. And time and again we still recognize (through faith!) signs of this lordship and of the power of his resurrection in our lives and in the world: deeds of deliverance, safekeeping, assistance in difficult times, healing, victory for truth and justice, strength to accept and forgive, reconciliation. Through faith we recognize these as his redeeming right hand. May he grant us to recognize these more readily and thank him more sincerely. But in the final analysis our faith is not grounded on experi-

ence, because history can be interpreted in different ways: what one person experiences as good news is for that very reason bad news for another! All these signs are recognizable as acts of God's power only through faith.

Through this faith, however, the church can live consoled and full of hope. And because the church needs this faith, the prayer for "enlightened eyes of the hearts" must be said continually. Only then will the church, through all affliction and in spite of all the powers seemingly rampant in the world, be able to cling to this power.

D. J. SMIT

The Sunday after Ascension: Psalm 87

Bibliography

Commentaries

Anderson, A. A. *The Book of Psalms*. Vol. 2. New Century Bible. London: Marshall, Morgan & Scott, 1972; Grand Rapids: Eerdmans, 1981.

Calvin, J. *The Book of Psalms*. Vol. 3. Grand Rapids: Eerdmans, 1949.

Kidner, D. *Psalms 73-150*. London: InterVarsity, 1975.

Knight, G. A. F. *Psalms*. Vol. 2. The Daily Study Bible (Old Testament). Philadelphia: Westminster, 1983.

McCullough, W. S., and Poteat, E. M. *Psalms, Proverbs*. The Interpreter's Bible. New York: Abingdon, 1955.

Sabourin, L., S.J. *The Psalms: Their Origin and Meaning*. Staten Island: Alba, 1969.

Weiser, A. *The Psalms*. London: SCM, 1962.

Homiletical

Koopmans, J. *Nieuwe Postille*. Goudriaan: de Groot, 1971.

Spurgeon, C. H. *The Treasury of David*. Vol. 4. New York: Funk & Wagnalls, 1882.

Additional

The New International Study Bible on Psalm 87. Grand Rapids: Zondervan, 1985.

Jager, O. *Opklaring*, 326-38. Bijbellezen met verbeeldingskracht. Ede: Zomer en Keuning, 1980.

Rothuizen, G. T. *Landschap*. Vol. 2. Kampen: Kok, 1966.

Since the church is a mission church, its preaching on mission should not be limited to a specific time of the year. At the same time, however, it should be kept in mind that, in terms of salvation history, the church received its mission immediately after Pentecost (cf. Acts 2). Thus proclamation concerning the missionary character of the church is ideally suited to the Sundays following Pentecost (e.g., a series on mission perspectives in Acts, in the Epistles of Paul, the prophets, or Psalms). However, since the mission of the church is so closely tied in with Pentecost, the Sunday between Ascension Day and Pentecost also offers an ideal opportunity for preaching on mission.

I. Exegetical

1. Psalm 87 is a song *(šîr):* a poem to be sung. It is also a psalm *(mizmôr):* it suggests the accompaniment of stringed instruments. Along with psalms such as 48 and 84, it belongs to a specific category of songs in praise of Zion, the city of the great King. And just as Psalms 44-49, 84-85, and 88, it is a song "of," and meant "for," the sons of Korah, Levite temple singers or musicians, and descendants of Korah, the great-grandson of Levi (Num. 16:1).

2. Many exegetes have so many problems with the Masoretic text that they attempt to rearrange sentences into their "original positions." These theories almost resemble jigsaw puzzles! Weiser (following Kittel), Gunkel, and Schmidt have each proposed their own scheme for rearranging the text. There is, however, no compelling reason for such rearrangement. Although it is written in an enigmatic, oracular style, the main line of thought, the actual meaning of the poem, is not as obscure as, for example, the patriarch Eusebius suggested. It is a song that praises Zion as the spiritual center of all the nations of the world (Lamparter; cf. Dahood). In addition, the prophetic element in the psalm cannot be ignored.

3. The date of origin is unknown. Some scholars reckon it to be before the Babylonian exile, perhaps during the time of King Hezekiah, when several nations came to Jerusalem offering gifts after the destruction of Sennacherib's Assyrian army (2 Chron. 32:23). Others are of the opinion that it is postexilic, perhaps during the first celebration of the Feast of Tabernacles after the rebuilding of Jerusalem under Nehemiah. According to some scholars, verse 7 suggests that the poem originated after the poet saw a procession of proselytes from different countries

on their way to Jerusalem to celebrate the annual feast of the pilgrims in the place that for them had become the holy city (Weiser). Other scholars hold that this does not necessarily indicate that the poem is postexilic, for proselytes are also mentioned before the exile (e.g., 2 Kgs. 5). When everything is taken into account, it seems quite probable that the poem originated in the exilic period, though whether shortly before, during, or just after the Babylonian exile is debatable (cf. Ps. 87:4).

4. When the structure of the psalm is studied, it becomes obvious that it consists of three parts, each revolving around the following central theme: "Glorious things are spoken of you, O city of God":

Verses 1-3:   Zion chosen, founded, and dwelt in by the Lord himself.
Verses 4-6:   Zion destined by the Lord to be the "mother city" of an
              incredible variety of nations.
  Verse 7:   Zion praised by this variety of nations as the city of
              salvation.

5. A few exegetical comments may prove helpful:

a. Verses 1-3: Verse 1 poses a question, Does the possessive form refer to Zion (cf. different translations) or to Yahweh (the opinion of Calvin, Ridderbos, Leupold, Smal et al.)? But it really does not make much difference. The idea is that Yahweh prefers Zion to be his place of dwelling rather than any other place he could have chosen, such as Shechem, Shiloh, Gilgal, Bethel, Hebron. Initially Zion had been a mountain fortress. It was captured from the Jebusites by David, and it became known as David's own city (2 Sam. 5:7-9). Later both the palace and the temple were built there.

Zion practically became a synonym for Jerusalem, as becomes clear when verses 2 and 3 are compared (cf. Ps. 51:18 as well), whereas the temple served as the expression or symbol of the presence of the Lord among his people. Yahweh's city is situated on the "mount" (lit. "mountains"). The plural may be a royal plural, but it may also refer to the fact that Jerusalem was situated on several hills. Mount Zion was, however, the central mountain (cf. Pss. 48:2-3; 68:17; 78:68-69; 102:16; 132:13-14; 147:2). Jerusalem's mountains are holy because the Lord has decided to dwell there. He has taken possession of Zion and destined it to be of service to himself.

Verse 2 says that the Lord loves the "gates of Zion." This may again simply refer to the city itself. However, in light of verses 4-6, it is probable that the poet intentionally referred to the gates of Zion because they are the entrance gates for all the nations (cf. Isa. 60:11; Rev. 22:14; see also Kirkpatrick, Moll, Smal). The expression "glorious things" (v. 3) is placed in an emphatic position in the sentence. It refers back to verses 1-2 while at the same time pointing forward to verses 4-6 and 7. The phrase "city of God" accentuates the glory of Zion, which is praised in verses 1-2 and 4-7.

b. Verses 4-6: Members of five nations that had been enemies of Israel at some time are now declared citizens of the city of God. Foremost are the two dominant world powers of that time, Egypt and Babylon. Egypt, Israel's arch-enemy for many a century, is called "Rahab" (lit., "anger," "vehemence," "arrogance"). Originally it was the name of a primeval mythological monster of chaos. Babylon, the enemy from the north, is the country of Israel's exile. Then follow Israel's neighbors to the west, Philistia and Tyre. Philistia was the bellicose enemy that caused many a page in Israel's history to be written in blood. Tyre, the rich and proud merchant city, represents the Phoenician coastal and merchant cities. It was from Tyre that King Ahab imported the cult of Baal (cf. 1 Kgs. 16:31-32 and relevant commentaries). Cush, or Ethiopia, probably lay to the south of Egypt and represented the most distant countries. Isaiah refers to the remote Cush as "a people feared near and far, a nation mighty and conquering" (Isa. 18:2, 7). Israel was on occasion attacked even by Ethiopia (2 Chron. 14:9).

Some exegetes (e.g., Davies and Kraus) are of the opinion that verses 4-6 refer only to the loyal Jews of the diaspora in the countries mentioned above. Although such Jews should not of course be excluded, it is most unlikely that the forceful expressions in verses 4-6 should be scaled down in such a way. Accordingly most scholars hold that the allusion is to proselytes from various countries on their way to Zion. There are even those who think that we have here a prophecy on a future conversion of all nations to the God of Israel (Kirkpatrick, Delitzsch, Noordtzij, Ridderbos, Leupold, et al.).

These two opinions actually complement each other (Lamparter): the proselytes are the first of a great number of people from the nations who, at God's own time, will turn to the God of Israel (Isa. 2:2-4; 44:1-5). Some exegetes see Psalm 87 as an explication of Psalm 86:9-10: "All the nations thou hast made shall come and bow down before thee, O Lord."·Of cardinal importance is the fact that Zion is the mother city for people from all nations, faithful Jews and faithful non-Jews alike. "It is as if the whole world had arranged to meet in this place" (Weiser). The Lord publicly states that these people from different nations are people who know him, i.e. they acknowledge him as God and obey him (v. 4). The recording of the nations in verse 6 reminds one of the keeping of a register for the inhabitants of a country (Ezek. 13:19) but especially of the "book of the living" (Isa. 4:3; Dan. 12:1). Whereas verses 4 and 6 refer to the nations as a whole, verse 5 puts it more individually and personally: each and every one (*'îš w^e'îš*). Interestingly enough, the first part of verse 5 ("And of Zion it shall be said") reads as follows in the Septuagint: *Mētēr Siōn, erei anthrōpos*—"Mother Zion, someone will say" (NEB: "And Zion shall be called a mother").

Although not directly expressed in the Hebrew text, the idea is implicit: Zion is a mother for people from every nation. And therefore *he* (the emphatic demonstrative pronoun), the most High himself, establishes Zion. "It is *he* who makes her what she is, *he,* the most High, Yahweh" (the Jerusalem Bible; my italics). The inhabitants of Zion are the Lord's family and he knows them by name because they are recorded in his book. The repetition in verses 4 and 6 of the expression "This one was born there" reminds one of adoption vows, where the parents solemnly promise to adopt a strange child as their own (Böhl).

c. Verse 7: This verse is very abrupt in the Hebrew, and is therefore translated in different ways. The main thrust of verse 7 is clear enough, however, and textual emendations are not really necessary. The springs of Zion suggest salvation, blessing, and joy (cf. Pss. 36:9-10; 46:4-5; Isa. 12:3). The city of Zion is simultaneously mother and fountain (spring). Grammatically, "in you" may refer to either Yahweh or Zion. Taken in its context it seems to refer to Zion. It does, however, include the God of Zion, since he has made Zion a spring of salvation for all nations. In his characteristically upbeat manner, Luther remarks on verse 7 that in this city serving God will be "ein Singen und Springen" ("a matter of singing and jumping")! The songs and choral dances of the new children of Zion express their unprecedented joy. Songs and choral dances formed part of the liturgy of Israel (cf. 2 Sam. 6:5, 14-15; Pss. 42:4; 149:3). "The psalmist intends to present the converted nations as coming in a grand procession, with songs and dances, to celebrate their admission to Zion" (Rawlinson).

II. Hermeneutical

1. It is important to see the psalm from a New Testament perspective as well. In Old Testament times people belonging to other nations had to go to Jerusalem in order to join God's people and to serve the Lord (Isa. 2:1-5). God's "permanent address" was: the temple, Zion, Jerusalem. Zion was the meeting place between God and humanity, between heaven and earth. With the coming of the Messiah everything changed. When the Samaritan woman wonders which mountain is the real place of worship, Zion's greatest son answers: "Woman, believe me, the hour is coming . . . and now *is* . . . when neither on this mountain nor in Jerusalem will you worship the Father" (John 4:21-23).

The new family of Zion no longer gathers on Mount Zion in Jerusalem, but in Jesus himself. He died and was resurrected in Zion, thereby fulfilling in himself everything that Zion stood for. *He* is the center of all believers, He is the center of all nations (Helberg). The old pilgrim city of Jerusalem, with its temple on Mount Zion and its temple offerings, has been replaced by a kingdom in which people from all nations are gathered in Christ by the Word and Spirit of God. Christ himself is now the meeting point between God and humanity, between heaven and earth. Thus God's intention is clear: to bring together from all the nations on earth a reborn people of God who will here and now profess the name of God with joy and who will ultimately gather around his throne with great rejoicing (cf. Rev. 7:9). *That* is the ultimate glory of Zion of which the poet sings in such a moving manner.

2. The central theme of the psalm is undoubtedly the glory of Zion, the city of God. A sermon on Psalm 87 should elaborate on one or more of the aspects of the glory of Zion. Indeed, a sermon on a song of praise such as Psalm 87 should breathe the same spirit, should be doxological itself.

How does the glory of Zion manifest itself?

Zion is glorious in that it is rooted in and protected by God's election and love (vv. 1, 5).

Zion is glorious in its holiness (v. 1).

Zion is glorious in its openness to the nations of the world (vv. 4-6).

Zion is glorious in the diversity of its reborn citizens (vv. 4-6).

Zion is glorious in its profession of joy (v. 7).

These five manifestations of glory may be reduced to two: Zion is glorious because it has been chosen by God, and because of the incredible diversity of its inhabitants. These two points may in turn be reduced to one cardinal point: the glory of Zion lies in the fact that God has chosen it to be the mother city of a new people coming from all nations. Rothuizen quite correctly asks Böhl why he places the idea of election alongside the idea of mission in his commentary on Psalm 87, since in reality these two concepts are two sides of the same coin.

3. There are two things that make the glory of Zion as God's worldwide city unique and significant: first, the fact that people who traditionally were irreconcilable are brought together; and, second, that it is presented as a spontaneous event.

a. Psalm 87 sings of a people of God consisting of faithful Jews as well as of people from nations that traditionally were their greatest enemies, such as Egypt and Philistia. What could have been worse for a proud Israelite? That is why Blauw sees verses 4-6 as a pronouncement so unprecedented, so daring that it could only have been made by God himself! And the Lord does this with great joy! As he sits by the gates of Zion, counting those coming in one by one and writing their names in his book, each entry is a source of rejoicing for him. "This one was also born there [in Zion]!" The joy of the God of Zion, because of the gathering of the "irreconcilables," forms part of the glory of Zion (cf. Isa. 19:24-25).

"A white person a Christian? I don't believe it," says a black man in apartheid South Africa. "A black person a Christian? I don't believe it," says a white man in apartheid South Africa. There are so many things that divide and aleinate them, so much that causes them to dislike, fear, and even hate each other. But in the city of God a different language is spoken, because the God of Zion thinks and speaks and acts differently. Here the church of Christ is put to the test: to share in the glory of the divine city of Zion is to share in the delight of the God of Zion who rejoices that the irreconcilables have found peace with him and with each other in Zion. This is the glory in which we ought to rejoice! Every congregation whose members have open hearts and whose church buildings have open doors thereby reflects something of the glory of the city of God with its multilingual inhabitants and its gates wide open to anyone wishing to enter.

b. The spontaneity of the entry of the nations makes the glory of Zion as God's worldwide city so special. Verses 4-6 show how free of problems the entry of the nations was: "Among those who know me I mention Rahab and Babylon." There is no forced proselytizing here. No, the entry is brought about by God. He wants it to happen and therefore it happens. And in this way the city of God holds firm (v. 5). As Valeton says: "How the seed was sown . . . who knows? But why ask, when anyone can rejoice in the plants that have sprung forth?"

Of course the entry of the nations is fraught with pain and suffering: in verses 4-6 birth is mentioned three times! In the light of the New Testament we know that God's method also includes "the sword of the Spirit" (Eph. 6:17). But here in Psalm 87 the emphasis is on God's electing love. In the light of the New Testament the emphasis is on the inscrutable regenerating power of the Holy Spirit. He who wishes to share in the glory of Zion must be able to take pleasure in the spontaneous ingathering of the nations by God himself.

4. When Psalm 87 sings the praises of the glory of Zion, it already sings the praises of the glory of the church of the Lord. And if the church is really the church, it will reveal something of the glory to which Psalm 87 attests. (As to the contents of this glory, cf. II, 2 above.) The foundation of that glory is given in the acts of the God of Zion. For the glory of the Zion of God is after all the glory of the God of Zion. The glory of the church is the glory of Christ through the Holy Spirit in the midst of his people. When this can be said of the church, the church will indeed bear fruit and the fruit will be such that each one who sees and smells it will say: How I long for it! (Rothuizen).

III. Homiletical

1. A sermon on Psalm 87 may take the glory of Zion as its basic theme and could then be structured as follows: (1) the glory of Zion as praised by the poet of Zion (vv. 1-3); (2) the glory of Zion as praised by the God of Zion (vv. 4-6); (3) the glory of Zion as praised by all inhabitants of Zion (v. 7).

2. For other outlines, consult again the two already give in I, 4 and II, 2.

3. Finally: Psalm 87, with its three parts, may also be used as the basis for a catechism sermon on the church (Heidelberg Catechism, question 54):

a. Verses 1-3, 5(b): "That the Son of God . . . gathers, protects and preserves for himself . . . a community chosen for eternal life."

b. Verses 4-6: "That the Son of God . . . out of the entire human race, from the beginning of the world to its end . . . gathers . . . a community."

c. Verse 7: When the inhabitants of Zion sing and dance in joyous praise of the foundations of salvation in Zion, the Catechism summons all Christians to join in the joyous belief that they "are and always will be living members" of Zion.

J. DU PREEZ

Pentecost: Romans 8:26

Bibliography

Commentaries

Barth, K. *The Epistle to the Romans*. London: Oxford, 1933 (Hoskyns's translation of the sixth edition).

Bruce, F. F. *Romans*. London: Tyndale, 1963.

Käsemann, E. *Romans*. Translated by G. W. Bromiley. Grand Rapids: Eerdmans, 1980.

Lekkerkerker, A. F. N. *De Brief van Paulus aan de Romeinen*. Vol. 1. Nijkerk: Callenbach, 1971.

Ridderbos, H. R. *Aan de Romeinen*. Kampen: Kok, 1969.

Homiletical

Swank, G. W. *Living in God's Power*. Valley Forge: Judson, 1983.

Additional

Minear, P. S. *The Obedience of Faith*. Studies in Biblical Theology, Second Series. London: SCM, 1971.

Versteeg, J. P. *De Geest en de gelouige*. Apeldoornse Studies No. 11. Kampen: Kok, 1976.

Versteeg, J. P. *De Heilige Geest en het gebed*. Apeldoornse Studies No. 6. Kampen: Kok, 1973.

I. Exegetical

1. In Romans 8:1-17 Paul reminds believers of the riches that the children of God already possess in Christ. This inheritance includes an objective as well as a subjective dimension: it is already assured outside of us, but must also be experienced within us; it is received and enjoyed in a continual tension— between the "already" and the "not yet"; we are saved, but only in hope.

Paul especially emphasizes what we may call the objective dimension of justification in Christ and of the new life. Faith is ultimately based on an objective reality outside of us, *extra nos,* on something already done. This forms the basis of our assurance. However, it is not to be detached from subjective faith and trust. Through the Holy Spirit, our assurance of faith becomes real *for* us and *in* us. Through the Spirit, believers now already take part in and therefore experience the content of faith. On account of the mediatory work of the Spirit believers already share in the mediatory work of Christ. What Christ has done for us, the Spirit now works in us, so that we can become what we already are in Christ.

Barth sees the growing process of the new life as follows: The Christian is the old person insofar as he or she had been one (Rom. 8:10a). The Christian is the new person insofar as he or she is already one (Rom. 8:10b) and will become one (cf. *CD* IV/1). Through the Spirit, we share in the fullness of the fulfilled promises of God: "heirs of God and joint heirs with Christ." This inheritance is received within the tension of the already and the not yet that this whole chapter reflects so dramatically.

2. Romans 8:1-17 deals with the wealth of our salvation from the perspective of faith. Romans 8:18-30 now deals with it from the perspective of hope. While 8:1-17 views the poverty of humanity from the perspective of "the law of sin and death" (v. 2; i.e. life in the flesh), 8:18-30 views the poverty of humanity from the perspective of "the sufferings of this present time" (v. 18; i.e. the time before the parousia of Christ).

Paul is fully aware of the fact that those who are (already) saved, are not (yet) completely rid of the devastating consequences of sin. Their lives are still filled to the brim with suffering, disruption, destruction, and pain. The decor against which Romans 8:18-30 is painted is that of earthly, day-to-day human suffering. In order, therefore, to use Romans 8:26 as text on Pentecost Sunday, the preacher has to take this background into full consideration.

3. The relevance of this pericope is that time and again the self-assured, technical, and rational people of today prove to be still disillusioned and perplexed by human suffering. With circumstances being what they are, we all despair at times and ask whether there will be a better future, a meaningful tomorrow. And, sometimes we ask whether there is indeed "life before death."

Something of this deep anxiety is found in Samuel Beckett's famous play, *Waiting for Godot*. In the midst of suffering and death, the characters become aware of the meaninglessness of their waiting. Beckett succeeds in putting into words the meaninglessness that so many humans experience in modern times. "We wait. We are bored. No, don't protest, we are bored to death, there's no denying it. . . . In an instant all will vanish and we'll be alone once more, in the midst of nothingness!" Despair sets in, because in Beckett's terms it seems as if Cain got the last say over Abel. Life is ultimately nothing but an open grave. "They give birth astride of a grave, the light gleams an instant, then it's night once more."

When the preacher puts Romans 8:26 alongside such an assertion, it seems as if Beckett could be right. It looks as if our weaknesses and our prayerlessness overwhelm us. Had the second part of verse 26 not been added, darkness would indeed have closed round the "prayerless prayer" of our text. According to Beckett, suicide seems the only "meaningful" alternative available to the person who, without any firm promises or hope, awaits Godot's arrival.

When we recall the desperate situation of the congregation in Rome depicted in this chapter, the question may indeed arise whether it is still meaningful to pray. The Roman believers were being threatened on every side—tribulation, distress, persecution, famine, nakedness, peril, and sword (8:35). This church was experiencing the reality of Psalm 44:22: "Nay, for thy sake we are slain all the day long, and accounted as sheep for the slaughter." They were "broken . . . in the place of jackals" and covered with "deep darkness" (Ps. 44:19). Does not the darkness of the grave seem to be the destiny of the prayerless prayer? And are we not all held captive behind similar bars of human suffering?

4. Suffering still creates many questions for believers. The church, like the woman in the wilderness, over and over feels the breath of the dragon on her (Rev. 12). The church cannot escape suffering and, accordingly, the existential problem of suffering. This surfaces in verse 26 in the form of weakness and prayerlessness. Therefore, one should first get some clarity about the meaning of "weakness" *(astheneia)*.

In verse 26 Paul does not distinguish between petitioners. It is not as if there is a category of "super-prayers" in contrast to "inferior prayers." Nor must this weakness be seen as some quality of human character. It does not refer to a psychological weakness or to an incidental weak moment, brought about through circumstances or a specific crisis. The weakness of this text rather refers to a total weakness, or incapacity. It suggests the totality of human existence in the midst of sin and guilt. The weakness is, of course, no inherent or natural human disability but, in line with Paul's general thinking, an incapacity called forth by human sinfulness.

This weakness is, in addition, related to "the sufferings of this present time" (v. 18). This weakness is part of the "futility" to which creation was subjected (v. 20). This futility points to the total barrenness of human existence, to the inability of creation, on account of "the law of sin and death" (v. 2), to serve its purpose. As a result, creation has been subjected to futility. Verses 21ff. deal with "the bondage to decay," and the resulting fear of death and ultimate destruction. The "groaning in travail" of the whole creation in verse 22 indicates the suffering of creation itself. With groans and cries of distress creation itself is yearning for deliverance. Subjected to this law of sin, futility, death, and guilt, we cannot pray at all. To a certain extent we are standing on the edge of the deep chasm of meaninglessness. Is there any hope?

5. Before one looks at how the text answers this question, the preacher should pay some attention to another problem. Verse 26 reads, "we do not know how to pray as we ought." The question arises, How should we understand this "hesitation" in prayer? Should we see it as something absolute and total?

It is difficult to see the inability to pray as only a temporary matter within specific circumstances. Then it would mean that often we do not know what to pray. Then our inability would not be absolute, but instead determined by circumstances. However, according to verses 18-23, the circumstances that Paul has in mind do not refer to a specific point in time or to momentary events, but rather to a situation in which believers continuously find themselves in this dispensation. He is thinking about the human condition when praying.

According to some exegetes, the words "as we ought" do not refer to "pray," but to the words "we do not know." Accordingly, we do not know sufficiently what we have to pray; in other words, we do not know the extent to which it is indeed necessary for Christians to know. However, the words "as we ought" do not refer only to our inadequate knowledge, but in fact also to our prayer. "We do not know" in verse 26 is in contrast with the expression "according to the will of God" in verse 27. Therefore, the text tells us that we cannot pray in accordance with the will of God. The believer is not capable of such a prayer, and because of this inability the suppliant needs the Holy Spirit.

One must therefore be careful, because all these attempts to understand the text may easily lead to an underestimate of our complete and utter inability to pray according to the will of God. Our inability to pray is absolute, because we do not know God's will and purpose (*prothesis*, v. 28). After all, true prayer could only mean prayer according to God's will, prayer serving God's purpose.

The deepest reason for our inability resides in the unbridgeable chasm between God and us, between our reality and God's intention, between our present and God's future. We simply do not have a technique for reading God's thoughts. We do not understand his future. We get accustomed to the status quo, even to the sufferings of the present. We accept that life is "like that." And we forget that God does not accept things as they are, that he wants to change them, that he plans a new heaven and a new earth, where there will be no suffering and tears. We do not long for this future because we understand too little of it. To be able to cry out and long for God's future and his purpose, we need the Holy Spirit.

6. In prayer, the Holy Spirit acts as a bridge-builder. The Spirit intercepts our prayerless prayer and transforms it into "sighs too deep for words." This means that Christ is not the only one to make intercession for us (Rom. 8:34). In our earthly suffering, the Holy Spirit also plays an intercessory role. The Holy Spirit changes places with us. The Spirit gets into our prayerless situation and transforms it into a powerful prayer. Through the Holy Spirit the cry "Lord, I can't pray. Help me!" becomes the most powerful prayer possible for Pentecost!

This assistance of the Spirit implies sympathy and support. This is underlined in the last part of the text, which mentions the intercession (*huperentunchanein*) of the Spirit. Intercession is acting "instead of," "in the place of," "on behalf of." This interceptive work of the Holy Spirit, of course, also reminds one of the paraclete, or advocate, motif in the New Testament. The term *paraclete* comes from the judicial sphere. Especially in John's Gospel the allusion is to a trial and to the person who stands next to the accused and defends this person's case before the judge.

In New Testament metaphors, Christ changed places with us the moment our death sentence was pronounced and took it on himself. The Holy Spirit now pleads our case on the basis of this work of atonement,

so that Christ's sacrifice can become our salvation through our re-
generation and repentance. What Christ has done objectively for us, the
Spirit works subjectively in us. The mediatory death of Christ is confirmed and applied to us by the Spirit. One result is that whenever we
are so overwhelmed by suffering and hardship that we become speech-
less before God, the Spirit intercedes for us and does what we are unable to do, namely to sigh and to pray according to the will of God.

7. In summary, one could say that in the midst of our sin and guilt
and suffering the Holy Spirit binds us to our mediator, Jesus Christ. Via
Christ we then have access to the will of the Father. On account of this
work of both Christ and the Holy Spirit, believers may now pray with
confidence and trust, forgetting our own inabilities and shortcomings.

Through the Spirit, Christ's prayer of intercession becomes our
prayer. Through the Spirit our prayerless prayer becomes a cry for salvation and redemption, heard and understood by him "who searches the
hearts of men" (v. 27). The words "sighs too deep for words" obviously
refer to God's character as well as to the content of the prayer of the
Spirit. This prayer does not spring up from us, from our insight and our
longings, but rather from the will of God himself, from the will and purpose of him who "works for good" in everything "with those who love
him" (v. 28)—even in our suffering.

II. Hermeneutical

During Pentecost, the ideas in verse 26 can be used in a special way to
remind the congregation of the assurance that believers already possess,
in spite of suffering and distress. Pentecost brings consolation. Pentecost breaks through the painful situations of our everyday lives and
offers hope! The church can look further than the present horizon of
death and misery.

Because the Holy Spirit binds the suppliants with their prayerless
prayers to the righteousness and power of God, hope and salvation enter
into our often hopeless and meaningless situations. "In this hope we
were saved" (v. 24).

1. This theme of hope, as focusing consistently on the fullness of
the salvation we already possess in Christ (cf. vv. 1-17), as well as on
the more complete realization that we shall experience at the second
coming of Christ, has already been mentioned in verse 18. In verse 18
the weight of our present suffering is contrasted with the "glory that is

to be revealed to us," i.e. the fullness of our salvation. In the scales of God's grace, the suffering and affliction of the present seem light when compared to that "eternal weight of glory beyond all comparison" (2 Cor. 4:17). These light rays of God's grace and of the resurrection triumph break through already in the present time—in hope!

2. Verse 19 speaks of an "eager longing." The picture here is of creation with "outstretched neck" straining to see what will happen in the near future, namely the coming of Christ and the fullness of the revelation of the conquering God. In verse 22 this longing is described as "groaning in travail," that is, the pangs of childbirth. It almost becomes a word play. The paradox is that the suffering that seems to us to be the last gasps of death (and therefore apparently signs of God's absence) become, from the perspective of the work of the Holy Spirit, the pains of birth—the promise of a wonderful new life!

The tragic futility and emptiness of life can be transformed by Christian hope into a symbol of approaching eternity, fullness, and ultimate meaning. Sorrow and suffering become windows to God's future. Through the intercepting power of the Holy Spirit, the experiences that at times seem to be the pitfalls of faith become the watchtowers of hope!

The perseverance of the believer does not depend on human strength, character, or effort, but rather on the fulfilled promises of God. To be saved in hope means to be saved already, notwithstanding the seeming contradictions. We expect the triumph of the coming Christ, because he has already conquered in the resurrection. Hope in the Holy Spirit ultimately means hope in the resurrection. Pentecost becomes a feast, because through the Holy Spirit believers have a part in the resurrection victory of Christ (Acts 2:36; 1 Cor. 12:3).

3. The idea of hope and resurrection victory corresponds with the central motif of the work of the Holy Spirit. The most important part of the work of the Spirit is to let believers share in the triumph of Christ's resurrection victory. Romans 8 therefore concludes in a song of victory. "In all these things we are more than conquerors through him who loved us" (v. 37).

The preacher should stress this aspect of hope and victory in the midst of suffering. It is through the Holy Spirit that the church can profess Christ as "Lord." "No one can say 'Jesus is Lord' except by the Holy Spirit" (1 Cor. 12:3). The title "Lord" is given to Christ as an indication of God's victory over death. It is also an indication of God's sovereignty over all destructive powers. Pentecost is the message of hope. God has made Jesus Lord. The God who has conquered death is in command of the suffering of the present time also. Through the working of the Spirit, the church shares in Christ's lordship.

4. The "first fruits of the Spirit" (v. 23) corresponds well with this theme of hope. This phrase should actually read "the Spirit, as the first gift from God." The Spirit, as the guarantee of our salvation, is also the guarantee of what we already are in Christ, and what we will one day be. "First gift" does not mean that the grace of Pentecost is only something preliminary. The gift of the Spirit is not simply a poor substitute for what is coming later. In the sermon on Pentecost Sunday it must be emphasized that in the Holy Spirit we already have everything. Whoever has the Spirit has Christ. And whoever has Christ has the Spirit (Rom. 8:9).

5. At times, and especially during the time of Pentecost, one hears people praying, "Lord, give me more of yourself." Or, "Lord, give me more of your Spirit." This may reflect an un-Pauline way of thinking about the gift of the Spirit, for God cannot give us more than what he already gave us at the outpouring of the Holy Spirit! Because of Pentecost, all believers now share in the fullness of God's salvation. All the fulfilled promises of God are at our disposal, including the Holy Spirit.

The intent of such prayers could also be that although believers already share in the fullness of God's salvation, this salvation has not been fully realized in this present dispensation, and believers must continuously plead for this to happen. This, of course, is legitimate and very necessary. Through suffering, believers have to grow into the fullness of salvation. To be able to do that, continuous surrender, daily conversion, and ongoing struggle are necessary. The only way to endure in this struggle is to cling steadfastly to our hope. With this hope, believers can look past the horizon of suffering and futility and look into the glory of God's victorious promises. To help us persevere in this struggle, the Holy Spirit offers the believer certainty and security.

The term "first fruits" *(aparchē)* originates in the cultic sphere. God gives to humanity the first payment or advance of what is to come later. The first part represents the whole.

It is important that the preacher illustrates this with the idea of "guarantee" *(arrabōn)* in Ephesians 1:14, where we read that we are "sealed with the promised Holy Spirit, which is the guarantee of our inheritance." In the first payment of the Spirit, God commits himself to pay the full amount later. The Holy Spirit becomes the guarantee of the glory to come. In the gifts of the Spirit believers already taste something of the future.

Being "sealed" with the Holy Spirit grants divine security, and it means at least three things. First, it guarantees the genuineness of our salvation, just as the seal on a document guarantees the authenticity of the writing. It is also an indication of ownership, as a seal tells of a document's owner. Finally, it means protection. Through the Holy Spirit God himself guarantees the safety of our salvation. All the attempts of evil and its powers cannot harm or destroy this salvation (cf. Rom. 8:37-39).

III. Homiletical

Romans 8:26 can be used on Pentecost to comfort the congregation with the assurance that God, in the Holy Spirit, is present in our suffering. This is true even though he does not take it away.

The popular idea that suffering forces us and sometimes even teaches us to pray is true only to a certain extent. It is also true that suffering sometimes leaves us unable to pray, because we lose sight of God and lose all perspective. Then the Spirit "teaches" us how to pray. Because the Spirit intercedes for us, our deepest prayer on Pentecost may be: "Lord, we cannot pray." By praying that, suppliants throw themselves into the arms of God. True prayer simply says at such times: "Lord, we believe; help our unbelief!"

The sermon could perhaps be divided into two parts.

1. In the first part one can focus on believers and churches in situations of suffering, futility, temptation. We are constantly threatened by suffering. Experiences such as death, disease, oppression, and violence fill human lives. And some suffer the special torment of hunger and poverty. The preacher can underscore the fact that throughout the ages active and obedient discipleship of Christ has been costly and has led to opposition and persecution. Because all of creation has been affected by sin, the church must be very sensitive to factors that increase human suffering. Because of the cosmic implications of the atonement of Christ, the church also has the responsibility to combat all forms of suffering. The church has to be God's bloodhound, moving with its nose "close to the ground" to ferret out suffering. The sufferers must then be strengthened and supported with the message of consolation.

The consolation of the Spirit, however, means much more. It is

God's radical intervention in our suffering. God brings enormous comfort to all believers who experience weakness and prayerlessness, who find themselves without perspective or vision.

2. In the second part one can focus on the contents of our comfort, namely that in life and death we belong to Christ. The preacher has to explain how the intercession of the Spirit is related to the mediatory work of Christ. The sermon can then concentrate on the prospects for believers in the salvation they already possess. The weight of the coming glory can be pondered. The perspective of daily victory, through the assistance of the Spirit, making suffering believers "more than conquerors," and the prospect of being saved in hope gives a festive, joyous character to the sermon on Pentecost Sunday.

Because of our incapacity, our prayers are always inadequate. This urges us on Pentecost to pray in the Spirit. The Spirit intercedes for us according to the divine purpose. Then the wealth of the fulfilled promises of God pours into the congregation. The strength of our prayer does not lie in the excellence of our words, nor on our enthusiasm as we pray. The Spirit liberates us from our anxieties and helps us pray boldly and confidently.

We do not get new perspective on life with our senses, but in faith. We start praying in the magnetic field of the Spirit. Life is no longer "giving birth astride a grave" (Beckett); it is the hopeful labor pains coming from an open grave, Christ's grave. The popular saying is, Where there's life there's hope. Because of Pentecost Christians know and experience, Where there's hope, there's life.

D. J. LOUW

Pericopes from
the Writings of John and Peter

Easter Sunday: John 20:11-18

Bibliography

Commentaries

Barrett, C. K. *St. John*. Philadelphia: Westminster, 1978.

Brown, R. E. *The Gospel according to John*. The Anchor Bible. Vol. 29A. Garden City: Doubleday, 1970.

Calvin, J. *Commentary on the Gospel according to John*. Vol. 2. Grand Rapids: Eerdmans, 1956.

Dodd, C. H. *The Interpretation of the Fourth Gospel*. Cambridge: Cambridge University Press, 1953.

Hendriksen, W. *Exposition of the Gospel according to John*. Vol. 2. Grand Rapids: Baker, 1954.

Morris, L. *The Gospel according to John*. The New International Commentary on the New Testament. Grand Rapids: Eerdmans, 1971.

Schnackenburg, R. *The Gospel according to St. John*. Vol. 3. New York: Crossroad, 1982.

Smelik, E. L. *Het Evangelie naar Johannes*. De Weg van het woord. Nijkerk: Callenbach, 1975.

Additional

Barclay, W. *The Gospel of John*. Vol. 2. The Daily Study Bible. Philadelphia: Westminster, 1956.

Berkouwer, G. C. *Het Licht der Wereld: Het Evangelie van Johannes*. Kampen: Kok, 1960.

Lüthi, W. *St. John's Gospel*. Richmond: Knox, 1960.

Moltmann-Wendel, E. *The Women around Jesus*. New York: Crossroad, 1982.

I. Exegetical

According to C. K. Barrett, in the two resurrection narratives of John 20:1-8 we find the "main statement of the church's Easter faith" and verses 19ff. is the "apostolic commission."

The very moving and genuinely human narrative of Jesus' appearance to Mary reaches its climax in verse 16. The tension culminates here. The initial scene with Mary and the angels ends with the dramatic statement that the weeping Mary "saw" Jesus but did not "know" him! Jesus then reveals himself to her in an equally dramatic way, calling her name (Schnackenburg; Iwand: "The preceding events were merely a prelude to this moment of actual revelation.").

Although detailed exegesis is impossible here, some comments may prove helpful:

1. Mary weeping outside the tomb. Exegetes differ markedly on the reason for her tears:

a. Barrett, Haenchen, and Strathmann refer rather negatively to her inconsolable weeping (cf. *imperfect,* therefore "incessant weeping") as her being totally overcome by sorrow. Smelik puts it even more strongly and calls it an egocentric sorrow in which tears symbolize blindness! All possible traces of hope are washed away by her tears, and all this "right next to the tomb"! Calvin, in a similar vein, contrasts her with the two disciples who had left the tomb seemingly feeling consoled (John 20:10), "but the women [according to Calvin there were other women with Mary] tormented themselves by idle and useless weeping. In short it is superstition alone, accompanied by carnal feelings, that keeps them near the sepulchre."

b. Iwand holds a quite different view. According to him Mary is weeping for her Lord. She cannot resign herself (as the disciples have done) to the fact that the Lord's body cannot be found. "In this hour, when the enemies are triumphant, when the disciples are beginning to be scattered and to fear, Mary is alone at the grave and doing what they all should have been doing," namely weeping. In this respect he agrees with the other Reformer, Luther, who says that Mary serves as a striking example to all believers of "how to wait for the Lord with one's whole heart. The risen Lord can only be received through tears" (*WA 28,* 448ff.).

c. Schnackenburg, Fürst, and Künkel all have a more balanced view. According to them this is neither "faithless" nor "holy" weeping, but rather an expression of personal grief and anxiety over the dead body of Jesus—and therefore over the inevitability of death. Fürst asks whether her weeping should perhaps be ascribed to the fact that death itself can never be a consolation, that one cannot be consoled when one is afflicted by the sorrow that death causes, that one can never be comforted with the knowledge of death alone, even though one may know where the body is!

2. The role of the angels (vv. 11b-13). Mary stooped forward to look into the tomb, but without actually entering. (Cf. John 20:5, where the same position was taken by John himself. According to Mark 16:5 and Luke 24:3 the women did enter the tomb.) The angels were obviously messengers from heaven, sitting in specific places *(hopou!)* within the tomb. Their presence and specific positioning, along with Peter's careful inspection of the tomb (20:6-7), seem intended to give credence to Christ's resurrection (Schnackenburg, Calvin).

Fürst paraphrases their question as follows, Why do you weep while here there is obviously no reason for sorrow? The angels were in fact sitting on the very spot where the Lord's body should have been, the body which Mary was seeking so fervently (v. 13). It was clearly not there! As opposed to the other Gospels, in John the angels merely put the question to Mary, but do not proclaim Christ's resurrection. John leaves this to Christ, perhaps to build up tension to such a degree that the appearance to Mary becomes the nucleus of the resurrection message (Schnackenburg).

3. The encounter with the resurrected Lord (vv. 14-16). "Mary turned around." The drama builds rapidly. Mary does not recognize the Lord (cf. Luke 24:16). The villain responsible for the disappearance of the body is now facing her! Bultmann rightly remarks that although Jesus may be present, we can fail to recognize him, because he has not yet addressed us personally (cf. also Künkel and Fürst). Calvin, Schnackenburg, and Strathmann state that her sorrow and fervor are the reason she does not recognize Jesus.

This detail has probably been inserted here to underscore the fact that the resurrection came as a total surprise! No one—not even Mary!—expected it in the least. His appearances are exactly the opposite of what we would expect. They do not see him because they expect to see him. On the contrary. They see him when they don't expect it at all, when they have no hope. Their earthly expectations are broken through from above!

As in his other early appearances (20:19, 26; 21:5), Jesus starts the conversation. He uses the question the angels have already asked, but adds: "Whom do you seek?" Is the way the question is phrased perhaps meant to focus all attention on the Person who is about to reveal himself? In any case, the tension is still mounting. At first Mary takes the man to be the gardener. Her answer reveals that she is searching for the Lord, and with great fervor. Although it is almost impossible for a woman to remove the body, she is prepared to try.

Then the resurrected Lord calls her name. "The sheep hear his voice, and he calls his own sheep by name and leads them out" (John 10:3). The name establishes a person's identity as a human being before God. Mary turns around when her name is called (*strephesthai*, "to turn to," "to turn towards"; Haenchen and Fürst say that in v. 14 she merely turns her head but here she turns her whole body). Many exegetes regard this expression as indicating much more than merely a bodily movement. Many see this as a symbol of an inner conversion (Schnackenburg; Fürst, e.g., calls it "a total turnabout, a conversion if one wishes: a turn from the pseudo-world of death into real life"). The calling of her name creates a new relationship, but also a new person, a new being, (another) new life!

Mary replies to this with "Rabboni!" (According to Strathmann this term was normally used only when addressing God.) Although Mary's response is more than one person's confession, it has indeed a very personal tone. Without such a personal confession the resurrected Lord remains distant and foreign (Berkouwer). But one should keep in mind that Mary's *pro me* is awakened and brought forth by the presence of the living Lord. Only the appeal by the risen Lord creates and sets free the faith that leads to profession (Fürst). Only in this correlation are we able to come to the true Easter faith and the Easter assurance that is built on more than belief in a mere fact. Mary's experience becomes the mirror image for faith that is awakened from above (Gal. 4:6-9). "Thus in Mary we have a lively image of our calling. . . . She renders to Christ the honor which is due to Him" (Calvin).

4. The instruction to Mary (vv. 17-18). Like the women in Matthew 28:9, Mary has apparently fallen at Jesus' feet. Jesus responds, *mē mou haptou*. Although this is often translated "Do not touch me," Schnackenburg, Strathmann, and Barrett all hold that this present imperative can best be translated, "Do not cling to me any longer," i.e. "Let me go." How should we understand this? Many exegetes have

tried to solve this problem, and we refer to only a few of them (for detailed accounts, cf. Brown, Haenchen, or Strathmann):

a. According to Bultmann, the Lord is telling Mary he should no longer be revered in the earthly way of prostrating oneself *(proskunē-sis)*. A new relation has to be sought with the risen Lord now that he is on his way to heaven. This theory, however, seems rather farfetched.

b. Smelik sees this as a somewhat defensive statement, as Jesus indicating his resistance to Mary's overly swift approach. He experiences her gesture and her response as restrictive, her excessive tenderness as a hindrance. He frees himself from this; he escapes from her cloying attachment to be free to continue on his way to glory. Calvin argues in the same way: "Their eagerness to touch Him had been carried to excess. . . . They fixed their attention on his bodily presence. . . ; by their foolish and unreasonable desire, they wished to keep Him in their world."

The purpose of the resurrection was not for Jesus to return to his previous bodily existence, in order to stay with his disciples, but to ascend, to build his kingdom, and to rule his church from heaven, seated at the right hand of God from where he would soon also send his Spirit in fullness.

c. M. Barth views the ascending to which Jesus refers (v. 17) as the coming glorification when the gospel will be proclaimed to the heathen. Mary is not allowed to touch Jesus because she is destined to take the message to the apostles (Israelites), but once they have touched him, they themselves proclaim the message to the heathen (1 John 1:1). "She may not yet kiss her Bridegroom like the bride of the end time."

d. It seems, however, much easier and far more convincing to deduce the meaning from the context itself, as Barrett, Strathmann, Fürst, and Schnackenburg do. Barrett says: "The ascending of Jesus to the Father (cf. 3:13; 6:62 where *anabainein* is used, and 7:33; 13:1, 3 . . .) was for John an essential act, completing what was done in the passion. . . . It was moreover a condition for the coming of the Spirit (7:39; 16:7)." Jesus now almost triumphantly tells Mary that this is what is happening! The promise of John 14:1-3 is being fulfilled!

"What emerges in the farewell discourse with the verbs of departing as the basic concern, namely, to show the importance of Jesus' departure for the disciples, is taken up in the saying of the risen One to Mary, and interpreted by John as the content of what Mary is to tell the disciples. The risen One keeps the promise which he gave to the disciples in the form of a prophecy as he was departing" (Schnacken-burg).

Christ needs Mary in all of this: not to tell them that he has risen (because they knew that already), but that he is already ascending! For them this would mean that immediately, very soon, they would almost receive the fruits of his departure (which have been promised in 14:12, 16ff., 21, 23, and summarized in 16:28). The breeze of the Holy Spirit starts blowing when Christ starts his ascension. In this way "the Easter event is brought into the theological line of the gospel and, on the other side, the announcements of the farewell discourses find their Easter confirmation and realization" (Schnackenburg).

The *anabainoō* therefore does not refer to the future, but to a process that has already started and still continues, a process that correlates with the promise that the Spirit will fill the earth!

5. The "remarkable formulation which sounds ceremonially solemn" (Schnackenburg)—"to my Father and your Father, to my God and your God"—deserves special attention. According to Barrett, the new and more intimate spiritual tie with the disciples (in which physical contact is no longer important) does *not* mean that the disciples' and Jesus' relationship with the Father are identical. Strathmann also notes that "our Father" is not used, and takes this to mean that some distance and difference here are maintained. Haenchen and Künkel, however, doubt that Jesus has this difference in mind here. What is rather emphasized here is that Jesus' Father is also their Father, that his God is also their God (cf. also Calvin). They have indeed received the right to be children of God through faith (John 1:12), and God has sent the Spirit into their hearts, "crying, 'Abba! Father!'" (Gal. 4:6).

6. In obedience, Mary goes to the disciples. She uses a word, "Lord," that sounds like an old Easter formula (1 Cor. 9:1; cf. Schnackenburg, Michaelis; Bultmann: "Here the Kurios title carries, for the first time in John, its true pathos!"). This is the name, now bestowed on him, that is above every name and that every tongue will have to confess (Phil. 2:9ff.). In this way Mary fulfills her commission: "Secure in her relationship with her Lord, filled with the joy and vision of his ascension, her piety does not choke in an individual salvation only, but starts moving" (Berkouwer).

Christ's ascension becomes the impetus for Mary's witness to the disciples. Thus the Lord's appearance to Mary explains the meaning of his resurrection to the disciples: from the ascending Lord they will receive the Spirit and they will be sent forth in his service, with the authority to serve him (vv. 21-23). Thus Mary's act of confession also prepares the next scene, in which the commission and the equipment with authority through the bestowal of the Holy Spirit is described in more detail. It is only in the church of Pentecost, with its message of the cross, on its way to the world (from behind closed doors!) that the resurrected Lord is truly glorified. This is what John's theology is all about!

II. Hermeneutical

1. The seemingly simple narrative structure of this resurrection story includes an entire theology, namely the question of what faith in the resurrected Jesus entails, and what faithful encounter with him means and can still mean today. It has important implications for the relationship between a personal or existential faith encounter with Jesus and the objective reality of the resurrection as a moment within the history of salvation. Because it is impossible to deal here with such a doctrinal question, readers are only reminded that one's theology and presuppositions will necessarily influence the way in which one approaches the narrative and the questions that one puts to it.

2. A much more specific question—but of great importance for understanding this account as narrative—is, What role does Mary's grief play? Is it the clue to understanding the plot? And does it provide the key for an existential interpretation of this pericope? That is, may we recognize our own sorrow, doubt, and hopelessness in that of Mary?

According to Schnackenburg, Mary's diligent search is a central motif. There even exists a tradition in which Mary is seen as a corrective of Eve's role in the temptation narrative (e.g., Gregory, mentioned by Iwand). Although Iwand does not agree with this view, he asserts that we have here someone whose grief prepared her for the message awaiting her. "Only through suffering can we develop the organ through which we experience the Lord's consolation." In fact, in the darkness of her faith she persevered, waited, and hoped, even when this no longer made any sense. That is why the Lord took this woman into his care, as he has done so many times in history with those who have persevered in lonely outposts, those who could never reconcile themselves with the "facts," those who could not believe with "reason-able" ease like the disciples!

Smelik and Calvin, however, take the opposite view. Calvin maintains that Mary did not receive the commission to go to the disciples because of her "faithful disposition." No, they who were so "tardy and sluggish to believe," deserved "to have women for their teachers. . . . The Apostles deserved to be more severely censured. . . . Yet it pleased the Lord by means of those weak and contemptible vessels to give a display of His power." Perhaps one must say that in both these approaches Mary receives too much emphasis. The real issue ought to be the transformation of a grieving and confused woman—someone without legal rights—to an all-important witness, the vanguard of the great events that are to take place: the mission of the church in the service of the ascended Lord.

3. It may be helpful to look briefly at the sermons of Bürkle, Iwand, and Fürst.

a. In a useful model for a mission sermon Bürkle points out the following:

(i) In non-Christian religions, death is often something terrible, which means that it has to be allayed by all sorts of rituals—but without any success! People without God do not want to resign themselves to death. They cannot accept or tolerate death. In Mary's story, however, the angels remind us that we cannot solve this problem from an earthly and human point of view. The resurrection is the only answer to this problem.

(ii) In the personal appeal made to Mary the triumphant events of the resurrection, which resounded through the entire cosmos, penetrated her private world. Now Mary no longer kept the name of the deceased Lord in remembrance, but—vice versa—"the resurrected Lord called the one still living on this side of death by her name and allowed her to share in the reality of his resurrection." The same call still reaches everyone *ad personam,* and faith in the resurrection is accessible only *ad personam.* That is why the message of mission is always brought personally. (This is clearly a somewhat artificial argument without a strong basis in the text!)

(iii) The new form of Christ's resurrected body, which we are able to "understand and grasp," is the *soma Christou,* i.e. his church. Only by sharing in this body can one encounter the Resurrected One. "Each personal relationship between the believer and the Lord should form a part of and remain subservient to this new body which came into being after the resurrection."

(iv) This section thus does not end with the resurrection itself, but only with the reality of the ascension and the resulting commission to the church to carry forth the message of forgiveness to all people. Along *this* way the risen Lord is not far away but, through his Spirit, remains close to his church, as the Lord of all humanity. John's version of the great commission results in the formation of the church: "In her unity with the risen Lord, the church, being an instrument of his service in the world, shares in his victory and reign. The preacher should point out this *proprium* (distinguishing mark) to the congregation."

b. According to Iwand the grave still represents the final "breach," the "ultimate interruption" within the neatly ordered world of science, technology, and human resources. Together with Mary we have been called as witnesses against the seeming power of death.

(i) Instead of the guards who were placed there *ex officio* by the authorities to guard the tomb, two witnesses belonging to the forces of victory were sitting there. They proclaimed the healing of the breach. From them Mary heard the liberating words that the gruesome attempt by the world to erect an impenetrable wall between lost people and God, between the Shepherd and his flock, was foiled! Mary became a witness of this. That is why she called out "Rabboni." She recognized him who, through crucifixion and death, had become Lord (cf. Acts 2:36)! These words contained a confession with worldwide impact, namely that no one can truly live without meeting him as personal Lord. Ultimately that is exactly what happened: this conversion spread throughout the whole world.

(ii) Mary wanted to hold this One whom she saw and loved! One can easily forget that the message of Easter is a miracle pointing far beyond the actual events themselves, a miracle to which one can testify, but which one can never keep to oneself. We can so easily cause the gospel to congeal!

(iii) The church was born where the risen Lord appeared. They received their new name of "brothers," brothers of the risen Lord. No church is possible without him. He makes people into children of the Father, into the family of God, into brothers and sisters.

(iv) Pentecost still had to come, but Christ would remain the One sending them out. Mary, the eyewitness, had to remain subservient to his message. "The message is the report of Jesus' ascension to the Father and of the *communio* with the congregation." That is the ultimate purpose of this pericope.

c. Fürst gives a good example of an Easter sermon that could also be used on Pentecost. His main idea is that the risen Lord revealed himself as the living One by calling disciples (like Mary) by their names, by giving them new life in his name, and by summoning them through the Holy Spirit to serve him. He points out:

(i) "Jesus does not depend on our faith to show himself as the living One, but our faith fully depends on him in order to remain alive!" Everyone who, like Mary, complains that Jesus "once came into their lives" but has since disappeared, is referred to him as the living Lord. Whoever says that remembering him gives them no consolation is advised to meet him personally.

(ii) There exists a dangerous longing within the church to return to the earthly Jesus and his physical presence alone. It manifests itself in diverse forms. All of them may impede the church in her fulfillment of the calling of the living Lord.

(iii) It is the risen Lord himself who at present delivers us from temptation in order that we may live lives of obedience. Such lives in themselves witness, through the power of his Spirit, to his authority over the world.

(iv) This leads to the theme of mission. We can only be children of God and brothers and sisters of each other when we proclaim Christ, the risen Lord, as Lord. We move from Easter, through Ascension, to the end of all times by way of mission.

This presents a workable model, but unfortunately it lacks structure and unity.

III. Homiletical

Another possible structure for a sermon can be offered:

1. Whatever Mary's reason for her sorrow, and whatever reaction we have to this, it is important to realize that the crux of this section is the meeting with the Lord (v. 14) and Mary's being addressed by the risen Lord (vv. 15-16). The Easter accounts are correctives for the sluggishness of the Easter witnesses, for their lack of joy, their anxiety and rigidness, which repeatedly threatened to congeal the message (Berkouwer). The believer and the church can so easily retard the progress of this dynamic, world-conquering message by sluggishness and stagnation. The church can so easily withdraw and only give attention to her own well-being, even her possessions and maintaining the status quo. Like Mary, Christians often display amazing zeal or bend their

knees piously, but in the wrong direction and motivated by inner stagnation and self-satisfaction! Only through an ongoing personal encounter with the living Lord and by taking part in his work in the world can we be liberated from the paralysis that characterizes so many of our religious activities.

2. The entire Gospel of John is aimed at the ascension, the lifting-up, the glorification—but a glorification or ascension that includes the cross, the resurrection, the ascension, and the promise of the Spirit all brought into one single focus. As the One who is "lifted up" (from the earth) in this way, Christ will "draw all men" to himself (12:32; cf. 3:14; 8:28). This means that world mission emerges from this comprehensive glorification or ascension. That is also the reason this section does not close with the message of Easter, but with the ascension of Christ. He wants to give his disciples a new vision and a new momentum to carry out the commission of their ascending Lord! This is how the message (via Mary) came to the disciples. They already "knew" about the resurrection, but were still confined to their small room, struggling with their own anxieties! Their sails were not put to the wind yet! Their seas were still too calm! They simply had to hear about his ascension, so that they themselves could be lifted up and set into motion! His resurrection was meant to make them rise as well, from their beds and their chairs, on into the world! Pentecost was coming!

3. The ascending Lord now called the circle of disciples "his brothers" and "children of the Father." We can be included in this circle only *through our personal relationship with him.* Without *that* relationship, true brotherhood or childhood—whether in the church or in the world—remains impossible! The church is the training ground for life: it should not only restore existing relationships, but should also initiate new ones. Without a relationship with the living Christ, we are most profoundly without God and without neighbors in a fatherless (and motherless), brotherless (and sisterless), inhuman world. That is the claim and message of the church!

4. This message is dramatically summarized in Mary's usage of *Kurios.* The pathos of the Kurios title demonstrates something of the horizon and of the ultimate purpose of the era initiated by the events of Easter. As the Kurios, the glorified Lord will draw everyone to himself and give them eternal life (17:3). He is still doing this through the sending of the Spirit and through the mission of his obedient church.

B. A. MÜLLER

First Sunday After Easter: John 20:24-29

Bibliography

Commentaries

Barrett, C. K. *St. John.* Philadelphia: Westminster, 1978.

Brown, R. E. *The Gospel according to John.* The Anchor Bible. Vol. 29A. Garden City: Doubleday, 1970.

Calvin, J. *Commentary on the Gospel according to John.* Vol. 2. Grand Rapids: Eerdmans, 1956.

Dodd, C. H. *The Interpretation of the Fourth Gospel.* Cambridge: Cambridge University Press, 1953.

Hendriksen, W. *Exposition of the Gospel according to John.* Vol. 2. Grand Rapids: Baker, 1954.

Morris, L. *The Gospel according to John.* The New International Commentary on the New Testament. Grand Rapids: Eerdmans, 1971.

Schnackenburg, R. *The Gospel according to St. John.* Vol. 3. New York: Crossroad, 1982.

Smelik, E. L. *Het Evangelie naar Johannes.* De weg van het Woord. Nijkerk: Callenbach, 1965.

Homiletical

Jager, O. *Zegen U zelf,* 77-89. Kampen: Kok, 1959.

Jager, O. *Opklaring,* 87-88. Ede: Zomer & Keuning, 1980.

Morgan, G. C. *The Westminster Pulpit.* Vol. 5, 126-39. London: Revell, n.d.

Noordmans, O. *Verzamelde Werken.* Vol. 8, 83-85; 319-21. Kampen: Kok, 1980.

Schillebeeckx, E. *Jesus, an Experiment in Christology.* New York: Seabury, 1979.

Additional

Barclay, W. *The Gospel of John.* Vol. 2. The Daily Study Bible. Philadelphia: Westminster, 1956.

Berkouwer, G. C. *Het Licht der Wereld: Het Evangelie van Johannes.* Kampen: Kok, 1960.

Lüthi, W. *St. John's Gospel.* Richmond: Knox, 1960.

Moltmann-Wendel, E. *The Women around Jesus.* New York: Crossroad, 1982.

Exegetical

1. The account of Christ's appearance to Thomas occupies a key position in the structure of the Gospel of John. If one assumes that John 21 is an epilogue, then John 20:24-29 is the last narrative in the "original" book. Most exegetes agree that this pericope is important, but they differ widely on John's purpose and message in this section.

a. According to Bultmann, verse 29 forms the climax and conclusion of this pericope and, in fact, of the entire Easter account in John. Verse 29 contains a reproach: it should not have been necessary for Thomas and the other disciples to see Jesus. His word alone should have been sufficient. The "word" is the essential element in the relationship with Christ. Appearances are less important, merely "a concession to the weakness of the disciples." This leads Bultmann to a further conclusion: verse 29 indicates that the Easter narrative as such has a very limited and relative value. Brown quite rightly remarks: "This exegesis of John reflects Bultmann's personal theology rather than the evangelist's thought."

b. Brown accepts Lindars's suggestion that John 20:24-29 is John's (final) dramatization of the important theme of doubt and skepticism. The synoptic Gospels already mention the disciples' doubt in connection with Christ's resurrection (cf. Mark 16:11; Matt. 28:17; Luke 24:11, 38). "We propose that . . . the evangelist had transferred this doubt to a separate episode and personified it in Thomas." Such a point of view naturally casts a shadow on the historicity of this account.

c. Dodd draws attention to the apologetic, even more specifically, the anti-Docetic, motif in this pericope. According to him, John wishes to emphasize the reality of the resurrection and, particularly, the reality of Christ's physically resurrected body. Although it is not possible to deny the presence of these themes in John's account, the question remains as to how important they really are in the pericope. From the fact that we are not told whether Thomas indeed accepted Jesus' invitation to touch his hands and his side, Schnackenburg concludes that John regards this question as of only secondary importance.

d. Barrett and Versteeg select verse 28 as the central verse in this pericope. "There can be no doubt that John intended this confession of faith to form the climax of the gospel." Thomas's confession of Christ as "God" refers back to John 1:1 ("the Word was God") and together these two verses form the climax and the keystones of John's entire christology. Versteeg also stresses the development that occurs during the Gospel: "What has been stated merely in general in John 1:1 is now focused into a very personal confession in John 20:28." According to him this confession forms the conclusion and climax of the entire fourth Gospel. "The fourth Gospel is meant to lead every reader to this very same experience that Thomas has undergone."

e. Schnackenburg, too, takes this very broad context for interpreting this pericope. The pericope of Thomas, he states, can only be understood from the perspective of the entire fourth Gospel's central motif, which is to help readers to attain a deepened faith in Christ. The purpose of this particular narrative is exactly the same, to create and strengthen faith.

2. If one wants to understand the entire message of John 20:24-29, Schnackenburg probably offers the best approach. The fourth Gospel's explicit aim is to persuade people to believe. In this pericope both John's paraclesis (consolation) and his paranesis (appeal, admonition) reach a definite climax.

This pericope offers an infinitely rich consolation. The crisis of the crucifixion is followed by the triumph of Easter! "The gospel always demonstrates its infinite strength in the breaking down of all resistance" (Berkouwer). Nothing can inhibit the progress of the gospel, neither the disbelief of the world nor the skepticism and doubt of the church! Furthermore, it becomes clear that the gospel brings hope for everybody. Versteeg quite correctly points out that "John here conveys the richest confession of Christ precisely as the confession of someone who over and over experienced the strongest doubt of all"! In view of this consolation, the urgent admonition can and should then be heard also: "Do not be faithless, but believing" (v. 27b). Christ indeed understands all our doubt—that is our comfort!— but he does not simply condone that doubt without questioning. He calls us to believe. That is the command!

3. Apart from the above-mentioned principal theme, the pericope also contains *a few secondary themes:*

a. The point has already been made that verse 28 forms the climax of John's christology (1d). John explicitly wants to induce the same faith that Thomas confessed when he exclaimed: "My Lord and my God!" It is a personal faith ("My . . . my"), the willing acknowledgment and appropriation of the different titles Christ (according to John's Gospel) claimed for himself (e.g., "I and the Father are one," as well as the "I am" expressions).

b. The problem of seeing and/or believing, which is touched upon in verse 29, is also a distinct minor theme, not only here, but in John's Gospel as a whole. It is impossible to deal adequately with this topic here. It is, however, quite obvious how important it is to John's mind. Accordingly, much has already been written on this subject. Verse 29 should therefore be seen in the context of what John writes about seeing and believing elsewhere in his Gospel.

John is not completely negative about the physical perception of Jesus, but he thoroughly realizes its limited meaning. Physical perception alone cannot induce faith. During Jesus' life on earth, many people have physically perceived him and all his works, and yet they have not believed (6:36; 12:37). He wants to emphasize this to his readers, who are living, of course, many years after the Jesus event. They are not in a disadvantageous position at all in relation to those people who have been eyewitnesses to all these events, because faith and communion with the living Christ do not depend on physical perception. To the contrary! One may see, yet not believe. And one may not see, yet be blessed! The contrast in verse 29 is further softened by Jesus' promise that he will soon return to his church in and through the Holy Spirit, in such an abundant way that he can even say: "But you will *see* me" (14:18-19; 16:16ff.). In any case one cannot conclude from verse 29 that Thomas's faith is the direct consequence of his physical perception. That would be alien to John's way of thinking.

c. According to Versteeg one also detects an intentional minor theme in the role of the community of faith, the fellow disciples. "Only from the moment that it could be said of Thomas that he was . . . 'with them' [i.e. in the company of the other disciples, where he belonged, and should have been!], did he fully understand the mystery of Jesus' identity." Put differently, it is only within the fellowship of the church that one can encounter the living Christ.

d. To what extent can John 20:24-29 be regarded as the final episode of a life story of Thomas, woven into his Gospel by John? John's two other references to Thomas (11:16 and 14:5) are sometimes used very confidently in sermons to paint a picture of Thomas as a particular type of personality, almost as if John has intentionally been giving biographical notes on Thomas. This is certainly not commendable and it lies completely outside John's intentions. On the other hand, many exegetes do acknowledge that it is contrary to John's style to make such references casually and completely without intention. The major problem, however, is that these two verses (11:16 and 14:5) are themselves not easy to interpret! According to some exegetes, John depicts Thomas as "skeptical by nature" (Brown), others view him as "a pessimist" (Bernard), and still others regard him as "a bit slow of understanding" (Barrett: "loyal but obtuse"). It is hardly possible to construct a biography on such scanty information, diverse theories, and obvious speculation!

e. It is important to remember that the narrative about Thomas forms part of John's Easter message. One should always be careful not to approach John's account of Christ's resurrection in a too dogmatic way. John operates with a christology in which it is not always possible to distinguish between incarnation, crucifixion, resurrection, and ascension. He does not so much stress the individual moments of the history of salvation, but rather the magnificence and glory of Christ himself visible in all these moments (through the eyes of faith)!

Accordingly one should guard against two extremes. For John, Christ's resurrection is less of a definite interruption within the entire history of salvation than was the coming of the Holy Spirit. The Holy Spirit introduces the new, "better" dispensation. On the other hand, the resurrection can, as is the case with Bultmann *cum suis,* be totally underestimated. This is unacceptable as well and will not do justice to John's intention either. The resurrection, after all, does indeed mean progress. After the resurrection Christ's glory is more fully and richly perceived than before. "Christ's true identity, although the same as during his life on earth, then dawned on the disciples much more clearly" (Versteeg).

As far as John 20:24-29 is concerned, it should be stated very specifically that it is the risen, living Christ who, through his mighty and creative word, leads the doubting Thomas to a steadfast faith. Here one encounters the deepest mystery of Thomas's faith. "Through all this John reveals Christ's glory: the powers of disbelief and doubt disappear in a personal encounter with Christ" (Berkouwer). The key to this narrative is found in verse 27b—the life-generating word of the risen Christ. "This is not just pious exhortation, but a word of power" (Barth).

II. Hermeneutical

1. In his analysis of preaching on this pericope, Kamphaus points out two very common types of sermons that, in his view, are exegetically not justifiable. These are the "psychologizing" and the "historicizing" sermons. By psychologizing he means the preacher who is more interested in reproducing the emotional atmosphere of the text than in its theology. By historicizing he means that this pericope is preached in an apologetic manner, as being an objective "proof of the fact" *(Tatsachenbeweis)* of Christ's resurrection. John 20:24-29 does give evidence of Christ's resurrection, and faith accepts and confesses this; but this is definitely not the primary intent of the text. The same criticism also applies to a dogmatizing sermon, such as a message on the deity of Christ based on verse 28.

2. In nearly all sermons on John 20:24-29, Thomas is subjected to an analysis of some kind (psychological, philosophical, theological). Apart from the more common psychological ("pessimist," "melancholic") and philosophical ("rationalist," "modern skeptic") approaches, there are a few theological analyses that deserve more serious attention.

Luther (as quoted by Diem) detects three sins committed by Thomas: he did not realize that Christ was much more than an ordinary human being; he did not want to accept others' testimony ("he considered his fellow disciples as clowns and only himself as being wise"); and he wanted to believe on his own terms. Noordmans asserts that Thomas was too much of an introvert. "Disbelief is the state of mind that is too isolated in itself." Thence also his desire to touch Christ's wounds, because for such a person faith means *"self-*assurance." According to Sauter, Thomas's mistake was the fact that he became fixated on (one could almost say: fell in love with) a theology of passion and the cross and that he was not willing to seek (and to find) Christ where and how the Lord chose to reveal himself to us. Thielicke points out the "gravity" of Thomas's doubt. It was much more than an absent-minded "blasé doubt." According to John 11:16 he was even willing to die with Christ.

Barth feels more positively about Thomas, saying that he only asked what had already been granted to the other disciples. They also believed only after having perceived (20:8). It was then granted to Thomas so that he could become a true apostle (i.e. someone who had heard, seen, looked upon, and touched, according to John's own definition in 1 John 1:1) and also for our sake.

How should we evaluate these analyses? It may tempt a preacher not to preach the gospel, but to have a sermon on Thomas instead! It should be pointed out that although many of these analyses are ingenious while still dogmatically correct, they are often based on speculation and therefore lead one's attention away from the actual thrust of the pericope itself. There are, however, examples where this type of analysis is done with responsibility and where the kerygma of the text is not lost (e.g., Thielicke's sermon).

3. Kamphaus holds that a sermon on John 20:24-29 should provide an answer to the question of how faith can still be possible in an era in which the risen Lord can no longer be perceived. The contrast in verse 29 makes it impossible to sidestep this thesis. This is indeed the question worshipers would expect to be answered. Everything depends on the way in which it is treated.

a. One gets the impression that some preachers (as a result of insufficient exegesis, cf. I, 3b) are themselves overwhelmed by the contrast in verse 29. The entire sermon is then fixated on the question of seeing and believing, and degenerates into an apology (mostly with popular, philosophical arguments) for the invisibility of Christ.

b. A more legitimate type of analysis directly raises Kamphaus's question, and answers it with reference to the history of salvation. Because he was destined to be an apostle, Thomas was granted to see and to touch. The disciples had to hear, see, and feel, also for our sake. This does not imply, however, that we are at a disadvantage, because we have received the written Word and the Holy Spirit. With this type of sermon the pericope is usually expanded to include John 20:19-23 (for the sake of the reference to the Holy Spirit) and John 20:30-31 (for the sake of the reference to the written Word).

c. There is a third possibility, which would deal indirectly with Kamphaus's question. Without directly posing the problem, the message of the pericope can be evolved positively (as opposed to the apologetic approaches of a and b), in such a way that it will liberate the worshipers from an incorrect understanding of the contrast in verse 29.

III. Homiletical

Perhaps the following scheme for a sermon could prove useful:

1. In an introduction one can mention the fact that Thomas has fascinated people throughout the ages. Many divergent answers have been given to the question of the real nature of this man, called Thomas the Twin. As a matter of interest, and also to introduce the worshipers to the problems presented by the text, two or three typifications (cf. I and II, 2) could briefly be explained, concluding with the strongly positive portrayal by Barth, who almost regards Thomas as a hero.

2. Secondly, one can point out that we should not try to make excuses for Thomas. That does not correspond with the facts in the text and, moreover, it can prevent us from hearing the gospel, the good news, in John 20. Thomas is not the central character in John 20:24-29. The central figure is Jesus, in his searching and condescending love. Jesus forgives his disciples for renouncing him, and he exerts himself in order to help them believe. The gospel of our text is that Christ completely understands our disbelief and doubt, and that his death on the cross and his subsequent resurrection bring hope for all people— even those who have difficulty believing, those without a "religious ability," "religious potential," and "religious affinity" (Versteeg)!

3. After having heard the gospel and the consolation of John 20:24-29, we should, however, also listen to verse 27b. After Christ has done everything Thomas asked of him, he is now justified in saying to Thomas, "Stop your doubting, and believe" (TEV). Christ says that because he knows us and realizes that one can fall in love with doubt. There is something fascinating and alluring about "serious doubt" (cf. the famous words of Lessing: "If God were holding all the truth that exists in his right hand and in his left hand just the one ever-active urge to find the truth, even if attached to it were the condition that I should always and forever be going astray, and it said to me, 'Choose!,' I should humbly fall upon his left hand"). The problem, however, is that it cannot induce faith in us. Although the Lord understands our doubts, he is not satisfied to leave it at that. He wants us to stop doubting and to believe so that we can openly profess, "My Lord and my God!"

4. How does one obtain such a faith? A superficial reading of our text and especially of verse 29 can create the impression that Thomas only came to believe after he had seen Christ. But this is not true. John explicitly teaches the opposite. Physical perception can make one admit the truth ("I admit that you were right, now that I see for myself that he is alive"), but it cannot induce faith and the confession of the truth ("My Lord and my God!"). Only Christ can do this: the resurrected Christ with his creative, life-giving word. Thomas is converted because he stands before the living Jesus and because Jesus speaks to him.

Because this is the case, we do not have to pity ourselves when we look at verse 29. Okke Jager points out that not Thomas, but we who do not perceive, are called "blessed"! "It is not necessary for us to do anything to become part of those who 'do not see.' We already are part of them. We are blessed, because we only have to read that we are blessed." We really do not have to pity ourselves, because we have everything and more that is necessary to make people believe. We have Christ's Word (20:30-31), we have the Holy Spirit, and in and through the Spirit we have Christ himself (John 14:18-19).

5. And, apart from that, we also have the church. To conclude the sermon, one can point out the role of the church. On the one hand, Thomas has to realize that his salvation lies within the church. His doubt began when he broke away from his fellow disciples, and he only comes to faith when he returns to the church. On the other hand, we observe how the Lord, for that very reason, uses and engages the church to go out and search for wandering doubters and return them home.

C. W. BURGER

Second and Third Sundays after Easter: 1 Peter 1:3-9

Bibliography

Commentaries

Beare, F. W. *The First Epistle of Peter.* Oxford: Blackwell, 1947.

Best, Ernest. *1 Peter.* New Century Bible. London: Marshall, Morgan & Scott, 1971; Grand Rapids: Eerdmans, 1982.

Bolkestein, M. H. *De Brieven van Petrus an Judas.* Nijkerk: Callenbach, 1963.

Cranfield, C. E. B. *I & II Peter and Jude.* London: SCM, 1960.

Hunter, A. M. *Peter.* The Interpreter's Bible. New York/Nashville: Abingdon, 1957.

Reicke, B. *The Epistles of James, Peter, and Jude.* The Anchor Bible. Garden City: Doubleday, 1964.

Selwyn, E. G. *The First Epistle of St. Peter.* 2d ed. Thornapple Commentaries. Grand Rapids: Baker, 1947/1981.

Homiletical

Blaiklock, E. M. *First Peter: A Translation and Devotional Commentary.* Waco: Word, 1977.

Jewett. *The Epistles of St. Peter. A Practical and Devotional Commentary.* Grand Rapids: Kregel, 1905/1970.

Koopmans, J. *Kleine Postille,* 72-73. Goudriaan: de Groot, 1971.

Overduin, J. *Niet ik . . . maar Hij,* 157-67. Kampen: Kok, 1971.

Van Ruler, A. A. *Het leven een feest,* 82-102. Nijkerk: Callenbach, 1972.

Additional

Elliott, J. H. *A Home for the Homeless: A Sociological Exegesis of I Peter, Its Situation and Strategy.* Philadelphia: Fortress, 1981.

Moltmann, J. *Theology of Hope*. New York/Evanston: Harper & Row, 1967.

I. Exegetical

1. The structure and the theme of the pericope are important. In the Lutheran division of pericopes verses 3-9 are taken together as one unit. Commentaries and translations, however, almost without exception, take verses 3-12 as the complete unit. In his structural analysis of the entire Epistle, Combrink maintains that verse 13 has a connecting function and that it therefore belongs to both 3-12 and 14-25, in line with Peter's typical construction. Du Toit, in the final version of his structural analysis, changes his earlier viewpoint and agrees with Combrink. When preaching it is unnecessary—and impossible!—to try to cover all the aspects of this intricate pericope, so verse 13 and to a certain extent even verses 10-12 will be ignored in the present discussion.

As far as the internal structure is concerned, almost all exegetes distinguish three sections, verses 3-5, 6-9, and 10-12. Goppelt, on account of the content, further divides the center part into two sections, namely verses 6-7 and 8-9, and by doing so he distinguishes four parts.

Du Toit, however, calls it a "structurally intricate section." He explains that the major differences of opinion reflected in commentaries and translations regarding the theme of the pericope are due to these difficulties. He is convinced that an intelligent reading of this section simply with the aid of traditional grammatical methods is not enough to discover the argument and the meaning. In a structural analysis he then tries to show that there are five separate parts, structured in such a way that the theme is first stated, then expanded on and worked out, before there is a return to the theme and a final conclusion.

The theme is formulated by Du Toit as: "From God you have received a glorious expectation of things to come: Praise God and rejoice in it in spite of affliction." Combrink adopts this and gives the theme as: "God gives new life and a living hope and reveals that this salvation is yours now. Praise God and rejoice in this." In view of this, Du Toit is of the opinion that many summaries of this pericope are inadequate, because they either overemphasize a secondary motif and ignore relevant aspects, or force a structure upon the pericope that is totally inappropriate.

2. There are sharp differences of opinion regarding the genre and background of these verses. Two theories are usually combined here

with many variations. On the one hand there is the well-known theory that the entire First Epistle of Peter (up to 4:11) is an ancient Christian address or sermon on baptism. Preisker, for instance, goes so far as to say that 1 Peter is the oldest known documentation of a Christian worship service in which baptism takes place (between 1:21 and 22), but this act is not mentioned at all, in line with the then widespread Christian practice of the *disciplina arcani*. This theory has been enlarged upon by Cross, for instance, in his *Pascal Liturgy*. He argues that 1 Peter reflects the liturgy that was used at the Easter festival with its characteristic baptismal service and eucharist celebration. Should these theories on the Epistle be correct, it will, of course, also cast much light on various motifs in this specific pericope, such as rebirth, resurrection, suffering, and inheritance.

The other theory, combined with the former, holds that some sections in 1 Peter, including this pericope or parts of it, were existing hymns. Thus Boismard regards these verses as a baptismal song (along with others in 1 Peter), Preisker sees it as a prayer psalm, Coutts views it as a liturgical prayer, and Windisch and Schneider also call it a hymn, due to the fact that verses 3-12 form one long sentence, made up of a series of subordinate clauses. Despite widespread support for these viewpoints, they are also much criticized and one should consequently be careful not to rely too much on them. And yet one thing is sure, even according to some of those who reject these theories: baptism is indeed an important background for both the motifs and imperatives in 1 Peter and in this particular pericope.

3. Many of the differences of opinion regarding the theme are due to the terse style, with various details following rapidly on one another, and to the heated differences of opinion surrounding several of these details.

a. In verse 3 much attention is focused on the words "new birth." While many are at pains to ascertain the religious background of the term *rebirth,* Brox is of the opinion that it is not very helpful. The first aspect that is, no doubt, expressed with this term is God's initiative in salvation. It is meant as "boasting in God's mercy." Iwand says, quite rightly, that his mercy differs from our sympathy because he does, in fact, act and save. His mercy is not only an attitude, but a way of acting. It is therefore more correct to talk about the regenerating God than about regenerated man (Brown)! This confession shows humanity's inability and does not wish to give occasion to either subjectivistic self-examinations (of a sectarian mentality: Are you sure you are born again?) or objectivistic sacramentalism (of an often lighthearted and superficial nature).

The idea of rebirth should not lead here to all kinds of doctrinal or, even worse, moralistic extremes. God's initiative and the accompanying human inability find expression in the fact that the rebirth takes place in the resurrection of Christ from the dead. The objective nature of the rebirth is thereby underlined. "Objectively, the correct answer to the question: 'When were you saved?' would be: 'Around the year A.D. 30.' It was when 'the place of a skull' was transformed by an open tomb that our salvation was effected. In this sense, we were saved twenty centuries before we were born, by an act of God's gracious mercy" (Miller).

It is, however, also stated in 1:23 that the rebirth takes place "through the living word," so that one can quite rightly say that it takes place "by word and faith, by means of an encounter with a person" (Bolkestein), but not in such a way that it gives reason for "an inner search, in which one looks for some visible changes" (Gollwitzer). For this reason most exegetes therefore quite rightly think of baptism as the background (cf. John 3:5 and Titus 3:5).

Goppelt remarks that it is therefore very relevant to say that the root of one's Christian being is described in doxological style, because the basis of Christianity is not of an anthropological nature and is not contained in human decisions or in the human acceptance of a divine offer, but in God's own merciful act of a second birth. That is why verse 3 speaks about baptism and not of conversion. He also adds, however, that this confessional pronouncement should be read as a "kerygmatic indicative" that cannot be understood fully and correctly without the imperatives that are later built upon it. The rebirth does not therefore lead to deification, but to humanization. It leads to hope, to a living hope. It places human beings in the *peregrinatio,* the state of being aliens.

Bolkestein and Büchsel explain that rebirth turns humans to God's future, so that rebirth and eschatology belong inextricably to one another. "One cannot understand Peter's thoughts on rebirth if one fails to see its eschatological nature" (Büchsel). Brox also emphasizes these two poles, of a new beginning through the mercy of God and of hope for the future, as the two key points of the entire message of 1 Peter and already of his view on the rebirth in this opening pericope.

From a totally different angle Wolff comes to the conclusion that the idea of exiles or strangers (which occupies such a central position in 1 Peter and is already mentioned in 1:1 and 2) implied mainly three things in the ancient world—strange descent, strange language and customs, and strange gods. According to him, Peter therefore starts immediately in verses 3-12 to relate the "strangerhood" of Christians to their strange new birth or descent and thus the idea of rebirth functions very centrally within Peter's message. In this way it also indirectly becomes part of the paranetic theme, that is, his exhortations and admonitions.

b. The rebirth issues in a "living hope" (v. 3). Neugenbauer's comparative statistical table of the use of theological terms shows the central role that hope plays in 1 Peter—more so than in any other New Testament writing. To a certain degree, therefore, Peter is quite correctly called "the apostle of hope" (over against Paul as "the apostle of faith" and John as "the apostle of love"). One does not do justice to this living hope if it is merely described as "a hope by which one may live; it sustains the soul after the new birth with the nourishment needed for a higher life" (Reicke). Or "not dead, that is insubstantial and unfruitful, but living, i.e. certain and therefore effective even now" (Kelly, De Villiers). It does not, to begin with, refer to an act or attitude, the *spes qua* (which is strong and alive), but instead to an object, to content, to the *spes quae* (which is safe and secure).

This hope is "alive" because the eschatological inheritance obtained through the resurrection has been secured beyond any doubt. Schrage accordingly warns that attempts should not be made to describe this living hope "psychologically" (contra Beare, for example). Peter is referring to a hope that stands over against any form of daydreaming, wishful thinking, and illusions. It is "not merely an indefinite longing" (Schelkle), "not vague nostalgia" (Neugenbauer), "not projection of something lacking . . . but fruit of a possession" (Berkhof). It is "solid ground" (Ruthsatz), "hope with a reason for existence that cannot be destroyed" (Delling), "security" (Brox). In the New Testament, hope is not an expression of uncertainty, but of certainty (Bolkestein). The living hope, says Brox, is related to the living word (1:23) and the living stone (2:4 and 5). It concerns the Christian life, which is certain, because it rests fully on the supposition of the resurrection of Jesus Christ. Thus Schrage adds quite legitimately that any (ordinary human) hope without *this* hope, that remains living even in the face of death and destruction, is, in the final analysis, still a form of hopelessness!

No one describes these relationships between hope and resurrection better than Neugenbauer. He says that Peter starts the Epistle with a repetition of the Easter experience. He compares it with the story of Emmaus and says that this is exactly what the first Easter experience was, dismay and hopelessness. And then, the birth and renewal of hope! According to him Peter is not interested in baptism, but in the first Christian Easter experience that all Christians share ("we," v. 3), "the catastrophe of doubt and despair in the dark night when Jesus is arrested . . . and then the wonderful, new future that is received in the resurrection." "Easter means the renewal of hope. The Easter experience is identical with the regaining of hope."

Van Ruler also makes some interesting remarks about living hope. He writes that early Christians were called "the third generation." Both Jews and Gentiles were old and tired and without any hope for the world, but Christians stood in the world with "a new and fresh courage," as if life, the world, history, everything was apparently worthwhile. The Christian's field of vision, says Van Ruler, is not limited to the visible horizons. We are not trapped in the boundaries and walls of matters as they mistakenly may seem to be. Behind all horizons other worlds, new worlds, loom up again. Behind all the inevitabilities loom the possibilities of God!

The rule that applies in the physical life is, Where there is life, there is hope. For Christians, the reverse applies in the spiritual world, Where there is hope, there is life. "This attitude is of crucial importance in the Christian life," says Van Ruler. "Christians always see 'a hole in the wall.' Christians know that nothing is ever utterly hopeless, not even when they are facing death itself." For this attitude, however, one needs to be born again, "our deepest thoughts and convictions" must be converted, for this is certainly no natural hope or optimism, inherent in human nature. It is not a worldly hope that comes to a conclusion on the strength of all available data, but a hope that is by nature foreign to the human heart and a hope at which one can only marvel.

c. This hope finds its parallel in the "imperishable, undefiled, and unfading" inheritance that is reserved in heaven for us. It is "reserved in heaven," says Calvin, so that we can know that it is out of all danger. This is a well-known Jewish motif and expression, and is used here to describe once more the firmness and complete security of salvation (Delling). Final salvation can only be described in negative terms (cf. the a- constructions in Greek, the *alpha privativum,* to say what is *not* the case, without attempting to describe it positively), for "what the eschaton brings can, from the perspective of this world, only be described by means of *via negationis* ('denial,' 'negation'; i.e. it will be completely different, it will be the exact opposite!)" (Goppelt).

Schrage comments that this figure of speech can still serve today as a good reminder that it was just as difficult at that time to give positive opinions on eschatology as it is today, and that the authors of the New Testament were also content with stating the *totaliter aliter* (completely different) nature and revealed great restraint when talking about the future. Hope, after all, does not live by images or figures. "Just as one does not worship and praise an image of God, so one does not delight in an image of hope!"

In a fine pastoral meditation Van Ruler uses the same logic. He does not try to draw a picture of this wealth of hope, but rather of the frailty and the perishability of the present dispensation, so that the splendor of hope can be emphasized by way of contrast.

d. Not only is the inheritance reserved *(tetērēmenēn)* but we too are safeguarded *(phrouroumenous)*. The two *participia* correspond. The second one evokes the image of a military fortress that is guarded by a garrison.

> The power of God, the Holy Spirit, surrounds us like a bodyguard. To live is extremely dangerous. . . . Who will not fall prey to depression, when seeing all the vanity of human life? Who will not lose oneself in sin, because of utter despair? Indeed: we are not able to keep ourselves, to keep our souls alive. Each day we will give up hope and surrender expectation. But the Holy Spirit surrounds us like a bodyguard. (Van Ruler)

Because the expression *dia pisteōs* ("through faith") is added, some expositors weaken the meaning by saying that "reserved" or "kept" should be translated reflexively rather than passively, i.e. as "we safeguard ourselves through faith" (Brox) or that they are kept or reserved "as a result of their faith" (Kelly). These opinions are, however, exceptions. Most exegetes agree that these words are still describing the certainty and the comfort of God's faithfulness. "God himself is shielding the believers" (Reicke). Peter says *dia pisteōs* ("by means of faith") and not *dia pistin* ("on account of, thanks to faith"), so there is no suggestion of human achievement that is rewarded by God with salvation. His protection includes salvation and its recipients.

Before the paranesis starts, believers are assured that those who are called are also safeguarded, says Goppelt. He does add, however, that it is not meant to be deterministic, as a kind of inevitable fate, but that those who are called are safeguarded as persons (Canons of Dort: not as sticks and blocks, but as people). According to Goppelt *dia pisteōs* therefore means "because their faith is supported." At the end of the Epistle, in 5:10, this indicative becomes an intercession, and between indicative and intercession lies the entire range of the paranesis, "because God wants the 'you' of faith" (Goppelt).

Calvin asks what benefit it will be if salvation is safely kept for us in heaven while we are tossed about as in a tempestuous sea. In the light of such possible objections, the apostle teaches that despite the dangers of the world, we are kept by faith. Due to the weakness of faith, even faith often falters, so that we would be afraid of tomorrow if the Lord did not come to our aid even in this regard. Calvin then adds that Peter does not wish to foster *securitas* ("false security"), nor to leave his readers in fear, but that he wishes to cheer them up and comfort them by teaching that they are safeguarded by the power of God. In this regard the fifth chapter of the Canons of Dort, which deals with the perseverance of the saints as a living comfort but at the same time as a dynamic attitude toward life, and Berkouwer's *Faith and Perseverance,* can be used to good effect.

e. Verse 6 presents various problems. The first two words, *en hō* ("in this"), present an infamous problem of translation. If it is masculine, it refers to the "last time" (v. 5) in which the church rejoices (Bigg, Windisch). If it is neuter, it refers to all the foregoing thoughts (this is the choice of most exegetes; many—Nauck, Schlatter, Knopf, Selwyn, Beare—even take it quite generally to mean "therefore").

The real problem, however, is the translation of *agalliasthe* ("you rejoice"). Some take it to be future tense, such as Origen and in many other ancient versions. There is even an alternative reading, "you will rejoice," but this has no support in the Greek manuscripts (also futuristic, *inter alia,* are Bigg, Windisch, Greijdanus, Moffatt, Bolkestein). In recent times Millauer has defended the futuristic meaning. He sets forth three views of the relationship between joy and suffering in 1 Peter and traces them back to three traditions. Here in verse 6, according to him, Peter refers to "joy after suffering" (and not to "joy because of suffering" or "joy despite suffering"). Bolkestein says: "The suffering the church has to bear, has a limit. . . . After the suffering comes the joy of the Kingdom. Then joy will be the part of the church." He admits that this joy of the kingdom is already experienced en route, within the present "strangerhood." "To be on one's way to joy is already joy. The church reaches for this joy in anticipation." According to him, however, this is not the primary meaning here. Goppelt also translates it as "you will rejoice," explaining that it is a technical term for joy in the end-time.

Most exegetes, however, see this joy as present (Nauck, Schelkle, Best, Kelly, Selwyn, Schneider, Knopf, Wohlenberg). In this case it can be either indicative, "in this you rejoice" (RSV and most exegetes) or imperative, "Rejoice . . ." (cf. 4:13, James 1:2; a frequent interpretation since Augustine). Most exegetes who accept the indicative admit, however, that it also implies an appeal or call. It is therefore a promise of comfort and joy that assumes believers will practice themselves in it. Bultmann is of the opinion that the choice between future and present cannot be made, since this ambiguity is bound up with the nature of faith itself. It is a present joy about the eschatological joy.

With this the problems in translating verse 6 are not yet over. The term *oligon* is also ambiguous. It can mean either that they are tested "for a little while" (RSV) to the end or that they are tested "a little bit" in comparison with the greatness of salvation in future. Goppelt combines both meanings when he says that our eschatological joy is emphasized "to make the church conscious of the *oligon*-value of the present temptation, namely that it is *small and,* in view of the future glory, *very short."*

The expression *ei deon* ("if need be," "if necessary,") has also given rise to differences of opinion. Some regard it as proof of the fact that the suffering is still only hypothetical here, in comparison with the real situation of suffering later in 1 Peter, and use this argument to defend the theory that either the letter contains a sermon on baptism or that 1 Peter must be divided into different parts. Others regard it as a typically apocalyptic description of the inevitable woes of the last days. Most exegetes see it, however, similar to 3:17, as an expression of God's will, as a typical, original Christian confession concerning God's plan of salvation.

For the distressed and suffering church, this means that they are not sold out to arbitrary whims of fate and that they need not seek martyrdom, but only the road of obedience. The suffering they do experience along the way can be seen as part of God's plan of salvation for them (2:20; 5:6). Neugenbauer says, quite rightly, that this does not mean that suffering is glorified. It is no "joy over suffering" (as with

Selwyn), but instead "joy in and through suffering." Brox remarks that 1 Peter will later offer other theological explanations for suffering, but here it is still dealing with the traditional Jewish belief that suffering comes from God and should be regarded as *peirasmoi* (trials), which can also become temptations and therefore an instrument in the hands of Satan, but which are primarily afflictions and thus an instrument in the hand of God.

Van Ruler calls the "if need be" a colossally audacious utterance. It says nothing less than that all the troubles of the ages are necessary and useful. Suffering does not befall humanity without meaning, like a sudden downpour, neither is it irrational nor the result of God's wrath; it comes instead from God's wisdom and goodness. If we can only cling to this assurance with our whole heart, this knowledge can offer end-less comfort. We are unable to calculate his wisdom and goodness, but with the heart we can continue to trust in God, even when we are af-flicted. And then we do not trust in him to remove the affliction, but we trust that he finds it necessary. This consolation, at least, removes the seeming meaninglessness from suffering.

f. Not only is this suffering not without end (v. 6) but it is also not without meaning (v. 7). The purpose of our trials and suffering is to de-termine the genuineness of faith. The image of the gold that is tested by fire includes both the purpose and the necessity of such tests (Goppelt). All secondary motifs should be purged, so that naive faith can be changed into clear and steadfast faith. Schrage, however, contrary to most commentaries and meditations, says that the image only contains the idea of the proof of pure faith and not that of purging and cleansing as well. "The author does not want to say that pure faith develops step by step in the fire, but merely that it becomes clear in the fire what is faith and what not." Seen in this way, the tests play a sifting role.

In meditative fashion Van Ruler, however, goes further:

> This image includes, it seems to me, two ideas. Firstly, the practice and secondly, the purification of faith. Faith always has to do with a certain contradiction. We often believe the opposite of what we see. And all of the time we see the opposite of what we believe. Things seem so far different from what God has said. . . . Well, now: *that* is the most essential element of temptation! The temptation is for us to give up our faith and to accept reality for what it seems to be. . . . In the troubles of life, this temptation is at its strongest. Then the question is whether we shall be able to cling to faith, in everything, through every-

thing and in spite of everything. And *then* it becomes a question of practice and training.

Gymnasts gather weekly in their gymnasiums to train. The full swing on the horizontal bar needs practice. It takes lots of practice and effort over periods of time to do it. In the same way, the hardships of life form the gymnastic exercises of faith. This sport of living strengthens the muscles of faith. But, in addition to such practice, the testing of faith also includes an element of purification. . . . Faith is always mixed with impure ingredients. We never put our trust completely in God and his promises. We always trust a little bit in ourselves and in the visible realities as well. That leads to a divided heart. Therefore we must pass through fire now and then. So that our faith can be purged. . . . Then it becomes faith and faith only.

g. It is important to realize that these verses mention a dual hardship. In the Greek both constructions run parallel: *arti . . . lupēthentes* ("though you may have to suffer," v. 6) and *arti . . . mē horōntes* ("though you do not now see him," v. 8). The "in this you rejoice" (vv. 6 and 8) apply in both cases. The first difficulty is the painful experiences they suffer, especially due to the animosity of the community in which they find themselves, experiences such as insults, discrimination, and persecution. The second difficulty is the admission that neither Christ nor salvation is visible. The nature of faith is such that our spiritual experience remains ambivalent and that salvation is never "on hand," never tangible nor demonstrable. Doubt is therefore always possible. Because the church does not live by Christ's teaching alone, but by fellowship with him, the essence of their anxiety is that they have not seen him and that they do not see him now (Goppelt). In this ability to see what the eye of flesh cannot see, to know the invisible, and to judge and understand everything in a different way lies, of course, the power of Christian faith.

It is this power that Luther so often praised, contrasting it with reason, the blind harlot of seduction. Calvin wrote similarly: "This is the nature of faith, that it is content with what our eyes do not see. . . . Faith does indeed also have eyes, but eyes which are such that they can penetrate the invisible kingdom of God and are content with the mirror of the Word." At the same time, however, it is the weak point of faith, the Achilles heel, the locale of temptation and doubt. Bolkestein titles his commentary *The Church Between the Times,* referring to this situation in which believers are en route as strangers, with many temptations and without seeing anything. Brox says quite rightly that Peter is here not speaking only in passing of *not seeing and still believing,* but that it is the central problem of the entire letter.

h. It is widely believed that "the salvation of your souls" (v. 9) is not to be understood in a Greek-Platonic way, but should be seen in the Old Testament sense, as indicating the whole person, the human being. In most of the six times that this term is used in 1 Peter, this is the most probable meaning. It was understood as the "salvation of souls" in church history, and in this process it received shades of meaning that differed quite substantially from those of the biblical worldview.

i. Although verses 10-12 (13) belong to verses 3-9 by structure, they form a slightly new unit thematically. Some exegetes, like Brox, treat this unit separately. The commentaries can be consulted for these questions.

4. Looking back, it can be said that in verses 3-12 Peter is proclaiming promises, "kerygmatic indicatives" (Goppelt). God is praised in a eulogy for the salvation ("hope") he gave to the church through the resurrection and the new birth (v. 3), especially because this hope ("inheritance") is being kept intact, while the believers are also safeguarded (vv. 4 and 5). This steadfast hope is much greater than all the temptations caused by animosity or all the suffering and doubt due to their not seeing what the church is experiencing now (vv. 6-9). These verses are still formulated as indicatives, as a song of praise, though with an implicit appeal that is expanded later in the letter, and it is meant to comfort and to strengthen. This steadfast hope is the fulfillment of the promises of the Old Testament, so that the church can be made even more aware of their privileged position (vv. 10-12). Van Ruler speaks about the "unbelievably great and strong self-awareness of original Christianity" that was surely rather irritating for the onlookers, because this tiny, persecuted group of strangers regarded themselves as being the bearers of God's salvation! Luther also writes that these distressed people may look *coram mundo* (before the world) like "lauter Bettler und Narren" (nothing more than beggars and clowns), but in judging themselves they see themselves as those who have received a steadfast and a secure salvation, the salvation for which the world has waited and hoped for so many centuries!

In the light of all this, it will make good sense if the fundamental role played in this argument by Christ's resurrection can be explained in Easter preaching. His resurrection leads to both the new birth and the living hope. Mention can also be made of the fact that this life that they have received through his resurrection is strong enough to conquer the dual form of temptation.

II. Hermeneutical

1. The preacher who wants to take a bit of trouble can profitably read Moltmann's *Theology of Hope,* especially the third chapter, which deals with the resurrection and future of Jesus Christ. The links between resurrection, hope, and new life are also dealt with in 1 Peter 1:3-12. The relationship between eschatology and ethics is very well treated.

2. It is also interesting that 1 Peter 1:3 was Bonhoeffer's text on Sunday, 8 April, 1945, when he preached his last prison sermon, on the day before his execution.

From the "Editor's Foreword" in *Letters and Papers from Prison* comes a final perspective, as told by Payne Best, an English officer and fellow prisoner.

> He always seemed to me to diffuse an atmosphere of happiness, of joy in every smallest event in life, and of deep gratitude for the mere fact that he was alive. . . . He was one of the very few men that I have ever met for whom his God was real and close to him. . . . The following day, Sunday, April 8th, 1945, Pastor Bonhoeffer held a little service [1 Peter 1:3 and Isa. 53:5] and spoke to us in a manner which reached the hearts of all, finding just the right words to express the spirit of our imprisonment and the thoughts and resolutions which it had brought. He had hardly finished his prayer when the door opened and two evil-looking men in civilian clothes came in and said: "Prisoner Bonhoeffer, get ready to come with us." Those words, "Come with us"—for all prisoners they had come to mean one thing only, the scaffold. We bade him goodbye. He drew me aside. "This is the end," he said. *"For me the beginning of life."* . . . Next day, at Flossenbürg, he was hanged.

This is indeed a moving illustration of many motifs from this pericope: deep joy in life with all its trivialities (so very striking in Bonhoeffer's letters from prison), the reality of God despite being unable to see him, the comfort gained from the gospel, the courage amid suffering, the care for fellow believers, the animosity of the world, the hope in the face of death.

3. It may be useful to have a brief look at a few good sermons.

a. Overduin titles his message, "How Far Does Our Horizon Reach?" He points out that humanity, unlike animals that know no future, is always living between hope and fear. The fact that we are always striving toward the future is our glory and our sorrow. Where there is life, there is hope. And, conversely, hope brings new life again. When all hope is gone, life comes to a standstill. Humanity is simultaneously part of nature and of history, of the impersonal laws of "it must" (nature) and of "I will, I can, I know, I do" (history), of fate and deed, and therefore of both fear and hope. The deed is often restricted by fate. Fate, however, is also restricted by the deed. Hope is sometimes swallowed up by fear, and then fear is again dispelled by hope. Because we can do much, we hope. Because we cannot do everything, we fear.

This restricted and tempted hope is common to all humanity. The deep-seated difference between this and Christian hope, celebrated Sunday and on Resurrection-day morning, is that the horizon of the hope of common humanity is restricted by death. He then expands on the question of who guarantees that this Christian hope is no illusion or wishful thinking, but "grounded expectation" and "reality."

He ends with a moving story from World War II. Several pastors had to conduct a funeral for 250 people who had been killed during a devastating bombardment. They hardly had the courage to ask the mourning crowd to sing, so they asked some of the family close by whether it would be appropriate to sing. One family member suggested they sing Psalm 89:1. They all sang as never before, with tears in their eyes and with trembling legs, but with an unknown emotion in their hearts. He quotes the words of this moving hymn:

> My song for ever shall record
>   The tender mercies of the Lord;
> Thy faithfulness will I proclaim,
>   And every age shall know thy Name.
>
> I sing of mercies that endure,
>   For ever builded firm and sure,
> Of faithfulness that never dies,
>   Established changeless in the skies.

This, says Overduin, is reality.

b. Iwand starts off his sermon by saying that Christ was not raised "for his own sake," but "for us." So his resurrection day is our birthday! The person who does not realize how deeply this reality has crept into our lives and changed us, does not understand anything of God's mercy. The temptation is great to regard the visible world as the only real and lasting reality. This kind of thinking was, however, buried at Easter and we must not return to it!

In early Christianity the expression *in aeternum renati* ("born again for all eternity") was a well-known epitaph on graves. Iwand says we too are travelers on our way to "the last things," to "the ultimate." We are people who can no longer be satisfied by the penultimate. Faith therefore brings something into our lives that has not been there previously; there is a definite "now" and a definite "then." The certainty of the future relativizes the present. Christians live by a steadfast, unshakeable expectation and therefore do not regard reality as it appears to be, but reckon with reality in Jesus Christ. In this way the resurrection brings to all of life a perspective that is called "hope" in 1 Peter.

In a second section he differentiates between this hope *(spes)* and an overeager confidence *(praesumptio)*. That which is yet to come, the entire future salvation, is concealed in hope. He reminds readers to be cautious of all images and descriptions of this future inheritance. He quotes Luther, who said that hope sweeps us on into an unknown world, in the world filled with unknown things, in the inner darkness, where one does not know what one hopes and, yet, knows what one does *not* hope. In this way, says Iwand, we are totally and altogether dependent on God. In him we have everything, even if we have nothing. Hope itself is the fortress into which we flee, the last post, the unconquerable. A Christian without hope, just like dogmatics and ethics void of hope, is an "impossibility"!

As the life of Christians is determined by what is coming and not by what has gone by, he warns against those who hold on to traditions and oppose church reformation, because we must not lose sight of the flames of fire during our sojourn in the wilderness and start longing for the flesh pots of Egypt.

In a final section he discusses how suffering and temptation keep hope true hope and safeguard it against all premature and presumptuous anticipation. Not in spite of suffering, but because of suffering our hope grows and we are increasingly liberated from the inclination to hold on to that which we love by nature. It is true of this hope that we rejoice in it with tears! Only the *renati in aeternum* can understand this. Among them there will be great rejoicing amid the most severe temptations and loneliness. He points out that it was not only true of the time that 1 Peter was written, but is still true today, quoting from a prison letter in which the writer says they are keeping well and that singing is the only thing lacking—because it is forbidden! The only possibility left to them is to raise a powerful *Deo gloria,* not on their lips, but in their souls!

c. Moltmann starts by saying that the resurrection of Jesus is controversial, because many people do not know what to think about it. First Peter, however, says that we should not start with "we and the resurrection," but with "God and the resurrection." The question is not what we can do with the resurrection, but what God wants to do with us and the world through the resurrection!

He points out the dangers that our "strangerhood" brings with it, especially that it lets people stagger between self-assertion on the one hand and adaptation or compromise on the other. This letter wants to teach us, however, to understand our "alienage" as the election of God and to regard our feeling of homelessness as small in comparison with the hope we have received through the resurrection of Christ.

He explains that in the New Testament faith is identical with resurrection hope. Every Sunday morning brings memories and therefore expectation. Unfortunately, in the course of history people often had eyes for only the cross and by so doing replaced hope with memory, the future with the past, and the history still to come with a timeless eternity that is always the same. When hope was lost, however, faith and with it the meaning of the resurrection changed. The true hope of the resurrection was exchanged for an expectation of "life after death" alone.

He is of the opinion that, contrary to these popular developments, the New Testament wishes to teach us that God's mercy is the act of breaking the iron ring of history and in so doing giving us hope, which breaks open all the limitations and restrictions of the possible, until the finality of death itself is broken down. In the resurrection God confronts the hardest facts of life and death. Christian hope is therefore abused if it becomes only the repository for all our unfulfilled wishes.

True Christian hope is based on Christ and his future. It becomes a living hope when it takes account in the present time of the power and the future of Christ. The resurrection is therefore not only comfort for the future, but also includes the protest of God against death and all distress and humiliation his people have to suffer in the present world, seemingly lost under sin and death.

In this sense, Christian hope does not make us patient, but impatient, not relaxed, but "unrelaxed." The deepest sin is hopelessness!

Chrysostom has already said that it is not so much our sin but our despair that lands us in disaster! We become guilty not only because of the evil we commit but much more by the good that we do not do. It is not our misdeeds that accuse us, but our omissions. They accuse us of lacking hope. Hopelessness comes in two forms, on the one hand as audacity, which cannot or does not want to wait, but wants to reach for the future prematurely, and on the other hand in the form of despair. Both forms are resistance against "the suffering of hope." Both want fulfillment immediately or nothing at all. Moltmann is of the opinion that a "laughing" form of despair is reaching alarming proportions in the modern world. Many secularized people live without hope and thus without meaning, but they do not seem to care.

Christian hope, however, sees what is hidden and invisible and therefore calls the poor and miserable blessed. This means that patience is required to be able to hope. It is not, however, the patience of resignation or surrender but the patience of hope. It grants time to the other person and gives him or her freedom. It always takes account of the possibilities in others, including those that are not as yet present but which God can cause to grow.

In this way hope gives one's fellow creatures a future. Hope does not pressure the other person with all kinds of claims of how they should be. Hope creates possibilities for others to change themselves, gives them "a chance," and thereby liberates them. It negates both a spirit of blind acceptance and a spirit of revolution. "The resurrection of Christ is the ground for the rebellion of patience and of confidence in an impatient and desperate world." He ends by saying that temptation teaches us to understand the Easter words of promise.

III. Homiletical

It should now be relatively easy to prepare two sermons that follow the argument of this pericope.

In the first one, the tremendous implications of the resurrection can be discussed. Mention can be made of the act of God's mercy, the objective and steadfast nature of the new birth, the living hope, and the fact that both the inheritance and the recipients are safeguarded and protected. This sermon can primarily be a call to be joyful and thankful.

In a second sermon, which expands on the first, it can then be made clear that this living hope is continuously being attacked or put to the test from two sides, both by suffering and by the fact that we do not "see" at the moment. These trials, however, have their limits and they do have meaning, for the joy of hope is kept intact in this way, and is also purified. Much relevant and useful material can be taken from the details given in the first two sections.

D. J. SMIT

Fourth Sunday After Easter:
John 11:25-26

Bibliography

Commentaries

Barrett, C. K. *St. John*. Philadelphia: Westminster, 1978.

Brown, R. E. *The Gospel according to John*. The Anchor Bible. Vol. 29A. Garden City: Doubleday, 1970.

Calvin, J. *Commentary on the Gospel according to John*. Vol. 2. Grand Rapids: Eerdmans, 1956.

Dodd, C. H. *The Interpretation of the Fourth Gospel*. Cambridge: Cambridge University Press, 1953.

Hendriksen, W. *Exposition of the Gospel according to John*. Vol. 2. Grand Rapids: Baker, 1954.

Morris, L. *The Gospel according to John*. The New International Commentary on the New Testament. Grand Rapids: Eerdmans, 1971.

Homiletical

Berkouwer, G. C. *Het Licht der Wereld: Het Evangelie van Johannes*. Kampen: Kok, 1960.

Lüthi, W. *St. John's Gospel*. Richmond: Knox, 1960.

Additional

Coenen, L. "Resurrection" in *New International Dictionary of New Testament Theology*. Vol. 3, 259-79. Edited by Colin Brown. Grand Rapids: Zondervan, 1978.

Guthrie, D. *New Testament Theology*, 375-89, 641-44. Downers Grove: InterVarsity, 1981.

Ladd, G. E. *A Theology of the New Testament*, 254-69, 298-308, 315-27. Grand Rapids: Eerdmans, 1974.

Smalley, S. S. *John: Evangelist and Interpreter,* 178-84. Exeter: Paternoster, 1978.

I. Exegetical

1. John 11 provides us with a broad perspective in understanding death and life against the background of Jesus' life, death, and resurrection. To preach from this chapter, and to apply it to the present, one must understand how the Son of God saw his own resurrection. In Jesus, the present time has become the time of salvation and therefore meaningful to every believer, though everyone must still die physically. One could say that the resurrection narrative of Lazarus is John's way of saying what Paul meant in 1 Corinthians 15:14 when he said, "If Christ has not been raised, then our preaching is in vain and your faith is in vain." John 11 forms an explanation-in-action of John 1:4, "In him was life, and the life was the light of men." As the culmination in the revelation of his glory, it can also be called a prelude to the resurrection of Jesus.

2. John 11 has a special place in the overall structure of the Gospel of John. It describes the seventh or last miracle in the first twelve chapters, which comprise a unit. The resurrection of Lazarus also became a direct cause of the death of Jesus. As a result of his resurrection the Jewish Council gathered (vv. 46-53), and at this meeting they decided to arrest Jesus (v. 57). The resurrection of Lazarus further dramatizes the Johannine theme that Jesus is the life (vv. 11-25), just as the healing of the blind man dramatizes the theme that Jesus is the light (8:12). It is noteworthy that, according to the prologue of this Gospel (1:1-18), especially these two themes, light and life, portray the relationship between the Word who became flesh and humankind. It is also definitely not by chance that when Jesus performed this supreme sign showing that he had power over life and death (11:43), the decision followed that he had to pay for this with his life (11:53).

John 11:1-57 can be seen as a single unit (though vv. 55-57 are sometimes excluded). The antagonism of the Jews (vv. 45-57) accentuates the miracle, especially when the christology of the Gospel as a whole is taken into account. It is possible that early readers of the Gospel of John also experienced antagonism or even hostility from Jews because of the break between church and synagogue. The purpose of this story is therefore to strengthen the faith of the Christian community, which had its roots in Judaism but were now living in a new milieu. To achieve this aim, the Gospel of John portrays Jesus as the Christ, the Son of God, and also attempts to Christianize certain Jewish doctrines and traditions. Within this overall purpose, the function of John 11 becomes clear. Jesus showed his power over life and death and in this way confirmed his identity as Son of God, clothed in all his glory.

In the course of John's story of Jesus one must, of course, pay attention throughout to the question of Jesus' identity. The acceptance by faith or the rejection by unbelief of his identity—such an important theme in the Gospel—is often called "the Johannine process of identification." Thus readers of John's Gospel are continuously kept involved as well. Ultimately it is their own acceptance or rejection of his identity that is at stake.

In chapters 7, 8, and 9 the skeptical, limited insight of the Jewish leaders is exposed. The Jewish leaders, who are blind, cannot lead the sheep (10:1ff.), whereas Jesus has just recently healed the blindness of one of his sheep (9:1-12). Jesus explains the significance of his oneness with the Father (10:30) and the Jews accuse him of blasphemy (10:33) and try to arrest him. One would now expect Jesus to stay far from Jerusalem and its surroundings for the sake of safety. Yet he returns and raises Lazarus as a culmination of his public ministry.

3. In the story line of chapter 11, one can identify various sections. The construction is not only of formal importance but also contributes to understanding the contents of the different sections. The story line can be summarized as follows:

Section	Verses	Story Line	Subject Matter
1	1-10	Introduction	Mention of Jewish antagonism
2	11-16	Problem unfolded	Lazarus is dead
3-4	17-19	Information	Jews come to console
5	20-27	Discussion	Interpretation of events
6	28-37	Information	Jews console; conversation with Mary
7	38-44	Problem solved	Resurrection of Lazarus
8-9	45-57	Conclusion	Jewish antagonism goes into action

One can see a clear pattern in the response and conduct of Jesus. First, he learns that Lazarus is ill (v. 3). Then follows his apparently negative reaction (vv. 4, 6). And yet he goes to Lazarus as soon as he has explained the significance of present events.

The exegetical focus is found in verses 25 and 27, but the context of the rest of the chapter should not be forgotten. For a complete exegesis, commentaries can be considered. I mention briefly only the following:

a. One should not relate the events of John 11 to the parable of Lazarus and the rich man (Luke 16:19-31). The expression "whom you love" in verse 3 has caused exegetes and therefore also preachers to think that Lazarus may have been the anonymous disciple whom Jesus loved very much (cf. 13:23; 19:26; and 21:7, 20). This must be rejected as well.

b. The repetition of the contents of verse 4 in verse 40 is very important. The reason for the raising of Lazarus, given in verse 4, is that "the Son of God may be glorified by means of it." Jesus thus interprets the event still to come in the light of his own calling and task. God's power to give life will be realized by Jesus. This happens according to the typical Old Testament revelation of the glory of God, i.e. through his powerful deeds enacted in a blaze of visibility. The resurrection of Lazarus as visible manifestation of God's glory is also the manifest announcement of the identity of Jesus as glorified Son of God. This is indeed what the Lazarus story is all about. Accordingly, this event is also a prophetic sign of the resurrection of Jesus himself.

c. The figurative language in verses 9-10 (referring to the "hours in the day") must, in the first place, be taken as a response to the disciples' question in verse 8. Jesus' time for ministry is limited, and he must therefore use it to do the work of his Father, namely to conquer the darkness. Death, which confronts Jesus now, is a visible part of this power of darkness. The power of God, however, which will be demonstrated in the raising of Lazarus, will be proved to be much greater.

d. In the mind of Thomas, misunderstanding is mixed with fear. In verse 16 he tells the other disciples that they must go "that we may die with him." He does not understand the words of Jesus (v. 15) and is therefore afraid. He also does not understand the true identity of Jesus. He only knows that their return to Judea will endanger their lives, because of the antagonism of the Jews. And he takes the reality and the finality of death very seriously. Faith in Jesus, on account of the raising of Lazarus, will, paradoxically, open the door to life instead of death. And eventually the resurrection of Jesus himself, to which the raising of Lazarus points, will help Thomas see the power of life over death when he finally recognizes Jesus' true identity as "Lord" and "God."

e. The finality of Lazarus's death ("already . . . four days," cf. vv. 17 and 39) serves to underscore the events that follow. The finality of life in Jesus is even more certain.

f. Jesus' conversation with Martha (vv. 20-27) is the key to the understanding of John 11. The sisters have as yet only expressed the general expectation they had of Jesus (vv. 22 and 32). He was, after all, the healer and could therefore have prevented their brother's death. These are words of faith and trust in the face of sorrow, and are not meant as criticism that he had not come earlier (v. 22). Martha acknowledges that Jesus has access to God. This was an established Jewish belief: God will not listen to a sinner but he will listen to someone who obeys his will (cf. 9:31). In verse 22 the narrator of the resurrection narrative is already suggesting a probable miracle, without it being consciously in the mind of Martha. This helps to build tension in this very dramatic narrative. The reader must look beyond Martha, who focuses more on her trust in Jesus than on procuring a miracle. She acknowledges that he is a Mediator from God (v. 22), but it does not really dawn on her that he himself is the life (v. 25) and that Lazarus can live again.

Martha misunderstands Jesus' answer in verse 23. She knows about the resurrection of the dead on the last day. According to late Jewish expectations (cf. Dan. 12:2) resurrection is a future gift of the end time. Jesus, however, clearly states that it has already become a reality that is experienced in the present (vv. 25-26). Martha's misunderstanding underscores the true meaning of verses 25-26. Instead of focusing merely on a future expectation, John 11 points to the person of Jesus himself. He himself is life and even now he gives life.

g. The christological meaning of John 11 is explained in verses 25-26, even before the resurrection happens. This is typical of John (cf., e.g., the farewell discourses in chapters 13-17, which serve as interpretation of the suffering, death, and resurrection of Jesus). The gist of verses 25-26 can be summarized as follows: Whoever believes in Jesus will live spiritually even though he or she may die physically (v. 25), and the believer who is spiritually alive will never again die spiritually (v. 26). Especially two things are underscored, "resurrection" and "life."

When Jesus says he is the resurrection, it is an explanation to Martha that what she expects on the last day is already a reality in the present (Schnackenburg). The future has already become the present in Jesus Christ. He is the resurrection in the sense that everybody who believes in him will live on spiritually, even though the body has died. To live spiritually is a gift from above, the gift of the Holy Spirit. If people accept the Son of God already in this life through faith, they will be in a constant relationship with Jesus, so that they already possess eternal life here and now. They have already passed from death to life and do not come into judgment (cf. 5:24).

The resurrection of Lazarus is a provisional demonstration or symbol of this, though the perfect embodiment will only be seen in the death and resurrection of Jesus himself. The concept of "life" places the raising of Lazarus in a christological perspective (cf. 6:35, 48, 51; 8:12; 14:6). Resurrection and life give expression to the functional relationship of Jesus to the believer. He is the revelation of the Father on behalf of humankind, *for* humankind *(pro nobis)*. The difference between ordinary, earthly life and eternal life, according to these verses, is to be found in faith in Jesus Christ. Through faith physical death comes to nothing and the believer's earthly life finds new meaning, a new dimension in Jesus Christ.

The powerful "I am" (v. 25) is of primary importance. It is the typically Johannine way of proclaiming the identity of Jesus as the One, sent by the Father, who also acts as the Revealer. Only through Jesus is life possible. Not only does he proclaim it, but he also gives indestructible life. He is the One to whom is given the power to give life. This finds ultimate expression in the resurrection of the dead. Just as striking as the "I am" at the start of the two verses is the question put by Jesus at the end: "Do you believe this?" The importance of faith does not only lie in its power of faith as such, but especially in the fact that it brings communion with Jesus, the giver of life, and through this communion with Jesus, the believer receives eternal life.

h. Jesus was truly moved as indicated by the Greek expressions in verse 33. The first expression *(enebrimēsato tō pneumati)* literally means that inwardly he burned with grief. His spirit was deeply moved. Another possible meaning for the expression is that he was angry, possibly because Mary and the Jews showed such lack of faith (Bultmann). The first meaning is to be preferred. The deep grief of Jesus goes further than mere sympathy at the death of Lazarus. One can again detect a moment of finality here. Jesus is confronted by death as the manifestation of the power of evil, knowing that soon he will have to make the greatest sacrifice, his own life, precisely so that the power of light can be victorious over evil.

i. The prayer of Jesus in verses 41-42 places the events in a theocentric perspective. Jesus does not pray for results based on who he is, but for a revelation of his true identity—that he and the Father are one and that the Father had sent him.

The poweful cry *(ekraugasen)* with which Jesus calls Lazarus in verse 43 is probably a symbolic echo of the cry with which Jesus, as the One sent by the Father, calls everybody to life, to believe in him. In chapters 18-19 the same word is used four times to describe the cry demanding that Jesus be crucified. What a contrast!

j. The application of John 11:25-26 is described in verses 45-57. Some believe and others antagonistically reject Jesus. Even the prophecy of Caiaphas (v. 51) unwittingly puts the proclamation of John 11 into a christological perspective.

II. Hermeneutical

The kerygmatic emphasis in John 11:25-26 is christological as well as eschatological. In Jesus Christ the future has become present. In him life has already started. His resurrection is the symbol of it. In preaching one should keep in mind that to John's way of thinking the coming of the Holy Spirit is already the eschatological fulfillment of the resurrection.

The oldest and most striking comment on the miracle of John 11 is made in John 5:20-21 (cf. also 5:25, 28). This also answers the question of the early church about believers who die before the second coming of the Lord (cf. Rev. 6:10; John 21:21-23). Throughout the ages Christians have never regarded the events of John 11 as simply the historical reason why Jesus had to be crucified. The resurrection of Lazarus was rather seen as a prophetic sign of the resurrection of Jesus. And his resurrection is the guarantee both of eternal life and of the day of judgment. When John wrote the story of Lazarus (after the resurrection of Jesus), he brought to the early church and the church of all ages a message of expectation and hope. The resurrection of Lazarus must always remind believers that they already possess life. Through faith the believers live in Jesus Christ!

John 11:25-26 can be used for a sermon only when the whole structure of the story is taken into account. Exemplary preaching focusing, for example, on the roles of Lazarus or his two sisters is dangerous. Berkouwer makes too much of "the Lord weeping." W. Lüthi places the emphasis beautifully on the appeal for faith to involve the reader existentially. This appeal for faith must, however, be built on a christological grounding.

III. Homiletical

1. The central figure is Jesus and, as a comment on the resurrection of Lazarus, the main thrust of Jesus' words in verses 25-26 is "life."

2. In the sermon, attention must be paid to the miracles done by Jesus as manifestations of his glory (cf. Brown), in order to place it within christological perspective. The revelation of the Son of God as the One sent by the Father is raised by the "I am" pronouncement (cf. Brown). The resurrection of Jesus certainly forms the climax of all theological exclamation marks (cf. Guthrie, NIDNTT 3, 259-79).

3. Based on the resurrection of Jesus, life is qualified by the Gospel of John as eternal life. John does not give a secret cure against mortality, but only testifies to Jesus, the giver of life. Sometimes John leaves out the qualification "eternal" when referring to this life because what he says is already qualified by the broader context of his christology. Eternal life belongs to the coming age, which has already dawned in Jesus Christ as the Messiah. This is why life is possible. Heaven on earth! For John "life" is the opposite of being doomed (cf. 3:16; 10:10). It also stands opposed to the wrath of God (3:36), to the judgment of God (5:24), and death (5:25). Life goes with abundance (10:10) because Jesus is the bread of life (6:35, 48, 51). Yes, the objective of the Gospel of John is defined as life through faith in Jesus Christ (20:31; cf. 3:16; 6:40). In proclaiming this passage one must also pay attention to "life" as deliverance from the judgment of God (3:36; 5:24), as knowledge of God (17:3), as fellowship with the Father and the Son (6:56-57; 1 John 2:24-25), as having love for one another (13:34; cf. 1 John 3:14-15), and as immortality (11:25-26; cf. 8:51-52).

4. In the closing appeal of the sermon one can especially stress the subjective condition for receiving this life, namely faith. How strikingly it is put at the end of verse 26. "Do you believe this?" John uses the verb *believe* instead of the term *faith*. He wants to lay the emphasis on believing as a dynamic, continuous act. Believing is to hear the Word

of Christ (5:24), to listen to his voice (5:25), to drink of the living water (4:14; 7:37), to eat of the bread of life (6:50, 51, 58), to come to him (5:40). In a sermon one must also stress the fact that to believe is not merely a human act. According to John, whoever believes has been given to Christ by the Father (6:37-39, 44; 10:29; 17:2).

5. Finally, love for one another is the visible sign of possessing life (13:35). Believers must therefore be visibly alive, especially now! The test of enduring life is the active manifestation of love (cf. 1 John 3:16).

J. A. DU RAND

Ascension: John 14:1-14

Bibliography

Commentaries

Barrett, C. K. *St. John*. Philadelphia. Westminster, 1978.

Brown, R. E. *The Gospel according to John*. The Anchor Bible. Vol. 29A. Garden City: Doubleday, 1970.

Calvin, J. *Commentary on the Gospel according to John*. Vol. 2. Grand Rapids: Eerdmans, 1956.

Dodd, C. H. *The Interpretation of the Fourth Gospel*. Cambridge: Cambridge University Press, 1953.

Hendriksen, W. *Exposition of the Gospel according to John*. Vol. 2. Grand Rapids: Baker, 1954.

Morris, L. *The Gospel according to John*. The New International Commentary on the New Testament. Grand Rapids: Eerdmans, 1971.

Schnackenburg, R. *The Gospel according to St. John*. Vol. 2. New York: Seabury, 1980.

Homiletical

Berkouwer, G. C. *Het Licht der Wereld: Het Evangelie van Johannes*. Kampen: Kok, 1960.

Van Gennep, F. O. *Postille 1966–1967* (No. 18), 83-92. The Hague: Boekencentrum, 1966.

I. Exegetical

1. The larger context of these verses is clear. John 14 is the beginning of Jesus' well-known farewell discourse (John 14–17). The composition of these chapters is of course heavily disputed.

Brown regards John 13:13-38 as an introduction announcing the theme of Jesus' departure. What follows is, according to him, a discourse about the problems raised by this departure and its implications. Much has been written about the sequence of these four chapters. This is because 14:30-31 leave the impression that chapter 14 contains the last words Jesus addressed to his disciples in the upper room. Various possible solutions have been offered to the problem of the continuation of the discourse in chapters 15-17, *inter alia* a rearrangement of the sequence of the chapters. Barrett may be consulted for a detailed discussion.

2. As regards the internal structure of John 14, the unit 1-14 is here chosen as a text for Ascension Day, though the whole chapter may be so used. Several aspects touched on in the beginning in fact reappear at the end. The central theme, Jesus is going away but will come again, is woven into the whole chapter.

There does, however, seem to be a point of demarcation between verses 14 and 15, so that 15-24 may be regarded as a new unit, one more specifically concerned with the coming of the Holy Spirit. Of course these two units are closely connected in that the Holy Spirit is sent by Jesus after his departure (cf. Brown and the beautiful Pentecost sketch on verses 15-23 by Bonhoeffer in *Herr, tue meine Lippe auf,* vol. 1, 184-89).

3. A complete verse-by-verse exegesis can be found in the various commentaries. A few relevant points are, however, discussed briefly:

a. The chapter starts with the immediate reassurance by Jesus: "Let not your hearts be troubled." *Tarassō* indicates deep distress. The same term is used to describe Jesus' distress at Lazarus' death (11:33) and his agony when announcing his own betrayal by Judas (13:21).

It is easy to understand that the disciples were deeply distressed at this stage. It was just after Jesus' announcement that he was going away. For them this parting was utterly inconceivable and very frightening. After all, they had relinquished everything to follow Jesus. What would become of them now? One can therefore understand Peter's reaction in 13:36ff.—he is willing to do anything as long as he is not separated from Jesus. Jesus' response, namely that Peter would deny him, as well as their bewilderment about Judas's betrayal, did not lessen their distress.

b. The call, "Believe in God, believe also in me," can be translated in various ways, depending upon whether the verb is treated as an indicative or as an imperative. Most exegetes, it would seem, prefer two imperatives. (Barrett distinguishes four possible translations!)

That faith in God and faith in Jesus are the same may seem obvious to present-day Christians. Yet, under these circumstances, Jesus' call to the disciples to believe in him "also" was not at all superfluous. There were many factors then, and later during the unexpected events that were to follow, that could cause their faith, especially in Jesus, to waver.

c. Jesus says that the purpose of his departure is the preparation of a place in heaven for his followers. "Father's house" undoubtedly refers to heaven. The image of "many rooms" indicates a permanent abode rather than a temporary stopping-place in this life. It does not refer to different degrees of perfection (salvation/blessedness) as the expression is interpreted by some scholars (cf. Brown, Barrett). The term "many" simply means that there is enough room for everyone.

d. Jesus' departure refers not only to his imminent death but also to his ascension, his return to the Father. The preparation of a place for them is not merely the consequence of his death and resurrection but also of his ascension. The question of what he is referring to when he says that he will come again (v. 3) is far more difficult to answer. It may refer to his resurrection, or to his return in the form of the Holy Spirit, or to his second coming in glory. Most exegetes prefer the last interpretation, though John does not often refer to this eschatological return of Jesus. In Jesus' resurrection and the coming of the Holy Spirit there is no mention of Jesus taking the disciples with him. Still, it should be made clear that the second coming by no means exhausts John's reference.

The expression may have "a surplus of meaning." After all, Jesus' communion with his followers is not merely deferred to the last day or even to the hour of the death of the disciples. Accordingly, Schnackenburg is of the opinion that the phrase "I will take you to myself" refers to a process already commencing at the resurrection and also experienced in our communion with Jesus, but that will only be fulfilled after death or with the second (eschatological) coming.

In this respect it is very necessary to take into account John's practice of not distinguishing sharply between the different phases of salvation but rather of combining these motifs. This simply means that for the disciples the comfort of his words was that his departure presupposed a new form of fellowship with him and was not a permanent separation. Paradoxically, only his departure could make this fellowship possible. What seemed like a catastrophe was a blessing in disguise. His departure thus became a promise.

e. Jesus' self-revelation in verse 6 is the heart of this pericope. Thomas's question gives rise to an opportunity to explain in more detail the way to the new experience of fellowship.

As with all the other "I am" statements in the Gospel of John, this one is a self-revelation. Jesus did not show the way to the Father only through his words and the life he led, but also through his death and resurrection. Thus he himself became the way for the lost sinner, the One through whom humanity now reaches God and the Father's house. Much has been written about the relationship between the three predicates, "way," "truth," and "life." Nevertheless, the context indicates that the accent is on Jesus as the *way* to the Father and that the concepts of "truth" and "life" serve to justify and to explain this statement. Since he is the truth (i.e. the revelation of the Father himself), he is the only way to the Father and only those who are on this way (i.e. those who believe in him), share in the eternal life in the Father's house. Thus Thomas's question is answered by a powerful self-revelation of Jesus. "Jesus confronts Thomas with the weight of his real identity" (Strathman).

f. The next few verses flow out of this central statement. Since Jesus is the way to the Father, it follows that if we know him, we know the Father also (v. 7, "know" in the sense of personal communion), and if we have seen Jesus, then we have seen the Father also (v. 8). He is the way because he and the Father are one (vv. 10-11). What is more, implicit in this pronouncement is the absolute claim of the Christian faith and, arising from that, the necessity of mission (v. 12).

The logic is clear. Jesus is the way for the very reason that he is going away. Thus, his ascension is at the same time good news (he is the way because he has completed his work of salvation!), an urgent call (Believe in me!), and a command (Proclaim the way!).

g. It is not clear what Philip has in mind with his question. And yet his question is typical of the desire of religious people to be able to see God. What Philip does not realize is that his wish has already been fulfilled! Jesus is the self-revelation of the Father himself and for a long time now they have seen God, heard him, experienced him! Jesus has often pointed out this identity between himself and the Father. The disciples have just not understood this! Now, however, it becomes extremely important. After all, this reference to the oneness between Jesus and the Father is no metaphysical speculation, but it throws light on his mission. All that he has been and said, and all that he was about to undergo—and that *they* were about to undergo!—only become meaningful in view of the fact that he himself is the way to the goal. Hence Jesus calls for faith in himself.

Faith is of central importance not only in these verses but in the pericope as a whole (and of course in the whole of John's gospel). The comfort the disciples now need and the comfort that is indeed offered by Jesus' departure is only received through faith in him. A proper understanding of Ascension means that one believes in Jesus in such a way that it not only brings comfort and peace but also leads one to activity.

h. Verse 12 is therefore crucial for a biblical understanding of the Ascension. "Belief in Jesus will bring to the Christian power from God to perform the same works that Jesus performs because, by uniting a man with Jesus and the Father, belief gives him a share in the power that they possess" (Brown). The "greater works" that the followers will do does not refer to deeds that are more spectacular, but deeds that are greater "because I go to the Father." It has to do with the changed situation after the resurrection of Jesus. Of course the disciples will achieve much more through their activities. These works are done solely on account of Jesus' fulfilled work of salvation, his ascension and sending of his Spirit. It is therefore done by people who are now his co-workers, his instruments. As ascended Savior Jesus himself remains the active One, the One actually doing these greater works through them!

The fact that Jesus' departure also implies a command to the disciples is therefore in itself reassuring! His departure is not the end of their service to him. In a very real sense it is only the beginning! The work of the disciples is directly dependent upon the completed task of salvation of Jesus, demonstrated in his departure. As regards their service to Jesus, their following of him, his departure therefore becomes an asset, it is to their "advantage" (John 16:7).

i. Precisely because of this dependence of the disciples on the exalted Jesus in carrying out the command to do greater works, we believe this pericope should also include verses 13 and 14. The prayer in the name of Jesus is an indispensable part of the accomplishment of the command. At the same time the Father's hearing and answering of the disciples' prayers depend upon Jesus' ascension.

II. Hermeneutical

1. When reflecting on this pericope the picture of a farewell scene comes to the fore. Jesus is here very explicitly preparing his followers for his departure. However, the decisive point is that here Jesus comforts his disciples by telling them his departure is totally different from a normal farewell. Unlike other farewells, this one is therefore not gloomy and final. Jesus does not turn his back on his disciples. They are not left behind on their own. His disciples do not lose him to death. No, his departure is a new beginning. He is going away because he loves them. He goes, only to come again. The nature of his departure must comfort and gladden his disciples, so that they will henceforth live in expectation.

2. Iwand neatly sums up the inner dynamics of this text when he speaks of two concentric circles. The first or inner circle is formed by the crisis and distress of the disciples. The imminent separation places them in a situation of crisis (*Anfechtung:* "temptation," "doubt," "trial"). This circle is, however, surrounded by an outer circle, the words of comfort and reassurance of Jesus, when he explains how his departure will change their lives. The outer circle completely encompasses the inner circle, the comfort overwhelms the crisis. This must also happen in a sermon. Where there is darkness, comfort should enlighten it. Where there is godforsakenness, faith in the presence of the Father through the Son must be experienced anew.

3. Berkouwer titles this chapter "The Great Reassurance" (cf. the beautiful discussion of John 14 in *Het Licht der Wereld*). He connects the content of this section to John 16 (it is advantageous for the disciples that Jesus is going away) and Romans 8 (nothing can separate us from God's love). The Ascension does not mean that God fails us, but it promises anew that he is for us. Jesus' words are indeed a comfort, capable of relieving deep distress. Not that the dangers of the interim period should be underestimated. There will indeed be many a struggle, but we always have the promise: there is a house; there is a way; "I will come again." That there will often be tension between what is and what will come is certain. However, the promise ensures that this tension will never lead to total breakdown.

4. This pericope (and indeed the whole chapter) is clearly dominated by the dialectic of coming and going. Jesus is leaving, because he loves us. His going away is in our interest. He goes away to prepare

the Father's house for his followers. His immediate destiny is their final destiny also. Hence his going away bears the imprint of the promise that he will come again. Since, then, Ascension is the feast of coming and going, the feast with a promise, this can be a cause for rejoicing. After all, in the light of the promise, there is no real farewell.

5. It is important that the emphasis in this pericope is not placed on the promise of Jesus' second coming. This is not the comfort arising from Ascension Day. If the church is here merely being referred to the remote future and to our heavenly home, the element of sadness would not be countered effectively. The importance of this text is that it sees the interim period, history up to the parousia, as meaningful. Jesus bestows history with a goal and the interim period with meaning. The interim period, the period of Jesus' seeming absence, is not empty. It is not meaningless. The meaning of the interim period is that it is the way to the ultimate goal.

6. First and foremost this means that verse 6 occupies a central position in the pericope. Jesus does not only comfort the disciples by referring them to the ultimate goal, the Father's house. He also categorically states that he is the way to that goal. In him the way and the goal are connected. Hence he can call for faith in himself. Whoever follows him is on this way and has at the same time already reached the goal. Hence his departure is indeed a new beginning and the interim period is meaningful, because it is full of him; through him, through his death and resurrection, a new path of life is opened. Faith in him as the way not only ultimately leads to the attainment of the final goal but it also allows humanity to share in communion with God in the present. It confers a new quality upon life in the interim period. Indeed, there is no real farewell (in this regard the coming of the Holy Spirit in the second part of the chapter is also relevant).

7. The meaning that Jesus' departure confers upon the interim period, however, also lies in the command that accompanies his departure. Verse 6 cannot be detached from verses 12-14. Jesus' departure does not mean that he is abandoning humanity. He is in heaven in our interest, so that we can be on earth in the interest of the world. His departure is not the end of the disciples' service to him, it is rather the beginning. The faith to which Jesus summons his disciples and through which he frees them from the distress caused by his physical absence is no passive faith. For now the believers are included in the history of him who reigns as Lord. Hence the mission command forms an essen-

tial component of the meaning of his ascension. Because Jesus is going away, the disciples are able really to do great things for God (v. 12). This is possible not merely because he fulfilled his task of salvation and as the exalted Lord now enables the disciples to carry out this command. After all, Jesus' departure does not mean that he is retiring. Jesus lives! He remains Lord of everything that is done in his name. The deeds done by his followers are in the final analysis *his* deeds.

8. Hence these deeds may be done only in a true and complete dependence on the exalted Jesus. The prayer in his name is the most forceful expression of this dependence. In these last verses (12-14) we encounter the most profound mystery of all church activity, and the Ascension reminds us of this. This mystery is given in the intercession in the name of Jesus.

III. Homiletical

1. As an introduction to an Ascension Day sermon on this pericope, one may point out that Ascension Day is very often the Cinderella of our church calendar. Not only do many church members neglect to attend the Ascension Day service, but most members have no idea of the meaning of Christ's ascension and what should be celebrated. John 14 can help to rectify this.

2. One may start with the fact that when one thinks of Ascension Day the overriding impression is one of a farewell. Our whole life is nothing but a permanent farewell and that is how we experience Ascension Day too. Some remarks on the distress of the disciples, who neither understood nor accepted his going away, may be helpful. A possible parallel between the experience of the disciples and our experience of the physical absence of Jesus may be to the point.

3. It will be very important to explain that the disciples did not understand Christ's ascension correctly, because they did not grasp the totally different nature of Jesus' farewell and departure. This difference is what makes his ascension unique. Jesus has gone away in our interest, on our behalf. He is in heaven for our good. His departure has taken place so that he can come again. Hence Ascension Day means promise and expectation.

4. However, the meaning and message of Ascension Day may never simply come down to an attitude of passivity, to the mentality that all that now remains is to wait. The comfort cannot only lie in what we

may receive in the future. On the contrary, the ascension of Jesus has fundamentally changed our situation on earth. It has given new meaning and a new urgency to the interim period. For the church this has a twofold significance.

a. Jesus himself is the way to the goal, and he appeals to us to believe in him. Our faith allows us to share in the presence of God now. It is because Jesus is away that the present time is full of him! Indeed, there is no farewell!

b. Once we have found this true way to life, then Christ's ascension becomes a command, for we must become witnesses to this way. The comfort of Jesus may never be understood merely as an inner experience, because it also implies an urgent and wonderful command. It is in carrying out this command that the promise, the hope, and the practice of the presence of the living Lord all become reality. Ascension anticipates Pentecost!

J. J. E. KOORNHOF

The Sunday after Ascension: John 16:4b-11

Bibliography

Commentaries

Barrett, C. K. *St. John*. Philadelphia: Westminster, 1978.

Brown, R. E. *The Gospel according to John*. The Anchor Bible. Vol. 29A. Garden City: Doubleday, 1970.

Calvin, J. *Commentary on the Gospel according to John*. Vol. 2. Grand Rapids: Eerdmans, 1956.

Dodd, C. H. *The Interpretation of the Fourth Gospel*. Cambridge: Cambridge University Press, 1953.

Hendriksen, W. *Exposition of the Gospel according to John*. Vol. 2. Grand Rapids: Baker, 1954.

Morris, L. *The Gospel according to John*. The New International Commentary on the New Testament. Grand Rapids: Eerdmans, 1971.

Schnackenburg, R. *The Gospel according to St. John*. Vol. 2. New York: Seabury, 1980.

Homiletical

Berkouwer, G. C. *Het Licht der Wereld: Het Evangelie van Johannes*. Kampen: Kok, 1960.

Morgan, G. C. *The Westminster Pulpit*. Vol. 1, 153-65. London: Revell, 1954.

Noordmans, O. *Verzamelde Werken*. Vol. 8, 349-51. Kampen: Kok, 1980.

Additional

Painter, J. *John: Witness & Theologian,* 64-70. London: SPCK, 1975.

I. Exegetical

1. Before looking at the exegesis of this pericope, we must give a short explanation of its division. There are chiefly three issues here on which opinions differ. Concerning the traditional division of John 16:1-15 (still used, e.g., by Barrett and Hendriksen) the following questions arise:

—Would verses 1-4 not make more sense when read together with John 15:18-27?

—Exactly where is the division—between verses 4 and 5? Or between verse 4a and verse 4b?

—How closely related are verses 8-11 and verses 12-15?

With regard to the first two questions, a vast majority of exegetes agree that a new pericope starts with verse 4b. With regard to the third, the minority viewpoint, held by Schnackenburg and Bultmann, is preferred here, mainly as a result of practical, homiletical considerations. If one should take verses 12-15 together with John 16:4b-11, the pericope becomes so full of themes that one cannot possibly do justice to them in a single sermon.

2. The pericope starts (4b-6) with a description of the disciples as dejected and without hope. Sorrow has filled their hearts (v. 6). In the farewell discourse (chs. 14–17), Jesus talks on more than one occasion about the disciples' grief *(lypē),* but especially in this chapter it functions as a main theme (cf. 16:20-21 and 22). Most commentaries mention two reasons for this grief. In the first place it has been caused by the expectation of hatred and persecution from the side of the world and the synagogue (John 15:18–16:4a). To make this much worse, they have now received the bad news of Jesus' going away, his ascension to go back to the Father. Much more than the possible hatred and persecution, this prospect of the disciples somehow managing without the physical presence of Jesus is the primary cause of their sorrow (v. 6). Further, because of the fact that in John's Gospel the ascension of Christ and his cross are very closely identified (cf., e.g., his ambiguous use of the expression "lifted up," which can refer to both events simultaneously), most commentaries admit the possibility that the prospect of the death of Jesus ("going away" then also means "going away into the grave") can be regarded as a further cause for grief on the part of the disciples.

3. In verse 7 we have the comforting answer of Jesus. He wants to

alleviate the bleak situation of the disciples. Schnackenburg points to the elements of comfort and consolation in calling this chapter a "consolatory discourse," that is "paracletic encouragement" in contrast with the "paranetic admonition" of the two previous chapters. The comfort given by Jesus, of course, means that a comforter (the Counselor, the Paraclete) will be sent to his people. How far-reaching and powerful the working of the Spirit will be is shown by the fact that Jesus commends this new dispensation of the Spirit as more advantageous than even his physical presence among the disciples. By virtue of the strong functional unity that John maintains between christology and pneumatology, it can rightly be argued that with the coming of the Spirit Jesus himself will return to his disciples, but now in power, having completed his task of salvation (cf. 16:7 with John 7:39).

Most commentators provide useful material on the origin and meaning of the term *paraclete*. In contrast to Bultmann's gnostic explanation, there now exists a growing consensus that the idea is of Jewish origin. Betz puts forward a very strong argument for its connection with the Qumran Scrolls, while Bornkamm discusses the concept in the light of the Old Testament "forerunner/finisher" scheme, in which the spirit of the forerunner falls on the successor (e.g., Elijah/Elisha, Moses/Joshua). Mowinckel seeks the origin in the Old Testament intercessor models, as can be found in Abraham (Gen. 18:23-33), Moses (Ex. 32:11-14), and Samuel (1 Sam. 7:8ff.), all acting as intercessors or mediators. Schnackenburg points to the connection with Mark 13:11 (when the believers are brought to trial, the Holy Spirit will teach them what to say) and pleads for a stronger legal and forensic interpretation of the work of the Paraclete.

4. There exists a near consensus among exegetes that such a legal and forensic view of the role of the Paraclete does indeed provide us with the best key for understanding verses 8-11 as well (described by Betz as "by far the most difficult" Paraclete text of all). For a detailed discussion of the questions of grammar and translation (e.g., how exactly to translate *elenchein peri* as well as the three following *hoti*-clauses), readers are referred to the commentaries. A few conclusions about the meaning of this fourth Paraclete text can, however, be drawn:

a. Exegetes generally agree that the work of the Paraclete with regard to the world, as it is described in verses 8-11, must be understood against the background of the Jewish expectancy of an apocalyptic-juridical conflict between God and the hostile "world" (another very important expression in the chapter). In line with John's general view of eschatology, it is here proclaimed that this conflict will not be resolved at the end of world history, but because of the coming of Christ it will be resolved *now,* in the course of history itself.

b. In the first round of this "legal battle" (Schnackenburg) it will seem as if the world is victorious when they succeed in finding Christ guilty, in convicting him, and even in obtaining a fatal judgment against him (John 18 and 19). With that the world may even hope finally to close the case against Jesus.

c. The promise of Jesus about the coming of the Paraclete must be seen against this background. The task of the Paraclete is in the first place to be a helper and intercessor (Advocate) for the church in distress. However, he also has a second function. With regard to the world and specifically in the juridical conflict against the world, the Spirit comes as if to reopen the closed court case of Jesus and to continue with it! The Spirit is going to enforce "a rerun of the trial of Jesus"!

d. In this new "cosmic trial" (Schnackenburg), the Spirit will play the decisive role! "In the Spirit who has been given to it, the community has an advocate of God who argues Jesus' case, exposes judgment on unbelief and helps the community towards victory" (Schnackenburg). The Spirit will change nearly every decision of the first trial. The Jews found Jesus to be the guilty party and the sinner (8:24; 15:22-25). According to verse 9 the Spirit will show that not Jesus, but the Jewish leaders themselves are the real culprits and that, ironically, their greatest guilt is precisely the fact that they did not want to believe Jesus. (For further discussion of this point see II, 3a). Moreover, the Jewish leaders were certain that in this case against Jesus they had "right" on their side. The Holy Spirit, however, will show that "they are wrong about what is right" (GNB)! (Consult the commentaries for a detailed discussion of the difficult problems in v. 10b.) Still, the biggest surprise will be that the Spirit will show that the Jewish religious leaders were also mistaken with regard to the sentence and its execution. Through the cross they thought to finally break the power of Jesus of Nazareth. What really happened was that in and through the cross the power of Satan, their chief, "the ruler of this world" was finally broken (3:18; cf. also II, 3b for further explanation).

e. Besides this legal explanation of verses 8-11 one must also keep in mind what some exegetes call the religious implications of these verses, namely that religion as such (sin, righteousness, and judgment are not only legal but also religious concepts) is totally redefined and that "in terms of Christ" (Roloff). After the Christ event, all religious concepts receive a totally new content and meaning. The Holy Spirit will convince the world that there is no sense in being religious outside of Christ: "By having this faith in the gift of the Paraclete . . . the community is encouraged in its distress both to bear witness to its faith and to resist unbelief" (Schnackenburg).

f. To the question of how the Spirit effects this task of convincing the world, the text gives no explicit answer. This question has, of course, already been evoked by the first Paraclete text (14:17) where it was stated that the world "cannot receive" the Spirit. On account of the other Paraclete texts, as well as the theology of John in general, it is generally accepted that the Spirit accomplishes this through the proclamation of the church and through the life of the church, its "proclamatory existence."

II. Hermeneutical

1. Perhaps it may be useful to summarize the expositions of three famous commentators, namely Bultmann, Iwand, and Berkouwer.

a. In his commentary, Bultmann offers a very ingenious (Kierkegaardian) explanation for the events of John 16:4b-7. According to him, the disciples had to be freed by the departure of Jesus from the misunderstanding and false assurance "which thought that it possessed the revelation in what was directly given." To make a possession of revelation is a basic human inclination. It is dangerous because the revelation then loses all power and value and becomes solidified. It retains its value only as long as it is something future. That is why Jesus was almost "forced" to leave his disciples—for their own good! "He can only be the Revealer as the One who always breaks in pieces every certainty, always breaking in from beyond and calling in the future."

Bultmann further expounds on this in a very famous sermon. The work of the Spirit, he says, is to open our eyes to the invisible realities beyond the visible things that normally monopolize our lives. "The world wants us to regard its realities as the only realities. It is its secret plan to try and make us believe that it can fill our whole life with its gifts and that it can 'engage' us wholly in its duties." The Spirit wants to help us withstand the power of the (visible) world. "It means that we shall tell the world that its power is not the ultimate power and that therefore it has no right to claim us for itself."

b. Iwand begins his meditation on John 16:5-15 with a discussion of Bultmann's exposition, evidently because it has been "beloved" and used by many preachers. Without denying its edifying character (he even acknowledges that Bultmann is justified to a certain extent in claiming Luther's support for his viewpoint), he maintains that Bultmann's interpretation has the fundamental weakness of not being biblical, but rather philosophical, when speaking about death. "Our text does not deal with an interpretation [Deutung] of death, but with victory over death."

Iwand believes that the "going away" of Christ means his death on the cross. In his view, this interpretation explains the depth of the disciples' grief. To their way of thinking, Jesus' work stopped with his death. It was the end of the road—for Jesus and for them. This is the kind of grief that can settle so deeply in a Christian's heart that it causes us not to hear the comforting words of Jesus any more. And when we look around then, we see nothing but the victory of death, "a victory even over God."

It is the task of the Spirit to deal with this bleak situation (v. 7). The Spirit does this by helping us understand the meaning, importance, and value of Christ's death on the cross. "Only in and through the death of Christ can one learn to believe in God. If we do not want to learn it at this point, we shall stay unbelieving and god-less all our lives." It only becomes Pentecost when the Spirit helps a sorrowful believer understand the death of the Lord correctly. Only thus can death be conquered.

Concerning the Spirit's task of convincing the world, Iwand considers this to be identical with his task of comforting the church. "It seems clear to me that this is one and the same deed; the comforted disciples become the bearers of the Spirit who convinces the world."

On the way in which the church should bring the message to the world, Iwand warns us: "One must guard against using the three issues mentioned here [sin, righteousness, judgment] in a sermon of judgment [Gerichtspredigt]. On the contrary, the sermon must proclaim the complete joy and consolation of salvation." Verses 8-11 must be lived out and preached as good news by the church. Even what the church has to say about sin, righteousness, and judgment must still sound "completely new and liberating" to the world!

c. Berkouwer pays special attention to verse 9 (sin as lack of faith) and verse 11 (judgment and victory over the evil one). These two verses seem to be of special importance in understanding the "good news" in John 16:4-11.

(i) If "sin" in verse 9 is narrowed down to disbelief or lack of faith, that, of course, does not disregard all other sin. Unbelief is here "the point of concentration" (Berkouwer) or the "point of culmination" (Durand) of all sin. Berkouwer says that this verse is intended to "prevent the church from a moralistic understanding of sin, applied as criterion in different ways to condemn human life." When the Bible calls for repentance it does not ask for moral improvement, but for faith. "But now that Jesus Christ has come, now everything becomes simple. Now it does not mean following the difficult way out of many sins along equally as many ways of moral improvement, but it is concerned with the one thing necessary, namely faith, surrender, and trust."

Civilized people are often tempted to change the gospel into merely a code of moral behavior. That is why we often find moral unbelievers more bearable than believers with a morality different from our own! Verse 9 proclaims to us (and through us to the world also!) a gospel that is certainly not immoral, but is more—infinitely more!—than just morals. "What we have in Christ is a sharp concentration, a condensation and simplification of all decisions to one only: faith."

(ii) With reference to verse 11, Berkouwer maintains that many churchgoers seem to believe that one day there will be an end to our domination by the power of darkness, but that at present we are ruled by the evil one. If this is true, there is something very wrong with the life and testimony of the church, because "the innermost secret of the Christian religion . . . lies in my being a child of God and in the perspective of a disarmed power, of a vanquished enemy."

2. In conclusion, three sermon outlines, based on the traditional Lutheran division of this pericope (i.e. John 16:5-15), are briefly mentioned:

a. Bauer's division is very common: (1) the situation of the disciples (vv. 5-7); (2) the Paraclete as Judge of the world (vv. 8-11); (3) the Paraclete as Helper of the church (vv. 12-15).

b. In Asmussen the emphasis is slightly different: (1) the blessing of the death of Jesus (vv. 5-7); (2) the coming of the Spirit as the start of a new history (vv. 8-11); (3) the new history as characterized by a growing knowledge (vv. 12-15).

c. Roloff takes as his starting point the bleak situation of the church and sees the answer of Jesus as providing a threefold hope. We may and must expect that the Spirit: (1) will pursue the mission of Jesus; (2) will guide us, his church, in truth; and (3) is working in the world through us.

III. Homiletical

1. The sorrow of the disciples (v. 6) is a good starting point for a sermon. Why this grief? Three reasons can be given (see I, 2) with special emphasis on the third, viz. that the departure of Jesus means his death. (Iwand's comments in II, 1b can also be used.) The depth of the disciples' sorrow is poignantly described in verse 5. They consider it useless to ask anything further about Jesus' departure! Why? Because nothing mattered any longer.

In their disillusionment they have already inwardly begun to distance themselves from Jesus and no longer expect anything from him. This gives a natural transition to the situation of present-day believers. How many of us have not deep in our hearts abandoned the cause of Jesus? How much do we *really* expect of him? Are we not all, in the long run, doing our own thing— living for ourselves and only expecting what we ourselves can accomplish?

2. The message of Jesus to his disciples is that his arrest, trial, conviction, and, in the end, his condemnation will not be the end of Jesus of Nazareth. The world will not be able to do away with him so easily! Someone is coming (the Spirit, v. 7), who will reopen the case of Jesus and will continue his cause. Here a simple and brief explanation of verses 8-11 can be given to the congregation, in line with I, 4a-e.

3. The line of interpretation given in I, 4f can now be developed. Since the world cannot receive the Spirit (John 14:17), the Spirit wants to use the church as medium and intermediary to bring Christ's message to the world. Through our words (preaching, witness, ordinary conversation) but also through our lives the Spirit wants to convince the world that Jesus has been right (v. 10) in everything he said and did. Our lives must be such that the world is led not only to a better morality (v. 9) but also to faith in Christ (cf. II, 1c for elaboration). Our lives should also reflect complete freedom (v. 11) because of Christ's victory over Satan (cf. II, 1c for further discussion). Pentecost means that the Spirit makes this message come true in the words and life of the church.

4. In conclusion the congregation can be asked directly whether

the world does hear and see this message of the Spirit in our lives. In line with Iwand's warning in II, 1b this can be crystallized into one question, Does the world experience our lives as "gospel"—as good news? Christ has not come to judge the world, but to save the world (John 3:17). We must know that the task of conviction by the Spirit is aimed not at winning the argument but at winning *people* for Christ. The Spirit therefore does not want us to witness to an "oppresive and terrifying judgment," but instead to proclaim the "liberating and joyful gospel."

C. W. BURGER

Pentecost: Revelation 22:6-21

Bibliography

Commentaries

Beasley-Murray, G. R. *The Book of Revelation*. New Century Bible. London: Marshall, Morgan & Scott, 1974; Grand Rapids: Eerdmans, 1981.

Caird, G. B. *A Commentary on the Revelation of St. John The Divine*. New York and Evanston: Harper & Row, 1966.

Ladd, G. E. *A Commentary on the Revelation of John*. Grand Rapids: Eerdmans, 1972.

Morris, L. *The Revelation of St. John*. Tyndale New Testament Commentaries. Grand Rapids: Eerdmans, 1987.

Mounce, R. H. *The Book of Revelation*. The New International Commentary on the New Testament. Grand Rapids: Eerdmans, 1977.

Van Hartingsveld, L. *Revelation*. Text and Interpretation. Grand Rapids: Eerdmans, 1985.

Homiletical

Bavinck, J. H. *En Voort Wentelen de Eeuwen*. Wageningen: Zomer en Keuning, n.d.

Mounce, R. H. *The Book of Revelation: What Are We Waiting For?* Elgin: Cook, 1979.

Additional

Barclay, W. *The Revelation of St. John*. Vol. 2. Revised Edition. The Daily Study Bible Series. Philadelphia: Westminster, 1976.

Berkouwer, G. C. *The Return of Christ*. Studies in Dogmatics. Grand Rapids: Eerdmans, 1972.

I. Exegetical

Because the epilogue of Revelation is really a resumé of the central message of the whole book (cf. Hendriksen), it is very important to keep the message of the book in mind when reading these verses. To quote Revelation itself, this is a "prophetic" book (1:3; 22:7, 10, 18) that is to be taken to heart (1:3; 22:7). It tells the church, which is suffering great oppression, of things that "must soon take place" (1:1; 22:6) because "the time is near" (1:3; 22:10). In their suffering on account of the gospel, the church can be encouraged by these things close at hand to persevere in her faith and to realize that this suffering is an essential part of God's scheme spanning the history of the world from creation to re-creation. It is part of the struggle against Satan, a struggle in which the Lamb triumphs in his own way, through the cross and the resurrection (5:5-6; 12:7ff.).

Mounce says strikingly:

> The Old Testament predicts the smashing of the nations with an iron bar, but the only weapon the Lamb wields is his own Cross and the martyrdom of his followers (ii.27; xii.5; xix.15). The seven spirits of God can be let loose into the world only as the eyes of the Lamb (i.4; iii.1; iv.5; v.6). The Red Sea through which the followers of the Lamb must achieve their new Exodus is the bloodbath of their own martyrdom (xv.2). The monster from the abyss can be conquered only by being allowed to conquer and so to burn itself out (xiii.7); and the perfection of the holy city, into which nothing unclean is allowed to enter, is achieved by allowing evil to exhaust its strength in unavailing attacks on the people of God . . . the repeated attacks upon the ungodly world order by all the armament of heaven, which occupy so large a part of John's book, are designed not to destroy or to punish, but only to penetrate the defences which the world has erected against the rule of God. The dethronement of the monster and the fall of Babylon are necessary parts of God's redemptive plan, if the vast populations they have deluded and seduced are to be set free for the kingdom of God. And the secret weapon by which God means to achieve this end is the death of his martyr servants. Only in this way can the nations be liberated from the deceptions of Satan (xx.3).

As conqueror Christ rules in the midst of his church (1:6, 9), through which he will bring history to a meaningful conclusion. That is why in the great "liturgy of the throne" (ch. 5) the twenty-four elders who represent the church (whom he "has made . . . priests," 1:6) lead the whole creation in worship and service to God (5:13). This heavenly liturgy is repeated in a great liturgy on earth that is found in the epilogue and can only be understood in its fullness as a liturgical dialogue initiated in heaven. In this liturgy the following subdivisions may be distinquished:

1. The liturgical introduction (v. 6): The process whereby the prophetic message is given to the church proceeds from God (literally from "the Lord, the God of the spirits of the prophets"). It is he who inspires the liturgy. The instrument and bearer of this message (the liturgist) is an angel who transmits God's message to his servants, the churches that stand "like lampstands" before the Lord of the earth to bear witness with their lips and their lives (11:4ff.). What is their witness? They are to prophesy concerning "what must soon take place." They must announce the summary, the quintessence, of all the messages from beginning to end of the long process of salvation that is now rapidly moving toward its divine realization. "The end and the beginning are but two perspectives on the same great adventure" (Mounce).

2. The liturgical denouement (vv. 7-11): The promise that this concentration of absolutely reliable prophetic utterances will "soon" be made known is answered from heaven by the first of three similar announcements: "Behold, I am coming soon!" (*tachus,* "quickly," "without delay"; cf. also 2:16; 3:11; 16:15). At this stage it is Christ who takes the place of the angel as liturgist. Now there is not simply a message coming from heaven, nor a tremendous event, but a Person—the living Lord is coming! He is at hand! This is the quintessence of all liturgy! This will sustain the church throughout the hell of persecution. This is the essence of the message that echoes round the world. This is the reason, the only reason, why each one is "blessed" who "keeps the words of the prophecy" (the words of the book must be kept in our heart).

This is the last of the seven blessings, addressed to those who must remain steadfast throughout the great oppression that is to come (1:3; 13:13; etc.; cf. Hendriksen). And because "the time is near" (v. 10), because the struggle lies ahead, the words of the prophecy must not be concealed (cf. Dan. 8:26; 10:14; 12:4—which refer to a vision concerning the distant future). This nearness serves as eschatological motivation and activation. This is what makes the message of the book so urgent and relevant, because the prophetic message is like a "lamp shining in a dark place"; "you will do well to pay attention to this . . . until the day dawns and the morning star [cf. Rev. 22:16] rises in your hearts" (2 Peter 1:19).

The nearness of the time therefore has a hermeneutical function: it opens the book! There is a grave danger that the church will fall under the fascination of the progressive history of the world if the book remains sealed. Then heaven will also remain sealed. Then the church's heavenward perspective will be dulled and the liturgy on earth silenced. Frey rightly warns against preserving this book between "two black pages" and meditating and speculating about its contents, and subjecting it to all sorts of demythologizing. "The church must teach from it and the church must preach from it."

The nearness of the time also functions hermeneutically in another way. It gives a specific effect to the message in the book: in light of the nearness of the time it will no longer be possible to change one's ways. The parting of ways has been reached. The wrong of evildoers goes rapidly and steeply downward; the road to holiness goes more rapidly and more steeply upward. (See Hendriksen for the meaning of "let" in v. 11—as a "positive exhortation" to continue with evil/holiness.) In the light of this nearness of time, previous decisions now become final (cf. 2 Peter 1:10). The parting of the ways is clear—there is no longer a middle of the road.

3. The liturgical gathering (vv. 12-14): Once again a liturgical wave starts with the heavenly cry, "Behold, I am coming soon!" And once again Christ is the heavenly liturgist. This time his coming sets in motion a tremendous reaction on earth: "I am . . . bringing my recompense" (v. 12). In order to understand this cry, one must turn back to a very interesting parallel in Isaiah 40:10: "Behold, his reward is with him, and his recompense before him." The prophet Isaiah has in mind the new exodus that God will accomplish as the faithful Shepherd leading his people out of exile. The reward that he is bringing is his flock, which he has ransomed for himself and which he will "feed" once he has "gathered" them in (Isa. 40:11; Caird).

From the context in Revelation it is clear that the Christ who is coming is expected to do exactly these things. When he comes, the blessed will be gathered together in the holy city (v. 14). Here again the events that will take place on earth are eschatologically initiated and motivated by the One who is "the Alpha and the Omega, the first and the last, the beginning and the end." In him God's great scheme of salvation will find its perfect fulfillment and its ultimate aim. Once again a blessing is proclaimed on those who "wash their robes" (continuing action, per the aorist form of the verb).

This section is often mistakenly interpreted in a one-sided, spiritualistic way, as though it had to do with purification from the uncleanliness that continually defiles us (cf. Hendriksen: "everyone wears a robe . . . that robe is your character"; cf. Morris, Schlatter: "Jesus died in order to give us that purity which we could never attain before God"). Along with Mounce, one must, however, much rather find the answer in the explanation given in Revelation 7:13-14: "These . . . in white robes . . . have come out of the great tribulation; they have washed their robes and made them white in the blood of the Lamb." Caird puts it strikingly: "That is, those who face martyrdom in the confidence that the Cross is the sign of God's victory over evil without and evil within."

Just as in the previous scene, the separation that is carried through is important, but now not only as regards their action, but also concerning their destination: the community of the faithful is gathered together in the holy city with access to the tree of life, while others, the "dogs" (v. 15), are left outside (cf. 21:8; concerning "dog" cf. Deut. 23:18; Matt. 15:26). They may rub shoulders in Laodicea, but in the light of eschatology they are either inside—or out!

4. The liturgical request (vv. 16-19): A cry originates on earth (Come . . . ! Come . . . ! Come . . . !). From the context it is clear that this is an answer to the double cry that has already come from heaven ("Behold, I am coming soon"). But why does this plea come now? Something must have triggered this cry from earth! It can only be the self-introductory words of the heavenly liturgist: "I am the root and the offspring of David, the bright morning star."

In the first place these names underscore Jesus' connection with the past: he is the king of Zion, the root and descendant of David. David is archetypal (Caird; also Frey; Schlatter) of the Messiah, the king to come (cf. Isa. 11:1; Hos. 3:5; Amos 9:11). Then the future is also included: the morning star heralds the passing of night, also the night of persecution, and the inexorable coming of a new day (cf. Rom. 13:12— "a new day so sorely needed by John's hard-pressed readers," Morris). Many people also see here a fulfillment of the prophecy of Balaam: "A star shall come forth out of Jacob" (Num. 24:17; cf. Bruce: "in the Qumran texts Num. 24:17 is a recurring testimonium of the messianic warrior of the endtime").

These names the heavenly liturgist uses to introduce himself thus call to mind powerful expectations that are echoed on earth when the Spirit and the Bride answer "Come!" But the question is: Who must come? Two answers have been given:

a. Some see it as an invitation to the world (Ladd), to the "outsider" (Morris). "The first come! is addressed not to Christ, but to all comers" (Caird). "It is the testimony of the church empowered by the Holy Spirit that constitutes the great evangelizing force of this age . . . the threefold use of the present imperative ('come/let him come') serves to extend the invitation until that very moment when history will pass irrevocably into eternity and any further opportunity for decision will be past" (Mounce).

b. Others see it as a desperate plea from the church awaiting his coming. The Spirit keeps this hope alive in the church (Rom. 8:16). It is not sufficient that the church merely know what forces control history and move it toward its fulfillment, she must also pray for the coming of the Lord, who will grant this fulfillment. They must long for him with a burning desire. It is the Spirit of the Bridegroom, the Spirit of Christ who dwells within the church (2:7, 11, 17, etc.) and teaches the church to pray "Come, Lord Jesus."

Perhaps, keeping in mind the liturgical nature of the epilogue, it is permissible to accept both these theories, to hear this "come" in both ways. The cry can have both a vertical and a horizontal dimension. The Lord has already said "Behold, I am coming" twice, and the church is replying with a passionate "Come, Lord Jesus!" inspired by the Spirit. But this liturgical cry of the church is, of course, also heard "on the sidelines of the world" (the Gentiles stood at the sides and back during early Christian worship services; they must be similarly motivated to pray for the coming of the King). So these cries from the church are also echoed to the "sides" and are passed on to others so that they will also "thirst" and then hear the invitation to come to the water of life. The Spirit testifies with our spirit (Rom. 8:16) and for us (8:26). There is also the testimony of the Word of God: that is precisely why the writings in this prophetic book may not be tampered with (vv. 18-19). The Word and the Spirit keep the crying voice alive!

5. Liturgical concentration (v. 20): The heavenly liturgist utters the third "I am coming soon" and it is embellished by the preceding "Amen"—so be it! Truly! No more is said, because no more *can* be said. The book, the gospel, the church, the history of the world, everything depends on these words. And then follows the church's last urgent reply

on earth: "Amen. Come Lord Jesus!" *(Maranatha!* cf. 1 Cor. 16:22). In the early church, worshipers uttered the Maranatha prayer at each communion service, thus binding the memory of the death of Christ *(anamnesis!)* to the future, a future that will not merely fall into the church's lap but is a day whose coming must be hastened on by the faithful and to which they look forward in hope (2 Peter 3:12; cf. Berkouwer, Maurer, Harder). The church cannot cry out anything more important or more urgent. This is the sum of all prayer. "It is the confession that the answers to the problems of life do not lie in man's ability to create a better world but in the return of the One whose sovereign power controls the course of human affairs" (Mounce). In the long run the church does not merely pray for something to happen or not to happen, but for *Someone* who must come—must come into the world and into history as he comes week after week, time after time in the liturgy. At the close of the epilogue one therefore finds liturgy in its purest form: it concludes with a divine promise that is the sum total of all promises, and with an earthly prayer that is the sum total of all prayers on earth (Schlatter).

6. The liturgy closes with a benediction (v. 21). Although there are many textual problems, it is most appropriate that this dialogue ends from heaven, with the granting of the rich grace and mercy of the Lord Jesus to all who wait for him and cry to him. Ultimately, the church can live only by grace while waiting for and crying to the Lord.

II. Hermeneutical

1. A crucial question is, of course, whether this liturgy reflects the spirit of *Naherwartung* (an expectation of events close at hand) to such a degree that this urgency and expectation are lost when this sense of imminence has disappeared. It would perhaps be a good idea to read what Berkouwer says about this. The book of Revelation itself seems to warn against turning a *Naherwartung* into a *Fernerwartung* (placing events far in the future), as if they will seemingly never happen!

Berkouwer states: "The believer is called to an attitude that does not *reckon,* but constantly *reckons with,* the coming of the Lord." He describes this as dealing with the "unexpected" and yet not "unexpected" coming. This is a subtle but important distinction, one that goes to the heart of Christian hope. "Unexpected" events tell us that the time is not known. Not "un-expected" points to the hope that must always be present in us. "In this context arises the familiar image of a thief in the night. . . . This suddenness will not present a danger for those who have expected the Lord's return. . . . The suddenness and incalculability demand constant vigilance and preparation. But the destructiveness in the analogy of the thief in the night disappears for the 'sons of the day.' . . . The danger lies in being unprepared for the coming of the Lord."

2. It is very important that attention is paid to the role played by the "nearness of the Lord" and the "end of time" in this section. The nearness of the Lord and therefore also of the end takes on many forms: in worship, in one's personal devotions, in the crises of life—sickness and death, in suffering and pain. But ultimately all these nuances of his nearness are grounded in the *reality* of the closeness of the Lord, the Morning Star who has risen and shines down upon us. The church does not experience the constant shadow of apocalyptic disaster but the closeness of the Lord, who stands before the throne holding the book of life in his hands. This is the closeness of the Bridegroom to the bride. *This* gives rise to all other forms of his nearness and his coming.

3. The close bond between the Spirit and the eagerly awaiting church must be preserved at all times. It is the Spirit through whom the individual is re-born and the Spirit who binds believers together in the new fellowship of the church. Through the Spirit one confesses "Jesus is Lord," and through the Spirit believers are united in one body (1 Cor. 12:3). We were all made to drink of one Spirit—that is, we have all absorbed one Spirit, "by one Spirit we were all baptized into one body" (1 Cor. 12:13). That is why the church cries out to the Lord through the Spirit: not as individuals, but together, with one voice, bound up in a living organism in which the same longing throbs: as the same pulse throbs through all the arteries of the body, so each part of the bride's body longs for the Bridegroom.

III. Homiletical

Perhaps the following outline can be used for a sermon:

1. By way of introduction can be mentioned that not only the world but also the church itself can become so tied up in the things of this world and its "passing form" (1 Cor. 7:31) that it all too easily forgets its destination. "One can sometimes become so entranced by the passing parade of daily life that one forgets where one is going" (Bavinck).

An experience of Karl Barth applies here. He was visiting a wealthy friend in a luxurious alpine lodge, and at one point he exclaimed: "Everything is so beautiful that there is no need here for eschatology!" This kind of sentiment may at times become a real danger to the church and to all Christians. They may have so many things near at hand that they believe they can do without the nearness of the Lord. There may be so many things to enjoy, to long for, and to cry out for that they no longer long for and cry out for the Lord. This often happens in prosperous times.

A similar thing can happen in times of suffering and distress. Believers may lose heart, they may lose faith and hope, they may lose their awareness of the nearness of the Lord because of overwhelming suffering and hardship. And again they may simply forget to cry out for the Lord. Faced with the enchantments of the world and/or the threatening forces of enemies, this book of prophecy may remain closed. Then heaven becomes vague, and our perspective upward and forward becomes clouded (cf. I, 2). Then our bank balances and our businesses, our comforts and our prestige, the rat race at home, work, and school, the burdensome toil of dehumanizing, oppressing circumstances, all of these become so important that heaven and the second coming grow vague. Then we all too easily become settlers on earth, no longer pilgrims. This danger also threatened the churches to whom Revelation was addressed. Because they were no longer living in the expectation that Christ was "near," and had made all sorts of adaptations in order to live at peace with the world, they were in danger of losing their awareness of his nearness. In this way many of them had avoided persecution, thus also losing their testimony (cf. Rev. 2 and 3).

2. What does it mean to hold on to the reality of "what must soon take place" (v. 6) and to participate in the powers of the coming age (Heb. 6:5)? Perhaps this can be illustrated through extending the metaphor of the bride used in this pericope.

a. Just as the bride applies her make-up, dresses in her wedding dress, and poses for the photographer, all in expectation of the bridegroom and her future life with him, so the whole appearance and behavior of the bridal church is determined by the Lord. The church yearns "to enter the city by the gates" (v. 14) with him. How onerous it would be for the bride to go through with all these responsibilities and preparations if she had ceased to yearn for the bridegroom and no longer joyfully anticipated a life with him! Is this not a disturbing, but at the same time true, reflection of a church and of Christians who no longer expect their Lord, and are no longer so sure of their heavenly citizenship? No wonder all the preparations and obligations become an intolerable burden for such a church! Where the Bridegroom is no longer expected, everything in and about the bride dies a slow but certain death!

b. It is a fascinating thought that the bridal robe of the church will be washed white in the blood of the Lamb and of the martyrs (I, 3). We would rather merely wash the robe in the blood of Christ, because we are afraid of the pain involved in resisting to the point of "shedding our blood" (Heb. 12:4). We are so quick to cry out in pain, and the result is that the bridal robe is not washed. It remains soiled by a negligent association with the things of this world. In the context of each particular congregation, these thoughts should be meditated upon, in order to make it prophetic, contextual, and to the point. The cost of discipleship comes in different forms in different situations.

c. Everyone knows the infectious enthusiasm of the bride on the way to her wedding: everyone is drawn along, caught up in the excitement—children, friends, family. Nothing seems too expensive or too much trouble. This is what the missionary zeal of the bridal church should be, because it is the Spirit in the bride calling to her bridegroom through the bride (II, 2). But through the eager congregation, which has a vision of the future, the Spirit calls urgently and fervently to the world: "Come . . . come!"

The calls of the Spirit cause both the congregation and the surrounding world to long for the Lord. Through the coming of the Bridegroom the thirst of the church as well as the torturing thirst of the world is quenched! This longing for the second coming gives rise to a contagious missionary longing in the church to include the world also. This longing for the world is instigated and kept alive by the Holy Spirit. "The Spirit and the Bride say, 'Come.'" In this call, the end of time and the end of the world, the return of Christ and the church's mission, are all linked together.

3. The words of promise, "Surely I am coming soon" (v. 20), give the members of the congregation the assurance that in their worship and in their lives, in their church and in their culture, they do not face a terrible future, but they face the Bridegroom! The church is waiting, suffering, calling, praying within this world, not in front of a closed door on earth, but in front of an open door in heaven. Every apparently

impenetrable wall on earth has a window that looks into heaven! And the church looks upward and to the side through this window: whoever notices heaven can never fail to notice the world. Revelation 22:6-11 simply wants to keep the church "posted," to inform them, no, to remind them of what is to come and what is (still) to happen.

B. A. MÜLLER